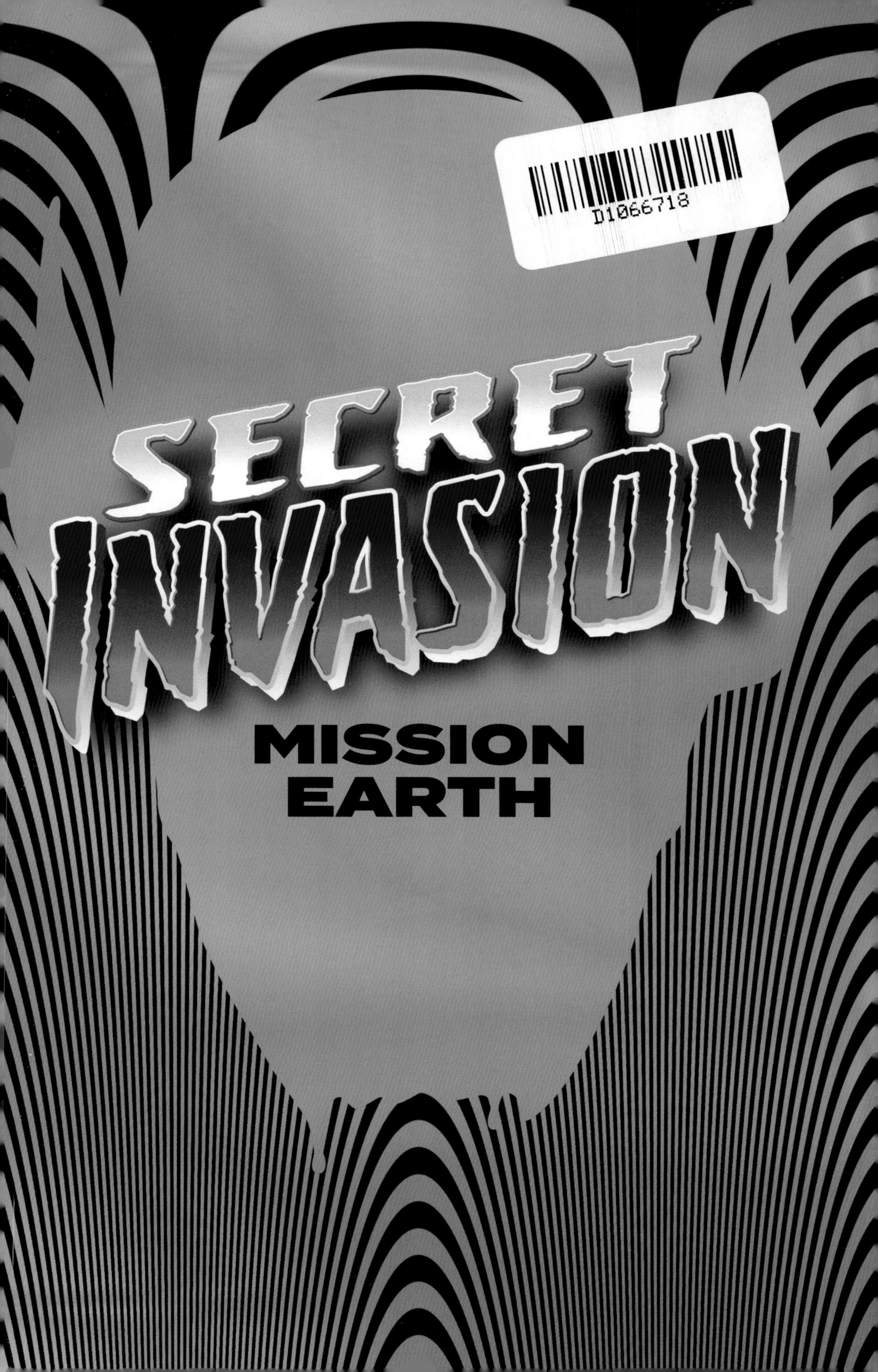
SECRET
INVASION
MISSION
EARTH

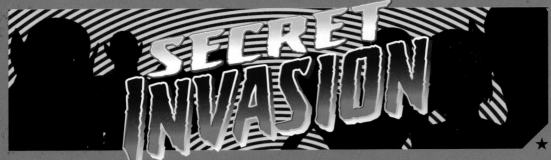

SECRET INVASION

MISSION EARTH

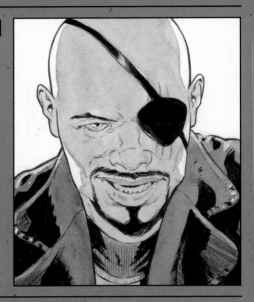

DISCIPLINE	AGENT(S)
WRITER	**Ryan North**
ARTIST	**Francesco Mobili**
COLOR ARTIST	**Jordie Bellaire**
LETTERER	**VC's Joe Caramagna**
COVER ART	**Matteo Lolli** & **Federico Blee** (#1); **Rafael Albuquerque** (#2); **E.J. Su** (#3); **Superlog** (#4); AND **Sanford Greene** (#5)
ASSISTANT EDITOR	**Martin Biro**
EDITOR	**Annalise Bissa**

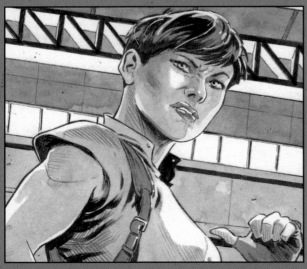

COLLECTION EDITOR **Jennifer Grünwald**

ASSISTANT EDITOR **Daniel Kirchhoffer**

ASSISTANT MANAGING EDITOR **Maia Loy**

ASSOCIATE MANAGER, TALENT RELATIONS **Lisa Montalbano**

VP PRODUCTION & SPECIAL PROJECTS **Jeff Youngquist**

BOOK DESIGNER **Jay Bowen**

SVP PRINT, SALES & MARKETING **David Gabriel**

EDITOR IN CHIEF **C.B. Cebulski**

SECRET INVASION: MISSION EARTH. Contains material originally published in magazine form as SECRET INVASION (2022) #1-5. First printing 2023. ISBN 978-1-302-93472-9. Published by MARVEL WORLDWIDE, INC., a subsidiary of MARVEL ENTERTAINMENT, LLC. OFFICE OF PUBLICATION: 1290 Avenue of the Americas, New York, NY 10104. **Printed in the U.S.A.** KEVIN FEIGE, Chief Creative Officer; DAN BUCKLEY, President, Marvel Entertainment; DAVID BOGART, Associate Publisher & SVP of Talent Affairs; TOM BREVOORT, VP, Executive Editor; NICK LOWE, Executive Editor, VP of Content, Digital Publishing; DAVID GABRIEL, VP of Print & Digital Publishing; SVEN LARSEN, VP of Licensed Publishing; MARK ANNUNZIATO, VP of Planning & Forecasting; JEFF YOUNGQUIST, VP of Production & Special Projects; ALEX MORALES, Director of Publishing Operations; DAN EDINGTON, Director of Editorial Operations; RICKEY PURDIN, Director of Talent Relations; JENNIFER GRÜNWALD, Director of Production & Special Projects; SUSAN CRESPI, Production Manager; STAN LEE, Chairman Emeritus. For information regarding advertising in Marvel Comics or on Marvel.com, please contact Vit DeBellis, Custom Solutions & Integrated Advertising Manager, at vdebellis@marvel.com. For Marvel subscription inquiries, please call 888-511-5480. **Manufactured between 4/7/2023 and 5/9/2023 by SEAWAY PRINTING, GREEN BAY, WI, USA.**

10 9 8 7 6 5 4 3 2 1

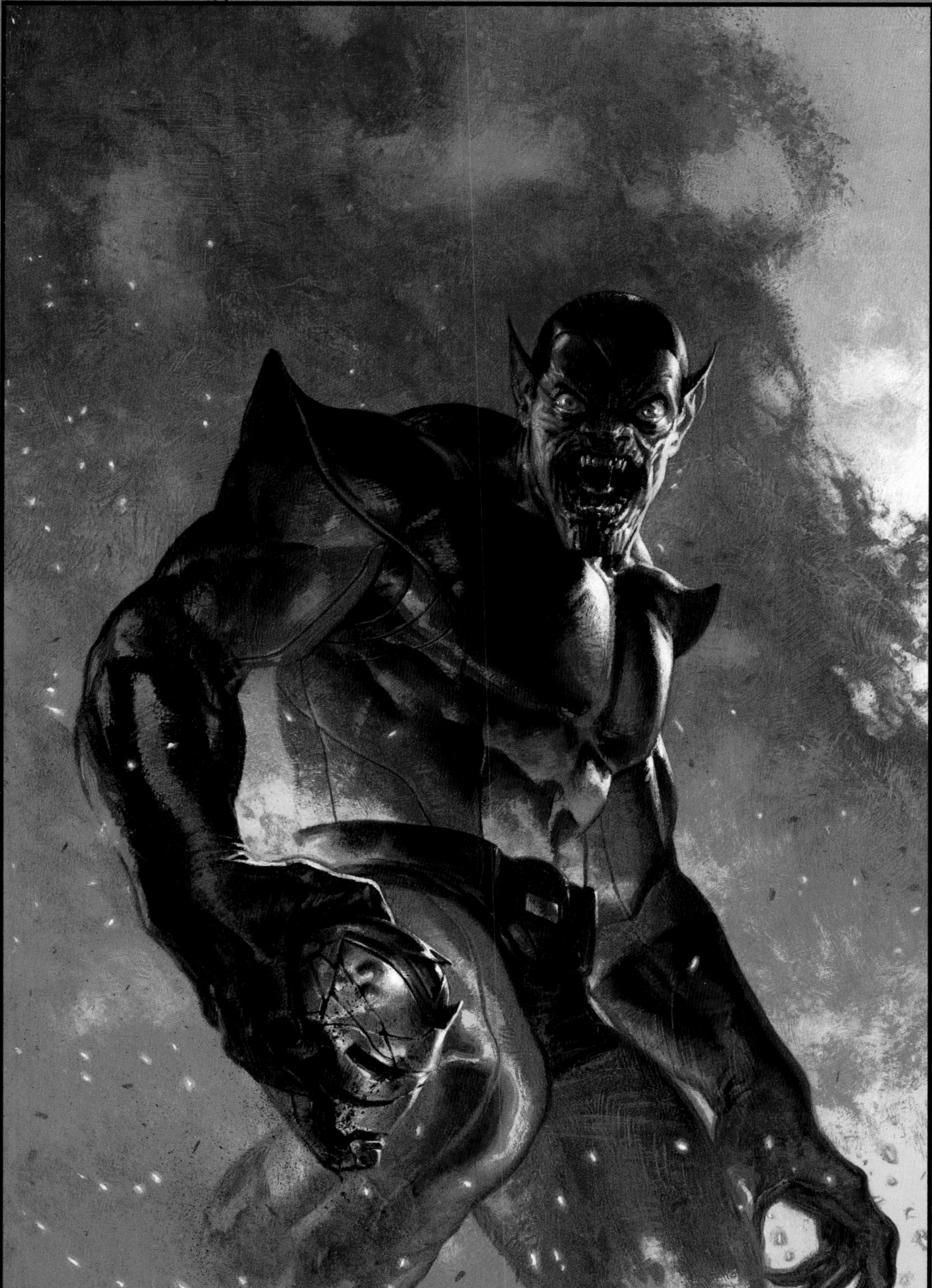

#1 variant by
Gabriele Dell'Otto

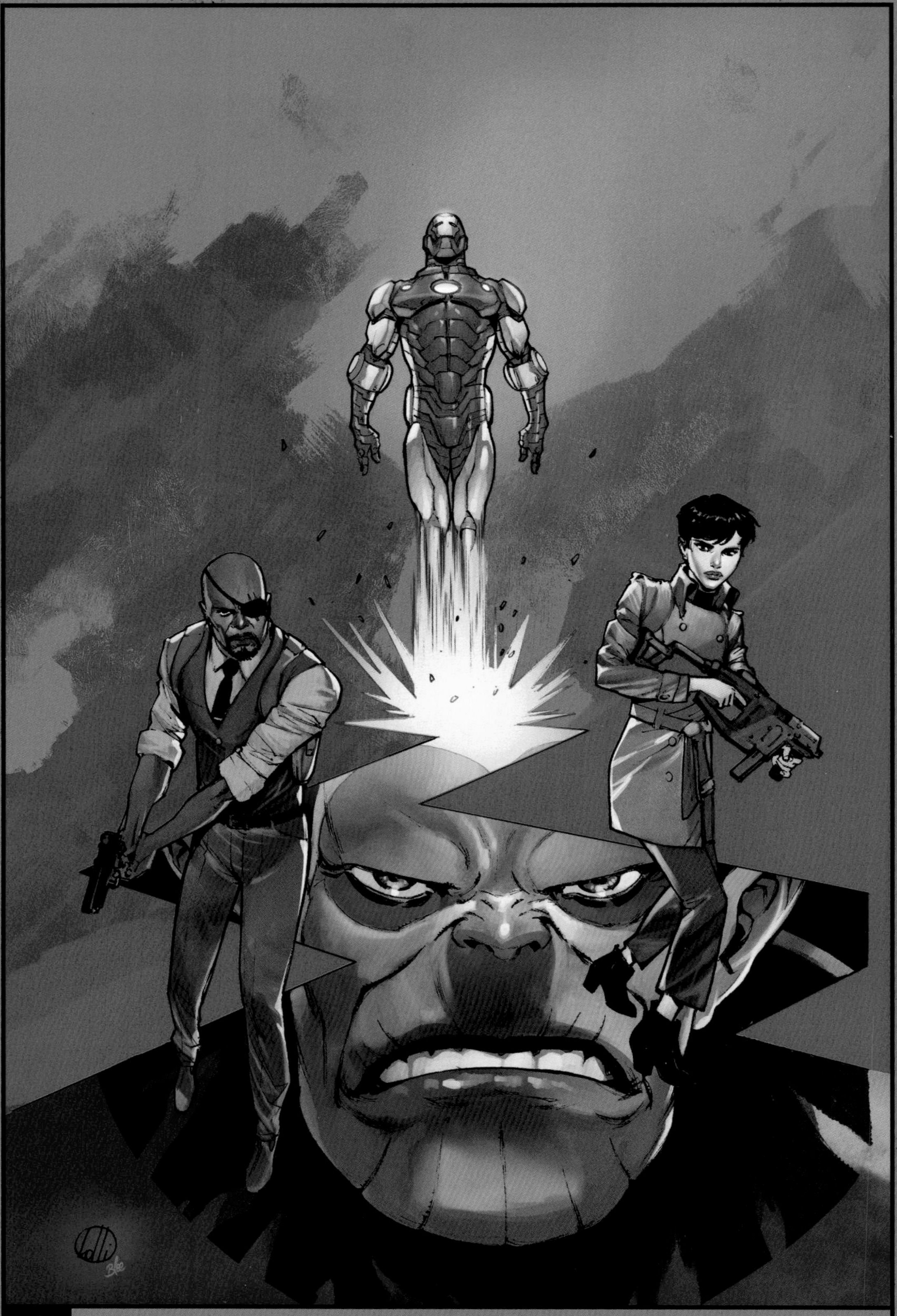

1

"Full of Surprises"

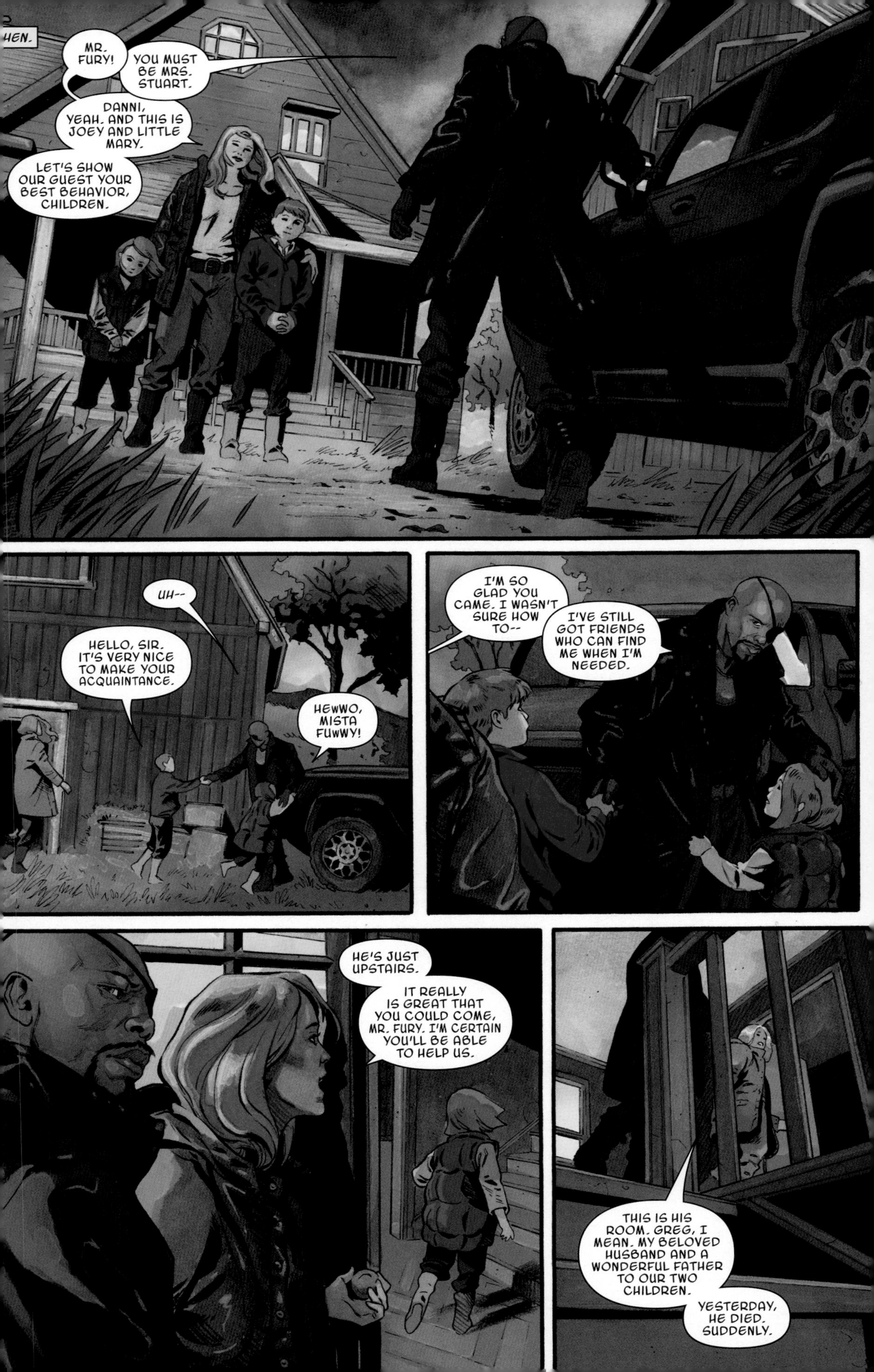
HEN.
MR. FURY!
YOU MUST BE MRS. STUART.
DANNI, YEAH. AND THIS IS JOEY AND LITTLE MARY.
LET'S SHOW OUR GUEST YOUR BEST BEHAVIOR, CHILDREN.
UH--
HELLO, SIR. IT'S VERY NICE TO MAKE YOUR ACQUAINTANCE.
HEWWO, MISTA FUWWY!
I'M SO GLAD YOU CAME. I WASN'T SURE HOW TO--
I'VE STILL GOT FRIENDS WHO CAN FIND ME WHEN I'M NEEDED.
HE'S JUST UPSTAIRS.
IT REALLY IS GREAT THAT YOU COULD COME, MR. FURY. I'M CERTAIN YOU'LL BE ABLE TO HELP US.
THIS IS HIS ROOM. GREG, I MEAN. MY BELOVED HUSBAND AND A WONDERFUL FATHER TO OUR TWO CHILDREN.
YESTERDAY, HE DIED. SUDDENLY.

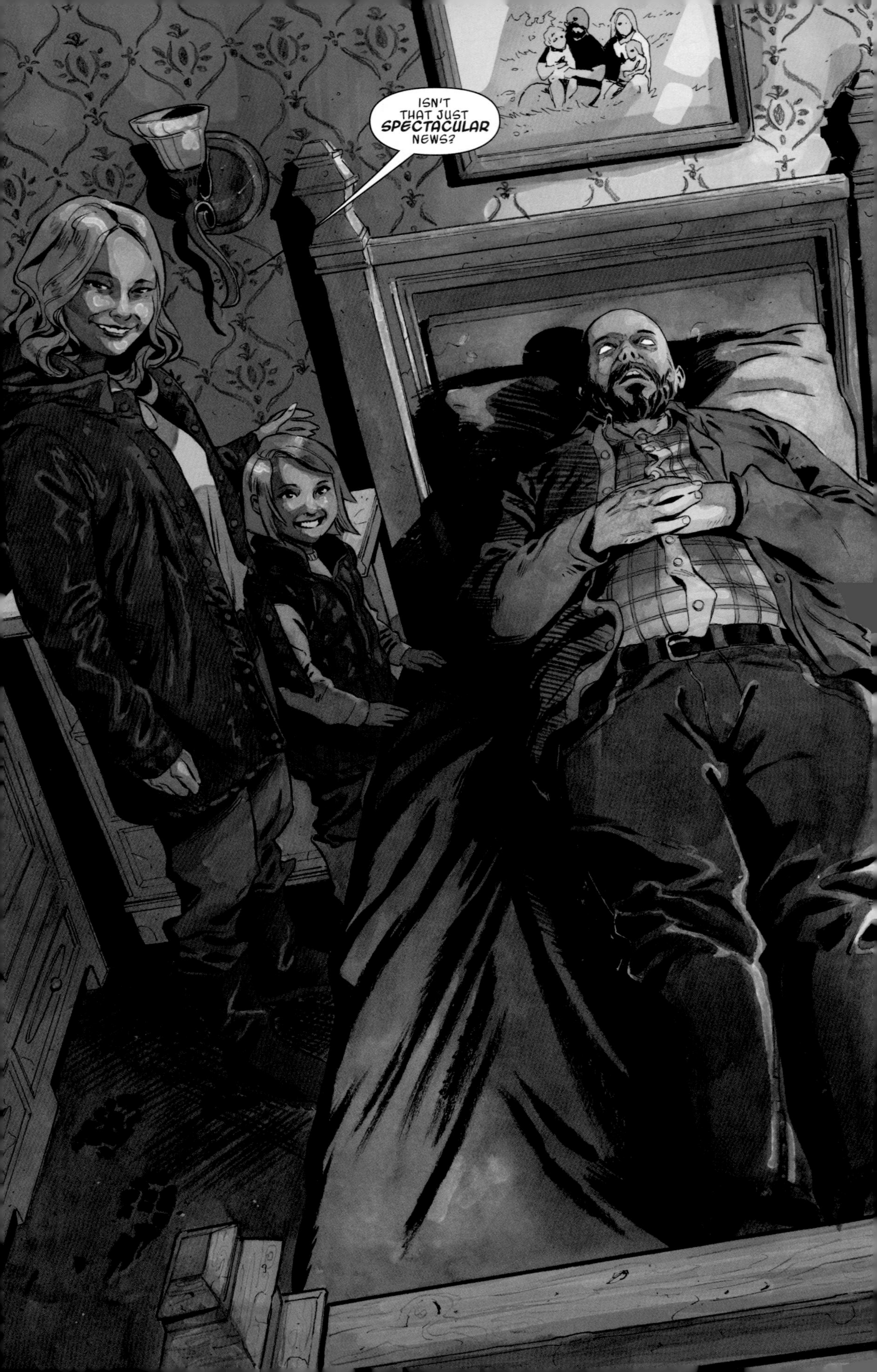
ISN'T THAT JUST SPECTACULAR NEWS?

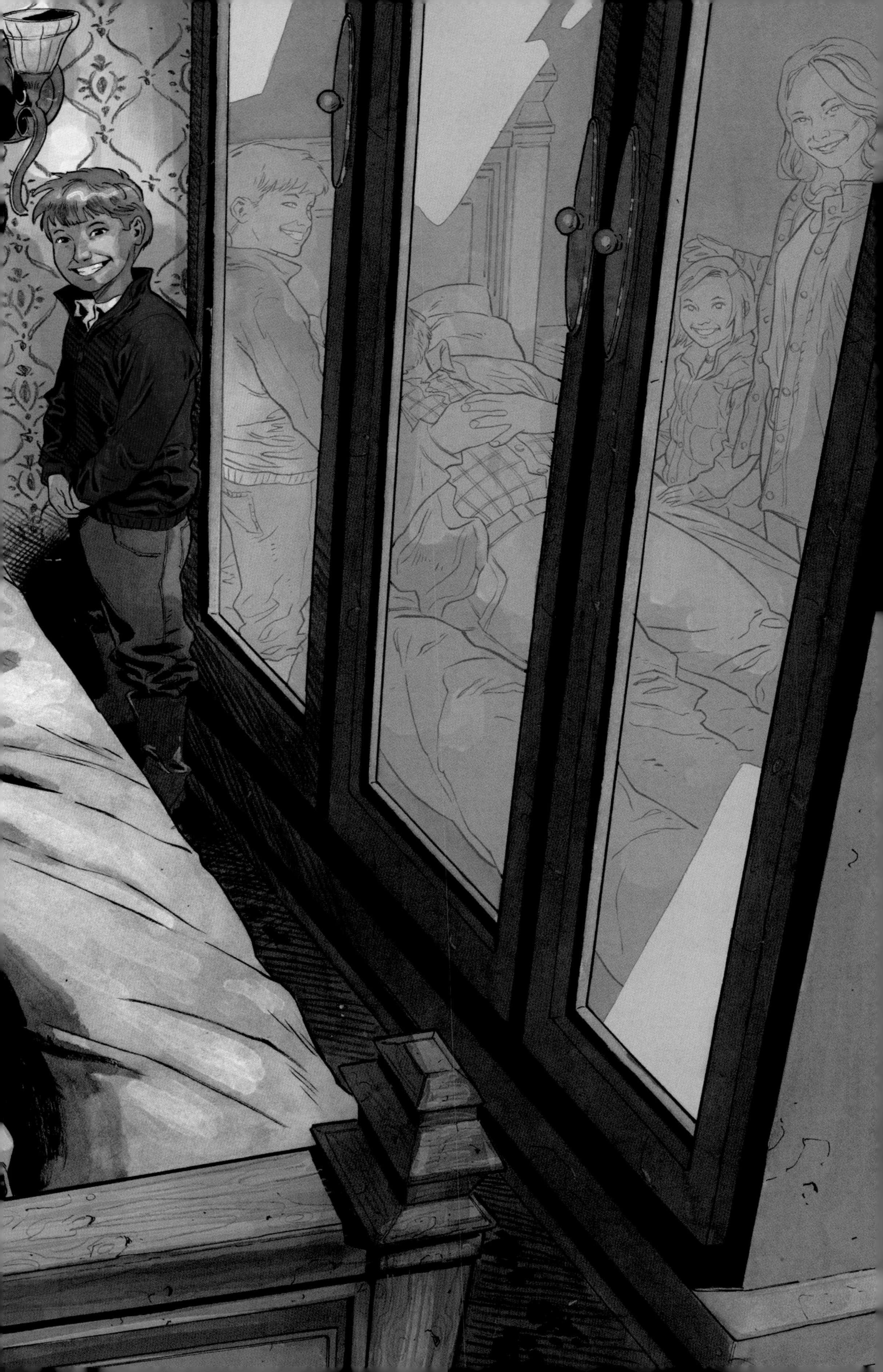

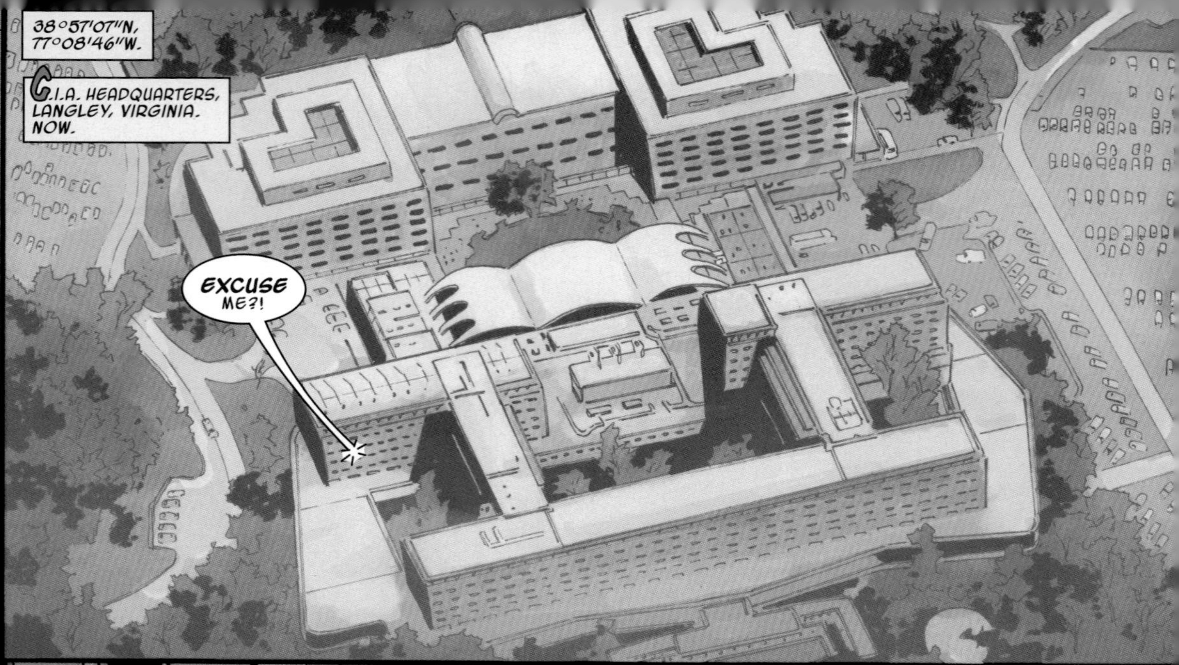
38°57'07"N, 77°08'46"W.
C.I.A. HEADQUARTERS, LANGLEY, VIRGINIA. NOW.
EXCUSE ME?!

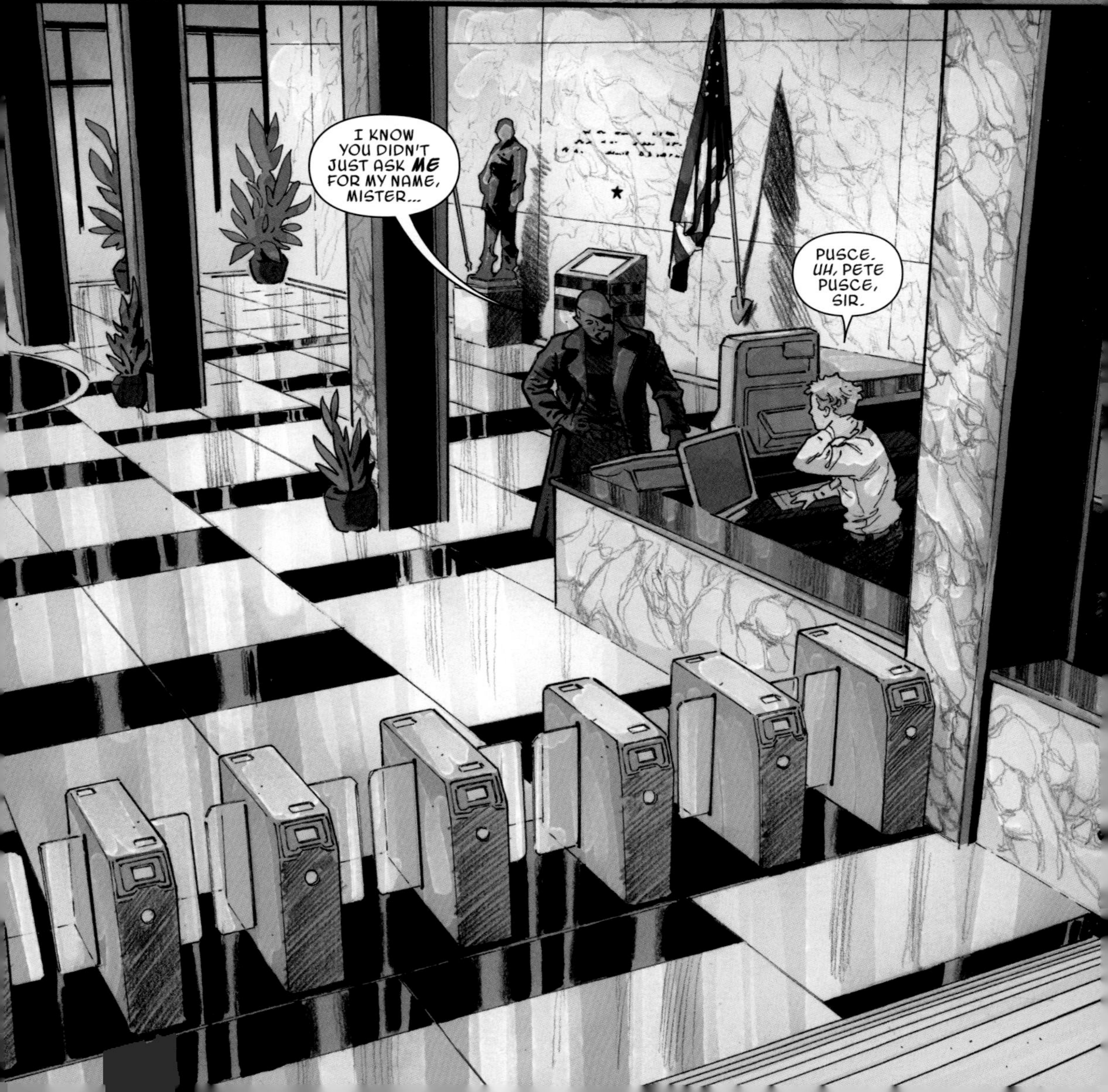
I KNOW YOU DIDN'T JUST ASK ME FOR MY NAME, MISTER...
PUSCE. UH, PETE PUSCE, SIR.

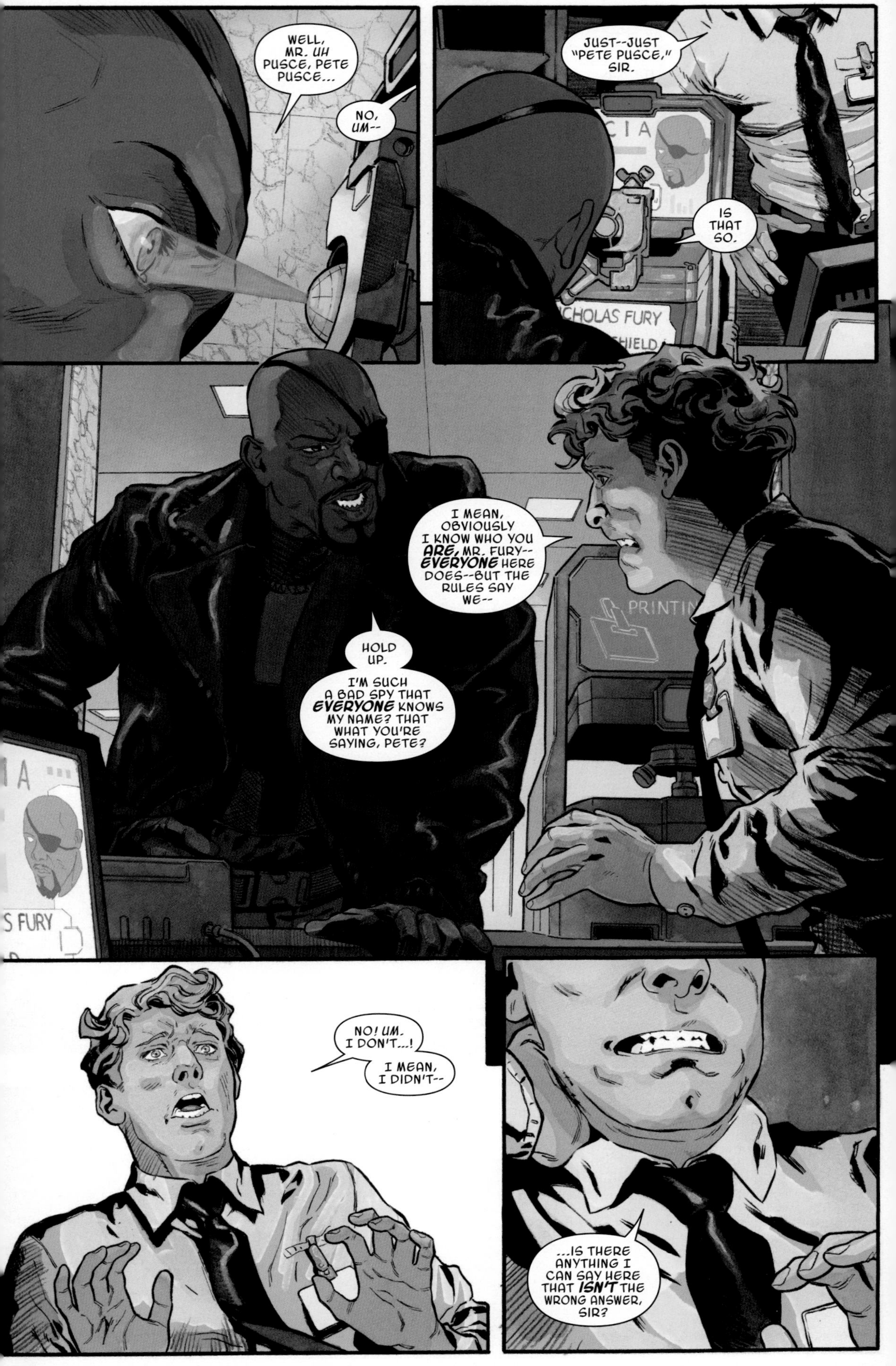
WELL, MR. UH PUSCE, PETE PUSCE...
NO, UM--
JUST--JUST "PETE PUSCE," SIR.
CIA
IS THAT SO.
NICHOLAS FURY
I MEAN, OBVIOUSLY I KNOW WHO YOU ARE, MR. FURY-- EVERYONE HERE DOES--BUT THE RULES SAY WE--
PRINTIN
HOLD UP.
I'M SUCH A BAD SPY THAT EVERYONE KNOWS MY NAME? THAT WHAT YOU'RE SAYING, PETE?
S FURY
NO! UM. I DON'T...!
I MEAN, I DIDN'T--
...IS THERE ANYTHING I CAN SAY HERE THAT ISN'T THE WRONG ANSWER, SIR?

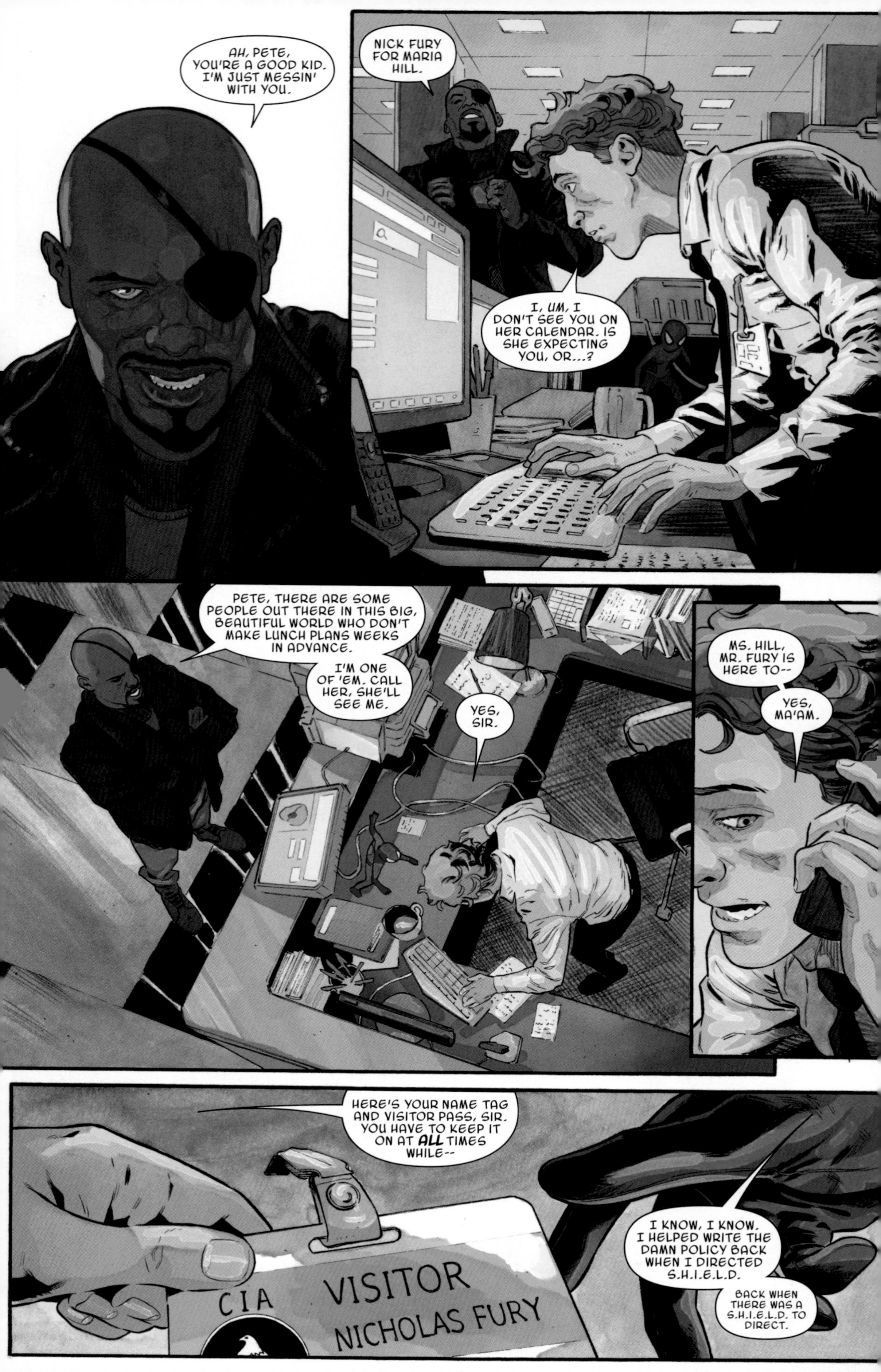
AH, PETE, YOU'RE A GOOD KID. I'M JUST MESSIN' WITH YOU.
NICK FURY FOR MARIA HILL.
I, UM, I DON'T SEE YOU ON HER CALENDAR. IS SHE EXPECTING YOU, OR...?
PETE, THERE ARE SOME PEOPLE OUT THERE IN THIS BIG, BEAUTIFUL WORLD WHO DON'T MAKE LUNCH PLANS WEEKS IN ADVANCE.
I'M ONE OF 'EM. CALL HER, SHE'LL SEE ME.
YES, SIR.
MS. HILL, MR. FURY IS HERE TO--
YES, MA'AM.
HERE'S YOUR NAME TAG AND VISITOR PASS, SIR. YOU HAVE TO KEEP IT ON AT ALL TIMES WHILE--
I KNOW, I KNOW. I HELPED WRITE THE DAMN POLICY BACK WHEN I DIRECTED S.H.I.E.L.D.
BACK WHEN THERE WAS A S.H.I.E.L.D. TO DIRECT.
CIA
VISITOR
NICHOLAS FURY

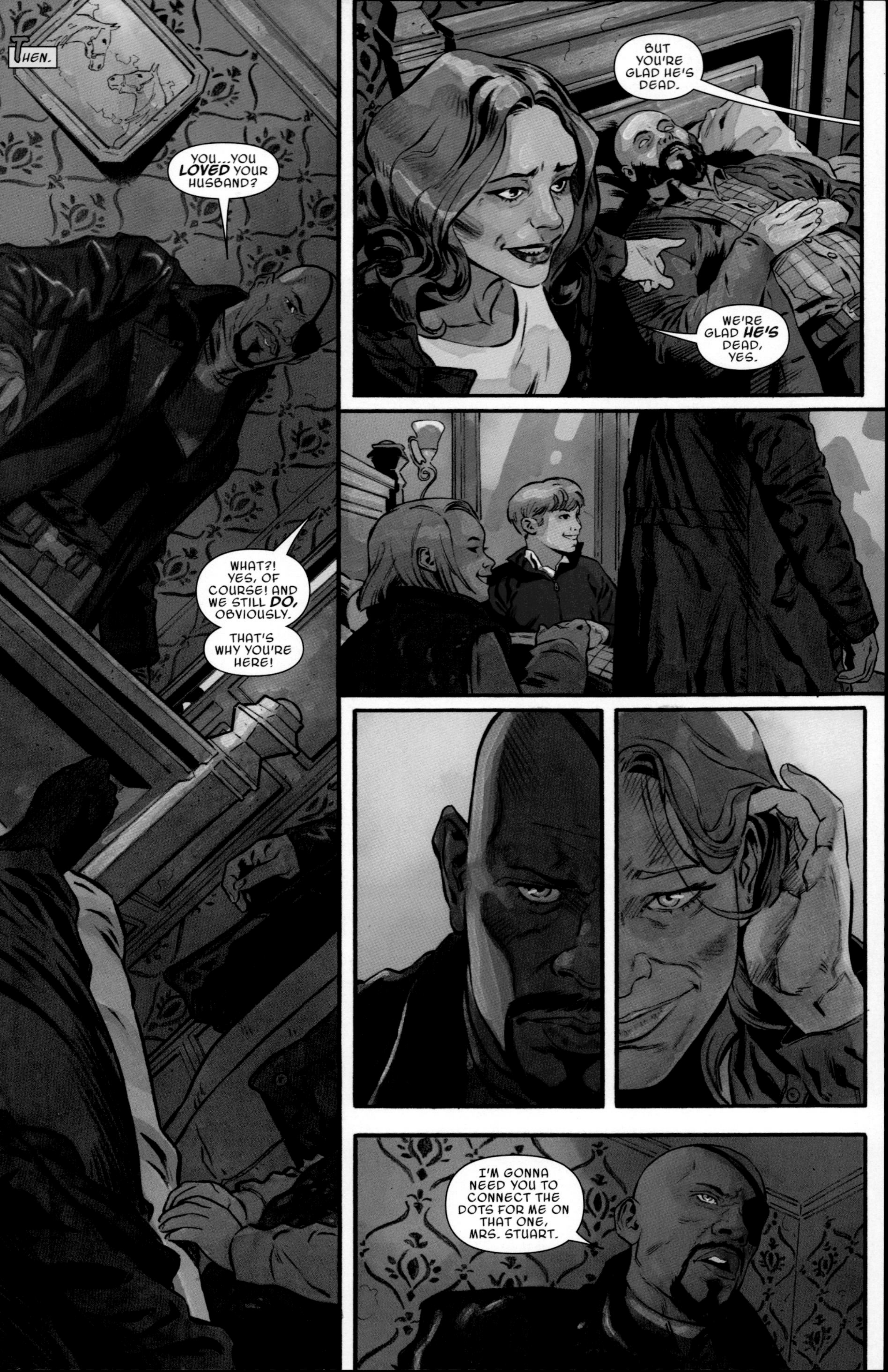
THEN.
YOU...YOU LOVED YOUR HUSBAND?
WHAT?! YES, OF COURSE! AND WE STILL DO, OBVIOUSLY.
THAT'S WHY YOU'RE HERE!
BUT YOU'RE GLAD HE'S DEAD.
WE'RE GLAD HE'S DEAD, YES.
I'M GONNA NEED YOU TO CONNECT THE DOTS FOR ME ON THAT ONE, MRS. STUART.

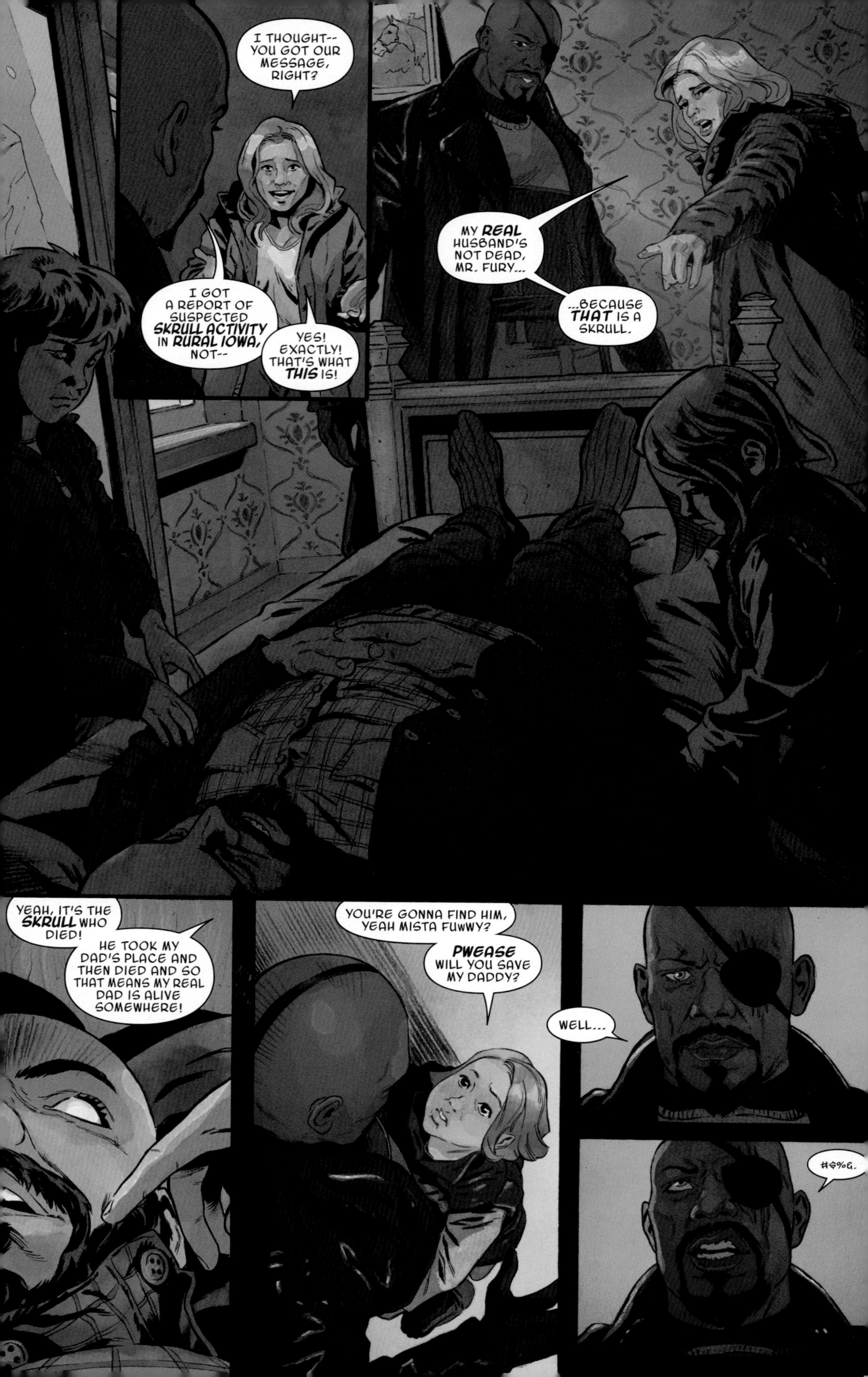
I THOUGHT-- YOU GOT OUR MESSAGE, RIGHT?
I GOT A REPORT OF SUSPECTED SKRULL ACTIVITY IN RURAL IOWA, NOT--
YES! EXACTLY! THAT'S WHAT THIS IS!
MY REAL HUSBAND'S NOT DEAD, MR. FURY...
...BECAUSE THAT IS A SKRULL.
YEAH, IT'S THE SKRULL WHO DIED!
HE TOOK MY DAD'S PLACE AND THEN DIED AND SO THAT MEANS MY REAL DAD IS ALIVE SOMEWHERE!
YOU'RE GONNA FIND HIM, YEAH MISTA FUWWY?
PWEASE WILL YOU SAVE MY DADDY?
WELL...
#$%&.

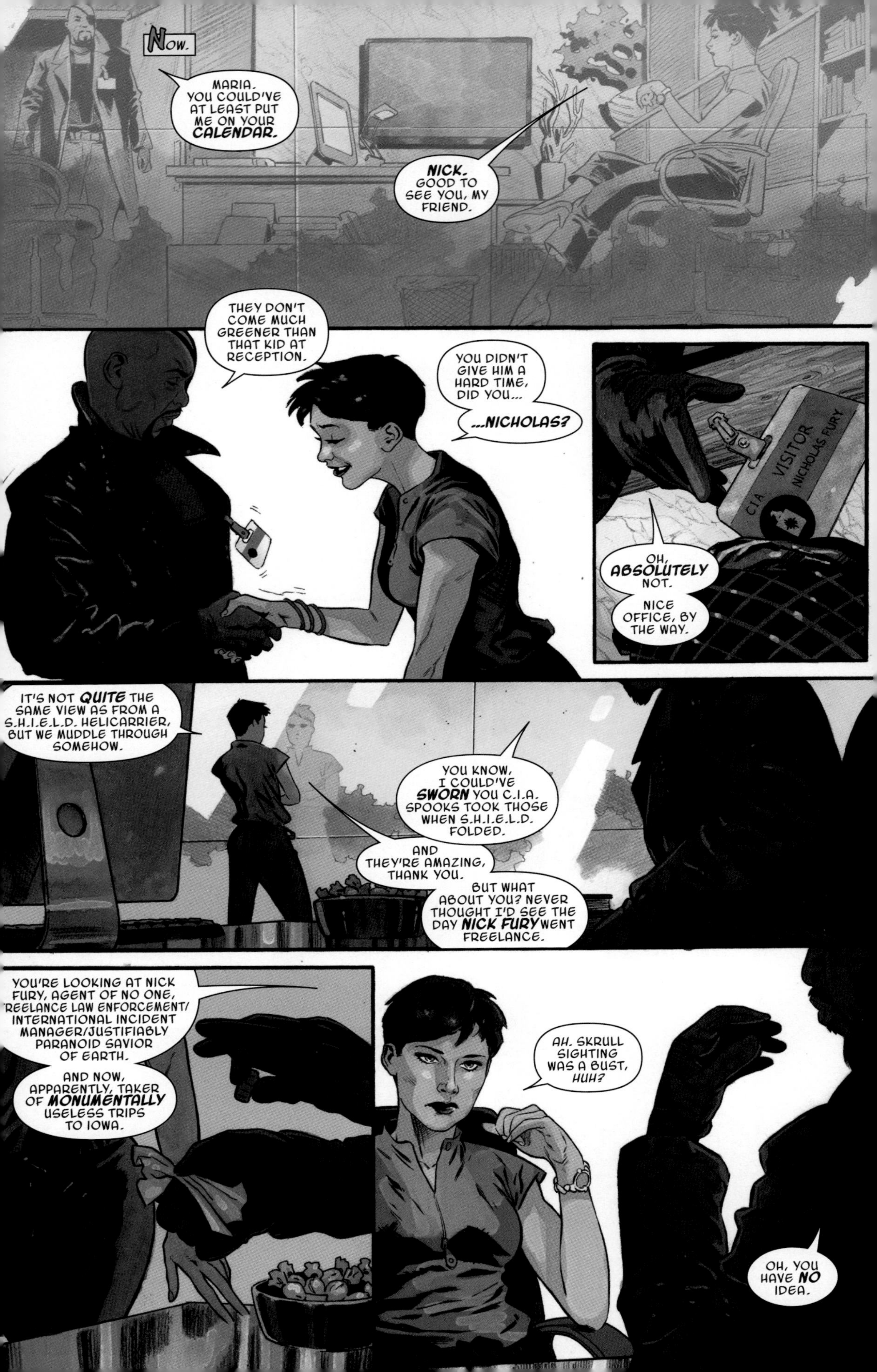
NOW.
MARIA. YOU COULD'VE AT LEAST PUT ME ON YOUR CALENDAR.
NICK. GOOD TO SEE YOU, MY FRIEND.
THEY DON'T COME MUCH GREENER THAN THAT KID AT RECEPTION.
YOU DIDN'T GIVE HIM A HARD TIME, DID YOU...
...NICHOLAS?
VISITOR
NICHOLAS FURY
CIA
OH, ABSOLUTELY NOT.
NICE OFFICE, BY THE WAY.
IT'S NOT QUITE THE SAME VIEW AS FROM A S.H.I.E.L.D. HELICARRIER, BUT WE MUDDLE THROUGH SOMEHOW.
YOU KNOW, I COULD'VE SWORN YOU C.I.A. SPOOKS TOOK THOSE WHEN S.H.I.E.L.D. FOLDED.
AND THEY'RE AMAZING, THANK YOU.
BUT WHAT ABOUT YOU? NEVER THOUGHT I'D SEE THE DAY NICK FURY WENT FREELANCE.
YOU'RE LOOKING AT NICK FURY, AGENT OF NO ONE, FREELANCE LAW ENFORCEMENT/ INTERNATIONAL INCIDENT MANAGER/JUSTIFIABLY PARANOID SAVIOR OF EARTH.
AND NOW, APPARENTLY, TAKER OF MONUMENTALLY USELESS TRIPS TO IOWA.
AH. SKRULL SIGHTING WAS A BUST, HUH?
OH, YOU HAVE NO IDEA.

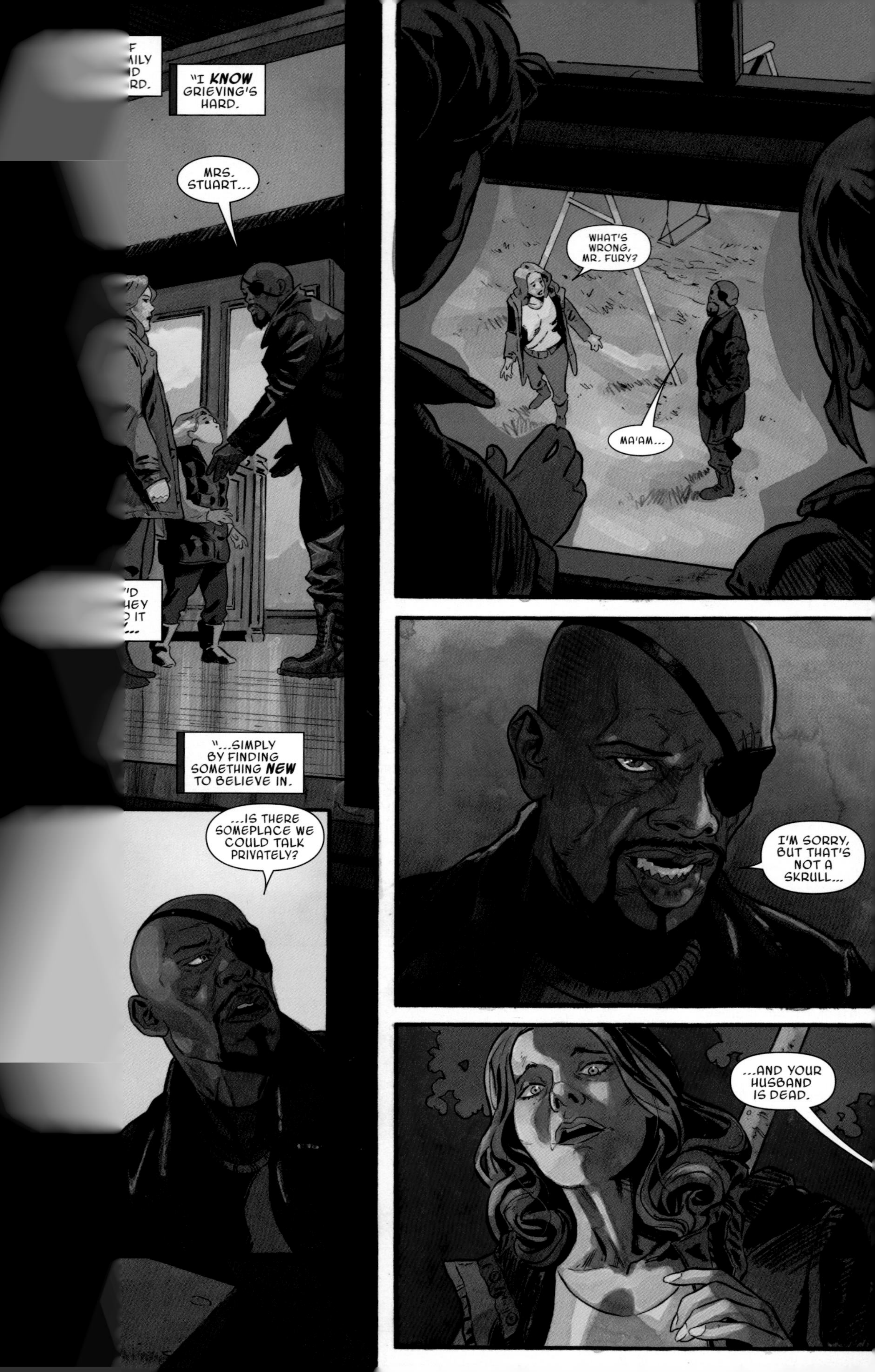
"I KNOW GRIEVING'S HARD.
MRS. STUART...
"...SIMPLY BY FINDING SOMETHING NEW TO BELIEVE IN.
...IS THERE SOMEPLACE WE COULD TALK PRIVATELY?
WHAT'S WRONG, MR. FURY?
MA'AM...
I'M SORRY, BUT THAT'S NOT A SKRULL...
...AND YOUR HUSBAND IS DEAD.

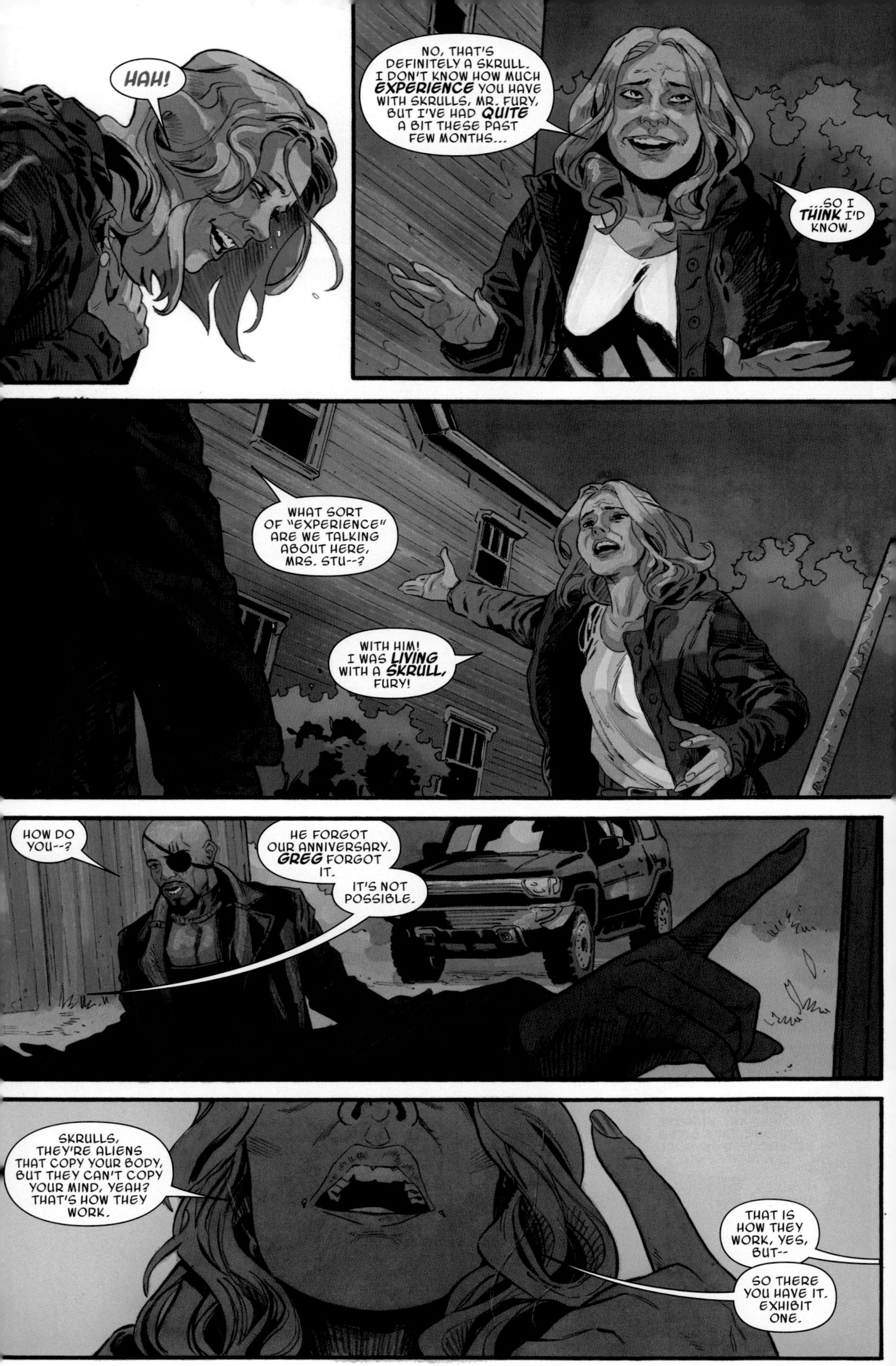
HAH!
NO, THAT'S DEFINITELY A SKRULL. I DON'T KNOW HOW MUCH EXPERIENCE YOU HAVE WITH SKRULLS, MR. FURY, BUT I'VE HAD QUITE A BIT THESE PAST FEW MONTHS...
...SO I THINK I'D KNOW.
WHAT SORT OF "EXPERIENCE" ARE WE TALKING ABOUT HERE, MRS. STU--?
WITH HIM! I WAS LIVING WITH A SKRULL, FURY!
HOW DO YOU--?
HE FORGOT OUR ANNIVERSARY. GREG FORGOT IT.
IT'S NOT POSSIBLE.
SKRULLS, THEY'RE ALIENS THAT COPY YOUR BODY, BUT THEY CAN'T COPY YOUR MIND, YEAH? THAT'S HOW THEY WORK.
THAT IS HOW THEY WORK, YES, BUT--
SO THERE YOU HAVE IT. EXHIBIT ONE.

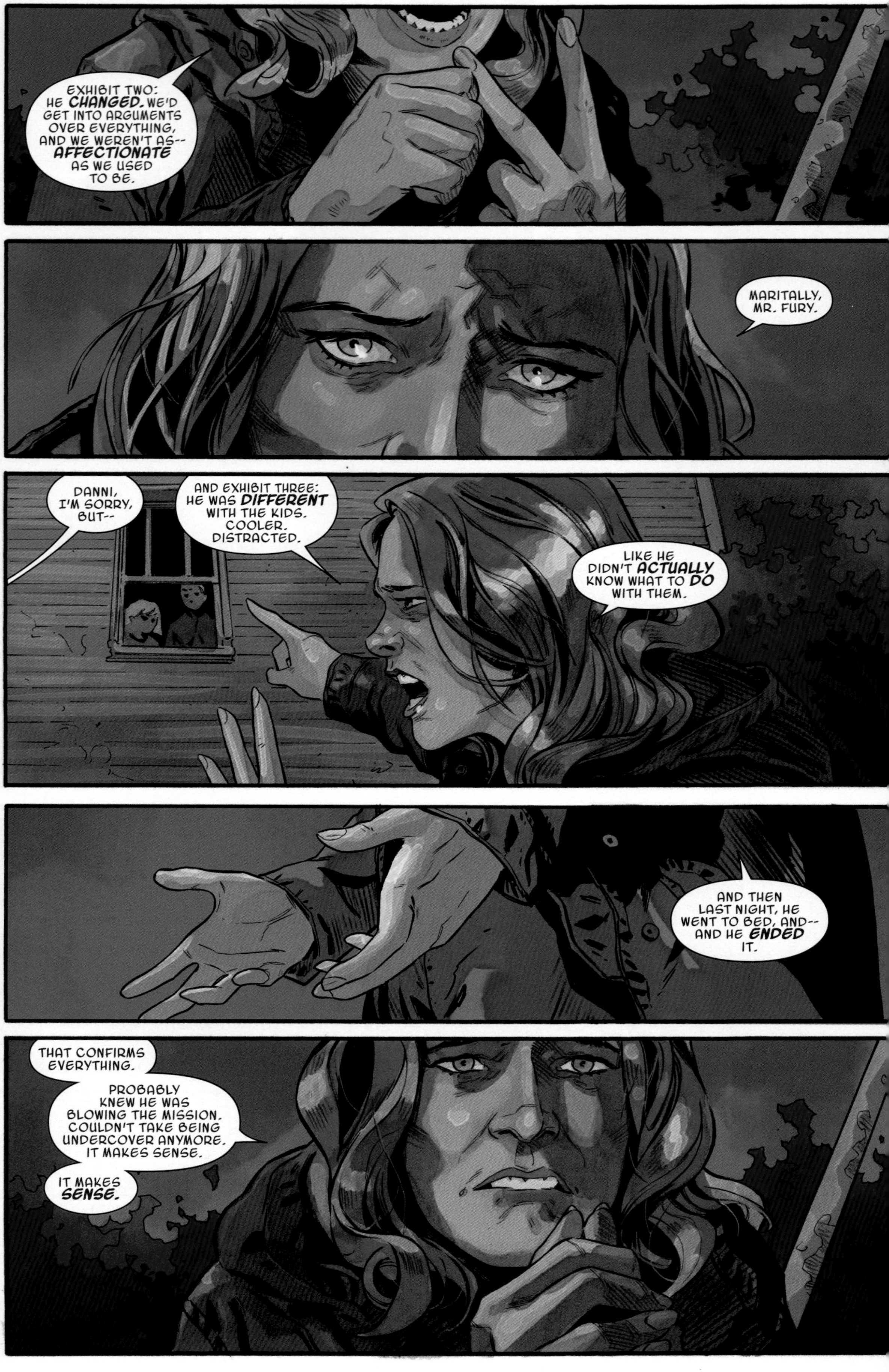
EXHIBIT TWO: HE CHANGED. WE'D GET INTO ARGUMENTS OVER EVERYTHING, AND WE WEREN'T AS-- AFFECTIONATE AS WE USED TO BE.
MARITALLY, MR. FURY.
AND EXHIBIT THREE: HE WAS DIFFERENT WITH THE KIDS. COOLER. DISTRACTED.
DANNI, I'M SORRY, BUT--
LIKE HE DIDN'T ACTUALLY KNOW WHAT TO DO WITH THEM.
AND THEN LAST NIGHT, HE WENT TO BED, AND-- AND HE ENDED IT.
THAT CONFIRMS EVERYTHING.
PROBABLY KNEW HE WAS BLOWING THE MISSION. COULDN'T TAKE BEING UNDERCOVER ANYMORE. IT MAKES SENSE.
IT MAKES SENSE.

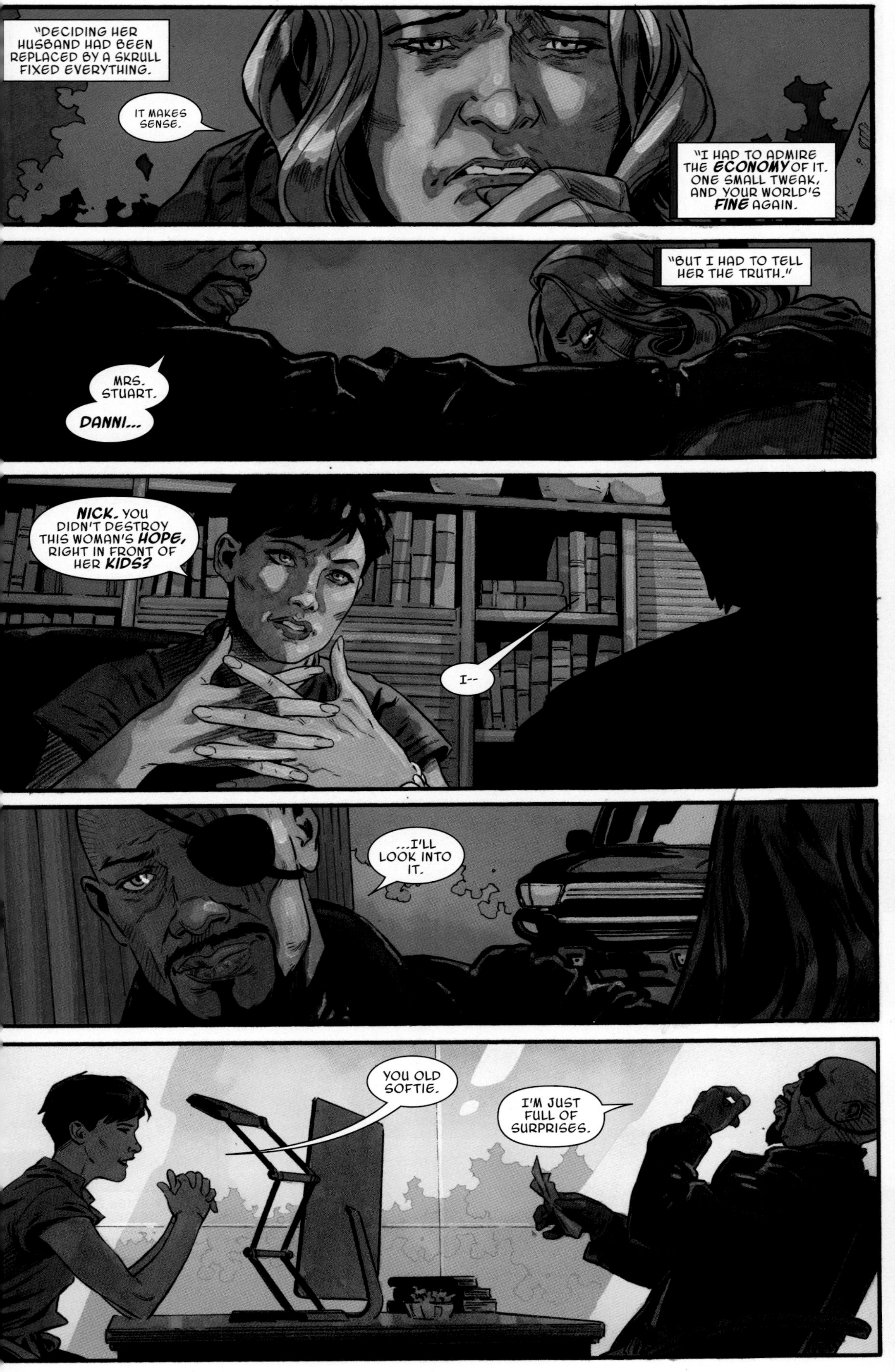
"DECIDING HER HUSBAND HAD BEEN REPLACED BY A SKRULL FIXED EVERYTHING.
IT MAKES SENSE.
"I HAD TO ADMIRE THE ECONOMY OF IT. ONE SMALL TWEAK, AND YOUR WORLD'S FINE AGAIN.
"BUT I HAD TO TELL HER THE TRUTH."
MRS. STUART.
DANNI...
NICK. YOU DIDN'T DESTROY THIS WOMAN'S HOPE, RIGHT IN FRONT OF HER KIDS?
I--
...I'LL LOOK INTO IT.
YOU OLD SOFTIE.
I'M JUST FULL OF SURPRISES.

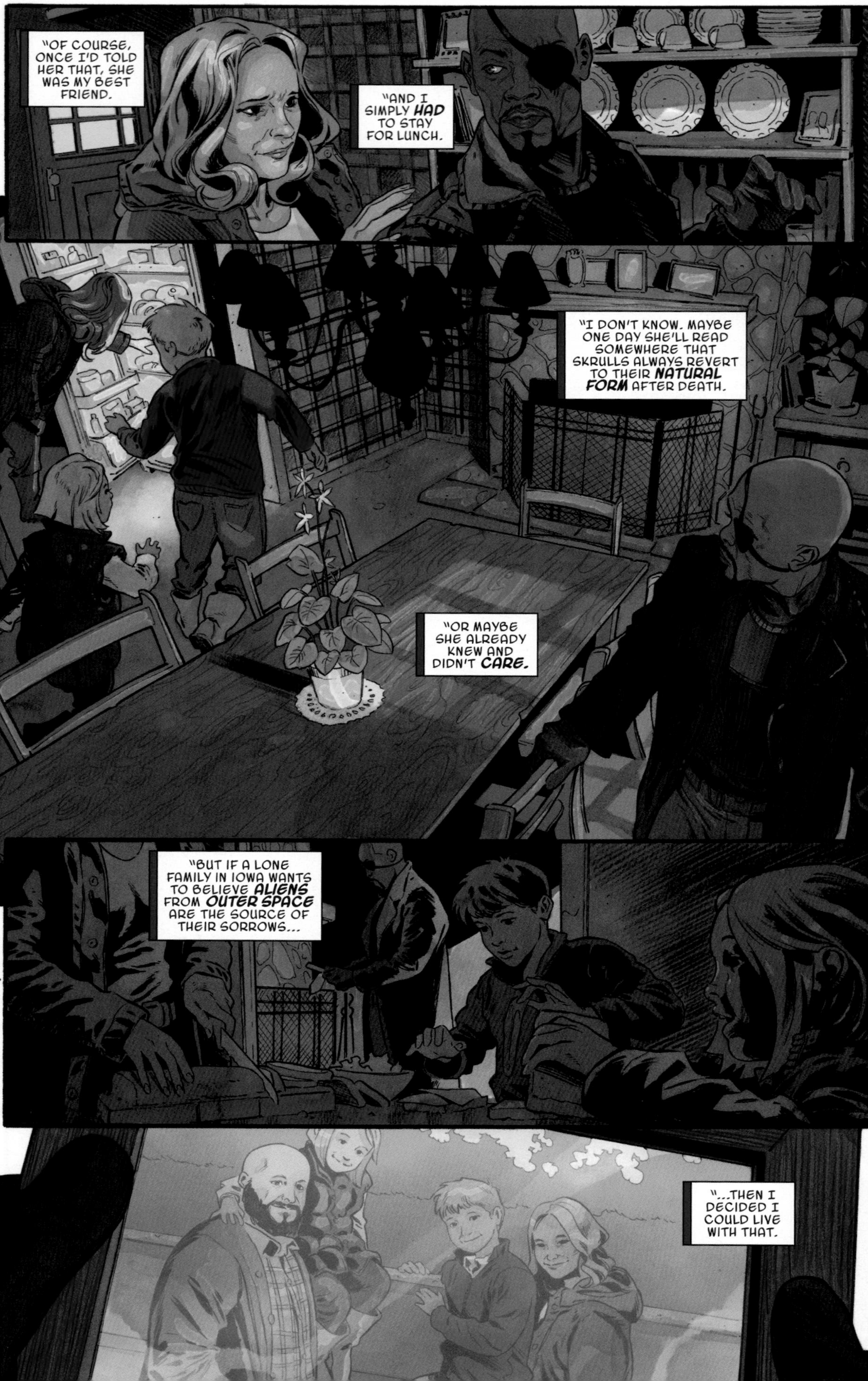
"OF COURSE, ONCE I'D TOLD HER THAT, SHE WAS MY BEST FRIEND.
"AND I SIMPLY **HAD** TO STAY FOR LUNCH.
"I DON'T KNOW. MAYBE ONE DAY SHE'LL READ SOMEWHERE THAT SKRULLS ALWAYS REVERT TO THEIR **NATURAL FORM** AFTER DEATH.
"OR MAYBE SHE ALREADY KNEW AND DIDN'T **CARE.**
"BUT IF A LONE FAMILY IN IOWA WANTS TO BELIEVE **ALIENS** FROM **OUTER SPACE** ARE THE SOURCE OF THEIR SORROWS...
"...THEN I DECIDED I COULD LIVE WITH THAT.

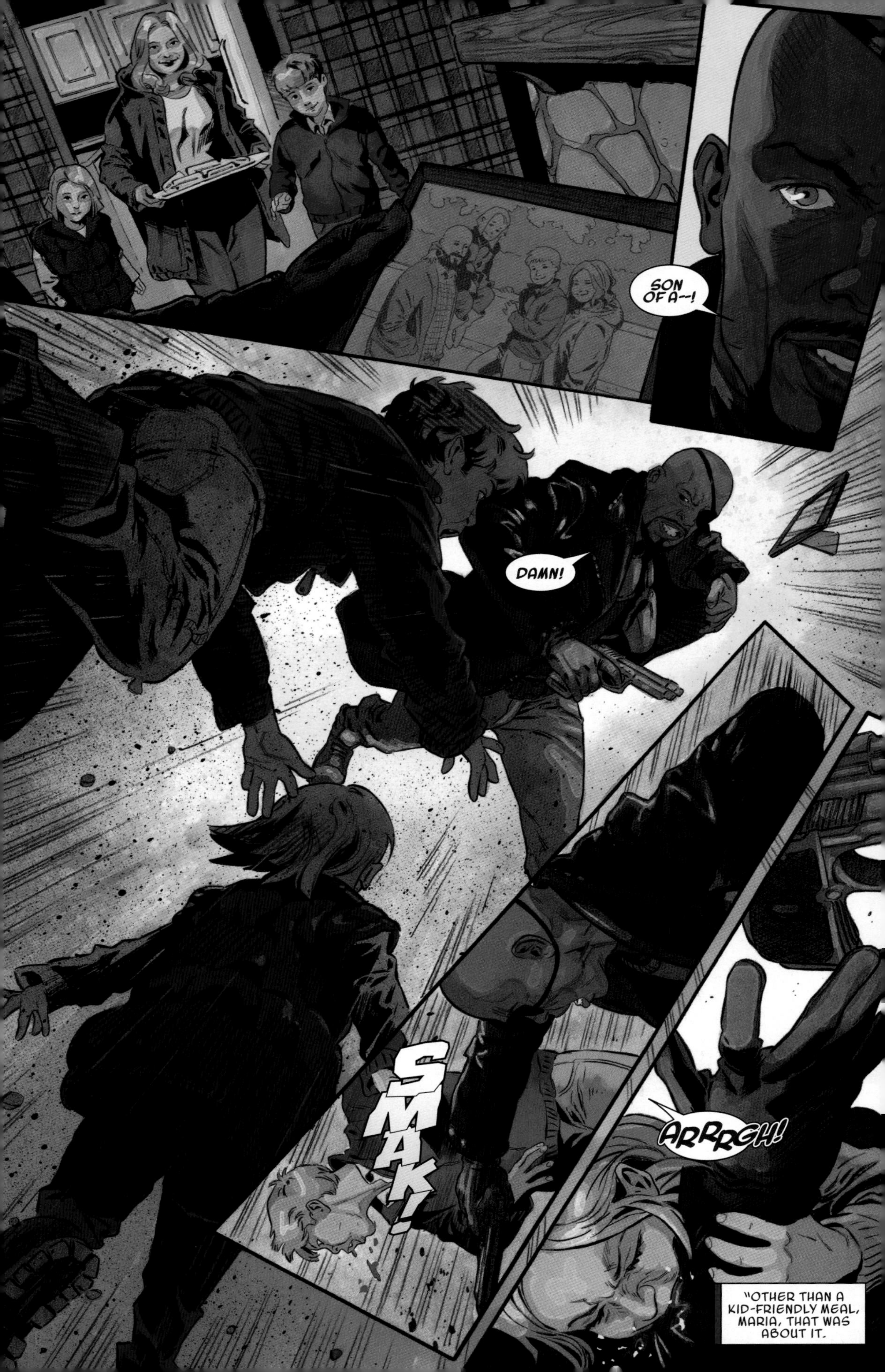
SON OF A--!
DAMN!
SMAK!
ARRRGH!
"OTHER THAN A KID-FRIENDLY MEAL, MARIA, THAT WAS ABOUT IT.

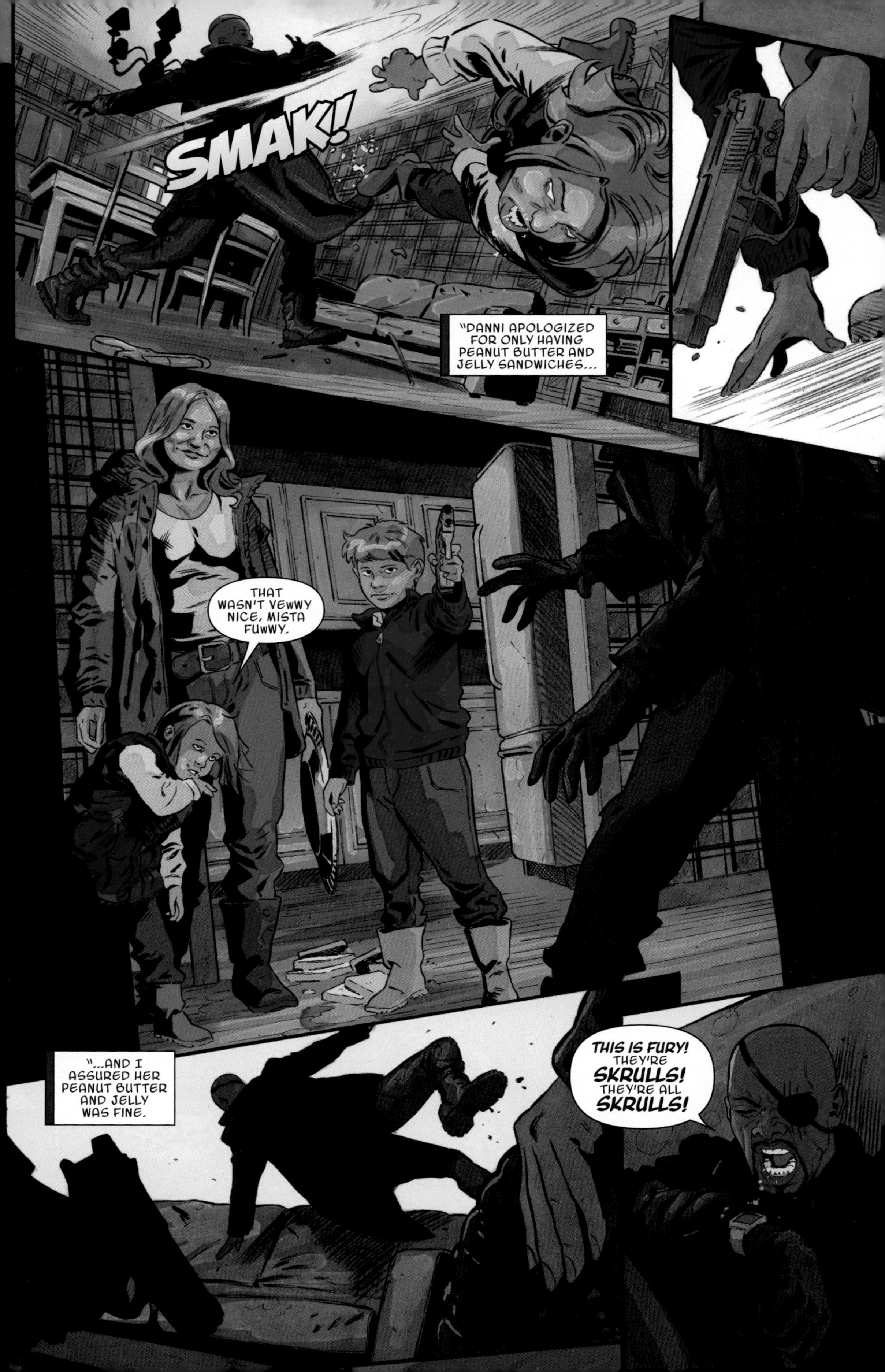
SMAK!
"DANNI APOLOGIZED FOR ONLY HAVING PEANUT BUTTER AND JELLY SANDWICHES...
THAT WASN'T VEWWY NICE, MISTA FUWWY.
"...AND I ASSURED HER PEANUT BUTTER AND JELLY WAS FINE.
THIS IS FURY! THEY'RE SKRULLS! THEY'RE ALL SKRULLS!

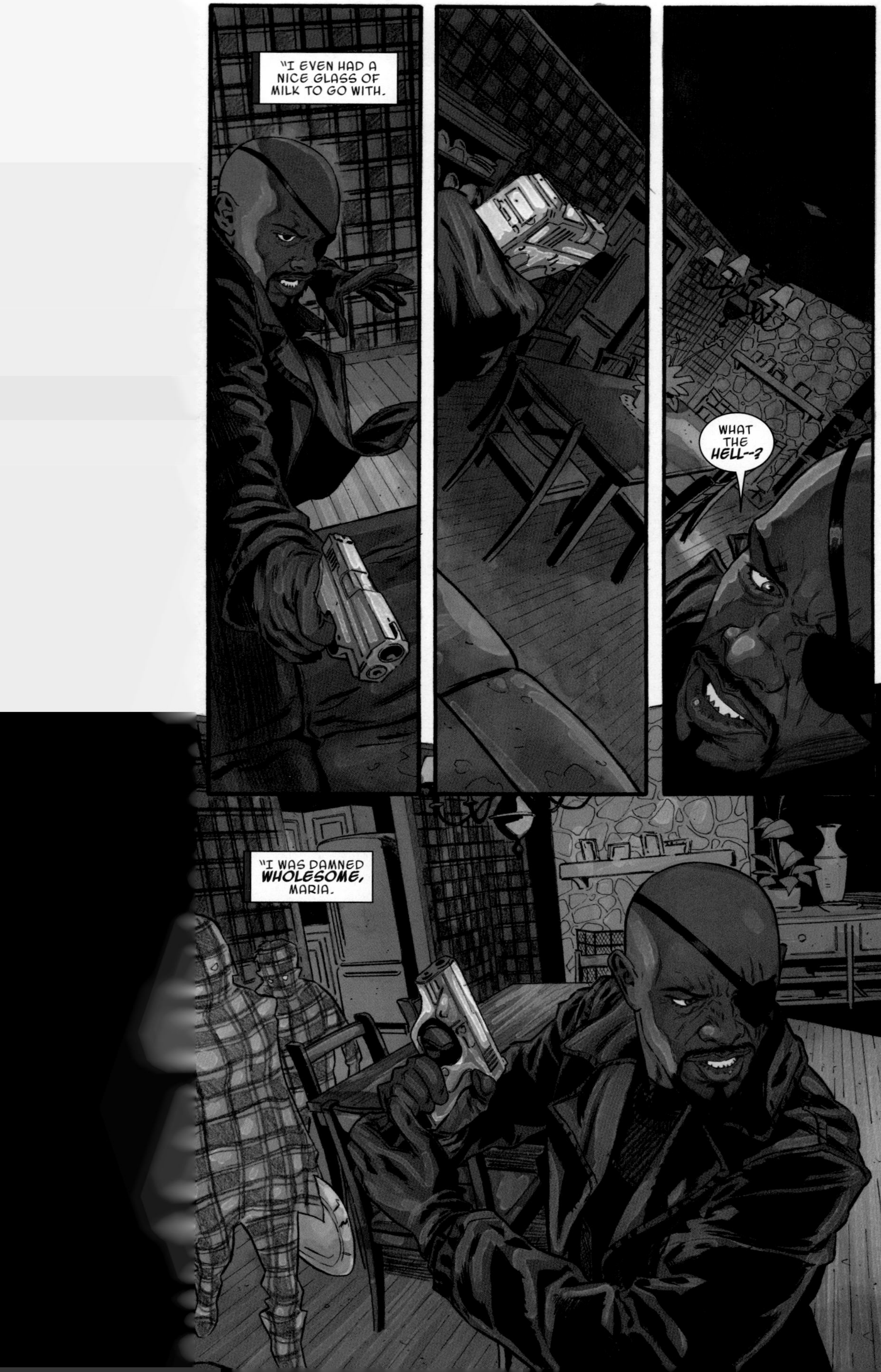
"I EVEN HAD A NICE GLASS OF MILK TO GO WITH.
WHAT THE HELL--?
"I WAS DAMNED WHOLESOME, MARIA.

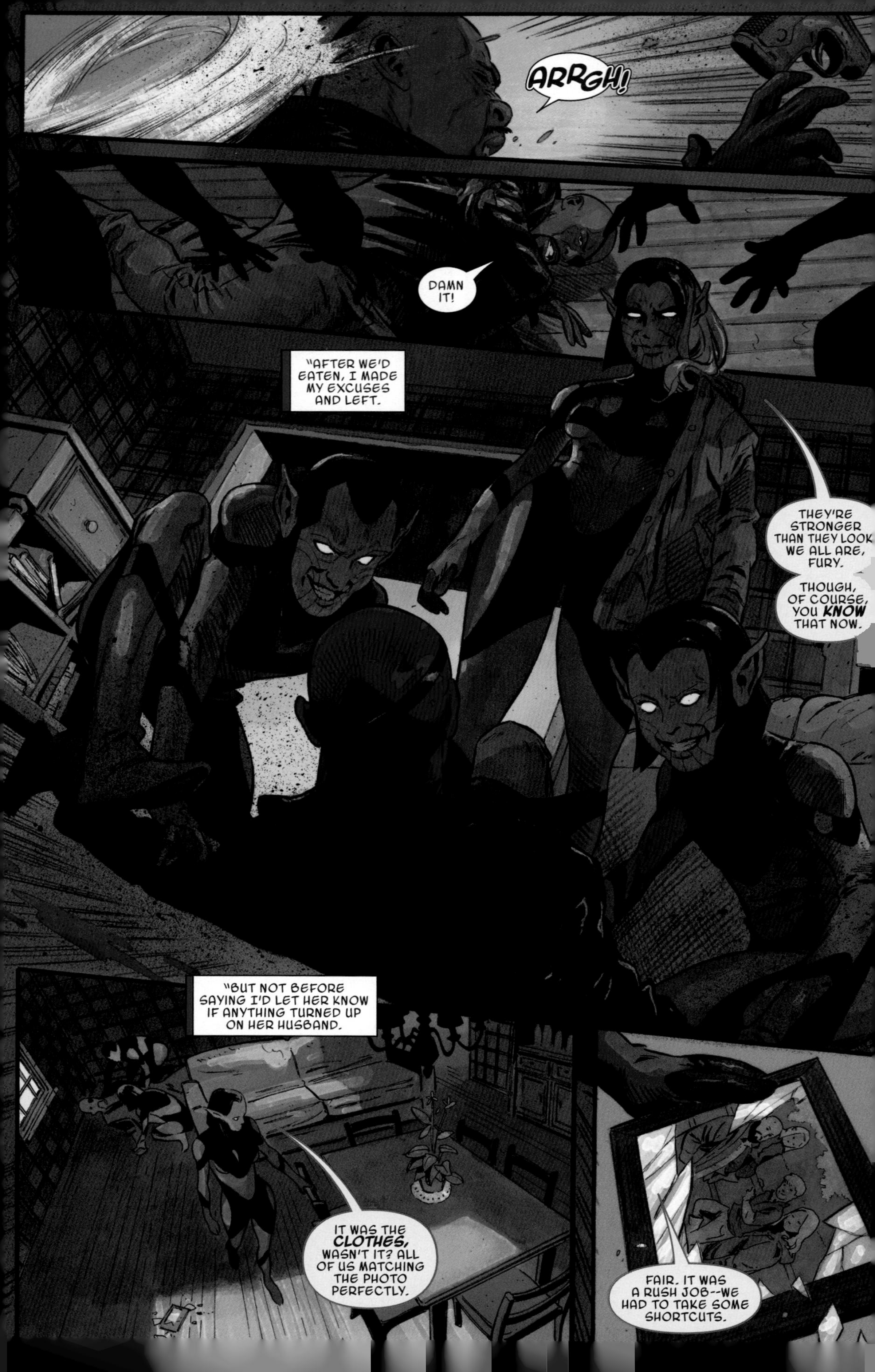
ARRGH!
DAMN IT!
"AFTER WE'D EATEN, I MADE MY EXCUSES AND LEFT.
THEY'RE STRONGER THAN THEY LOOK WE ALL ARE, FURY.
THOUGH, OF COURSE, YOU KNOW THAT NOW.
"BUT NOT BEFORE SAYING I'D LET HER KNOW IF ANYTHING TURNED UP ON HER HUSBAND.
IT WAS THE CLOTHES, WASN'T IT? ALL OF US MATCHING THE PHOTO PERFECTLY.
FAIR. IT WAS A RUSH JOB--WE HAD TO TAKE SOME SHORTCUTS.

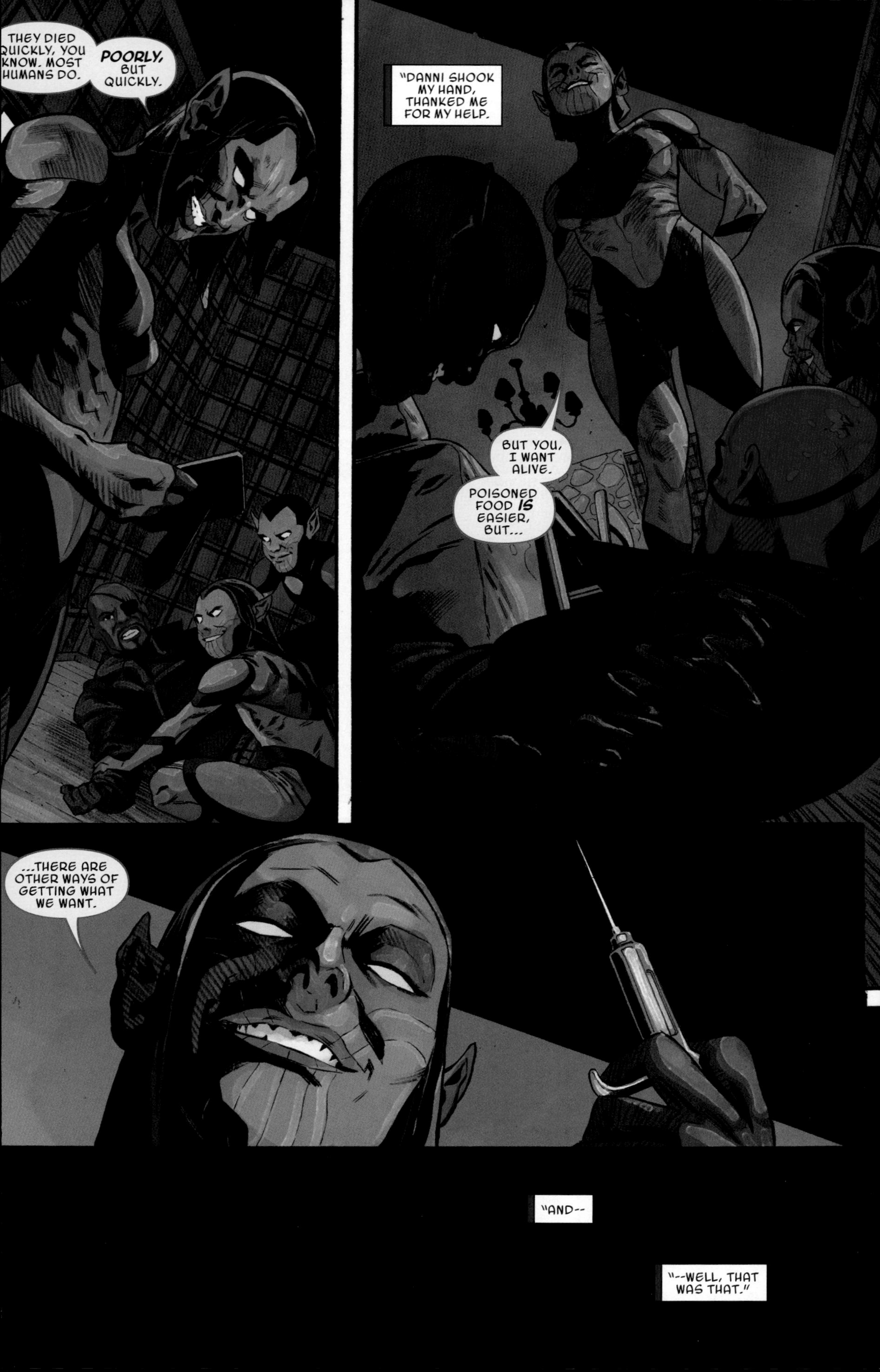
THEY DIED QUICKLY, YOU KNOW. MOST HUMANS DO.
POORLY, BUT QUICKLY.
"DANNI SHOOK MY HAND, THANKED ME FOR MY HELP.
BUT YOU, I WANT ALIVE.
POISONED FOOD IS EASIER, BUT...
...THERE ARE OTHER WAYS OF GETTING WHAT WE WANT.
"AND--
"--WELL, THAT WAS THAT."

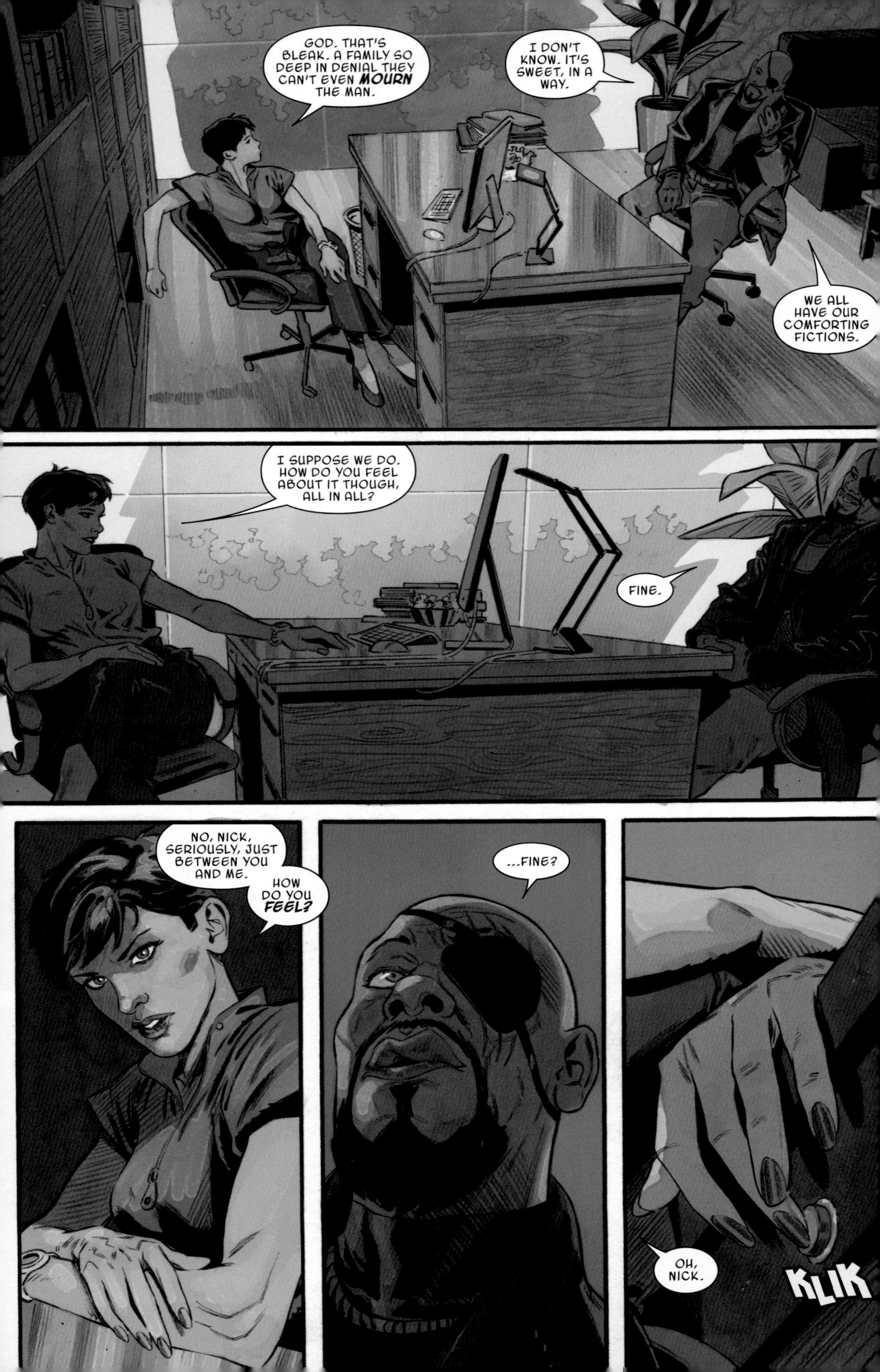
GOD. THAT'S BLEAK. A FAMILY SO DEEP IN DENIAL THEY CAN'T EVEN MOURN THE MAN.
I DON'T KNOW. IT'S SWEET, IN A WAY.
WE ALL HAVE OUR COMFORTING FICTIONS.
I SUPPOSE WE DO. HOW DO YOU FEEL ABOUT IT THOUGH, ALL IN ALL?
FINE.
NO, NICK, SERIOUSLY, JUST BETWEEN YOU AND ME.
HOW DO YOU FEEL?
...FINE?
OH, NICK.
KLIK

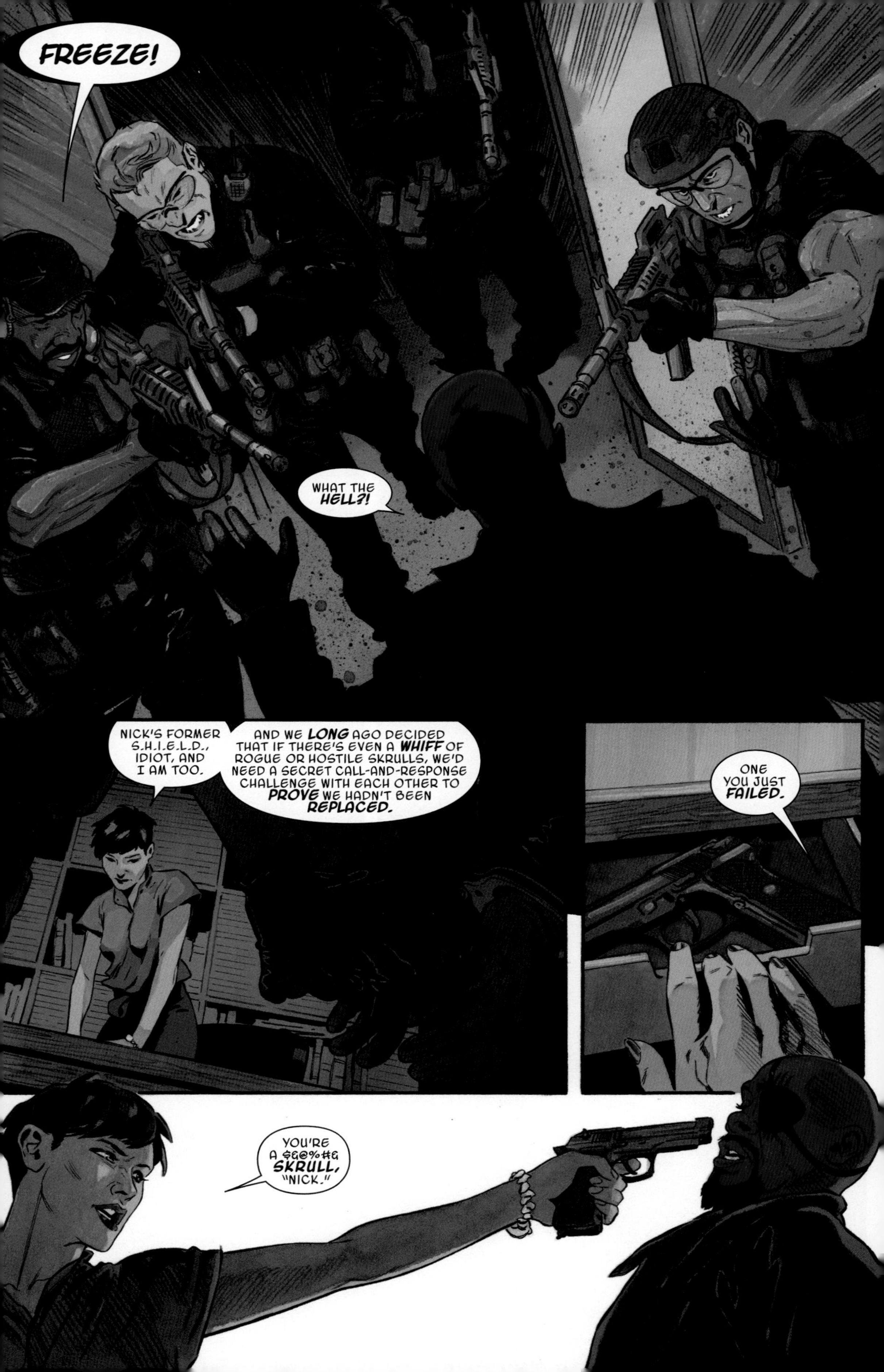

FREEZE!
WHAT THE HELL?!
NICK'S FORMER S.H.I.E.L.D., IDIOT, AND I AM TOO.
AND WE LONG AGO DECIDED THAT IF THERE'S EVEN A WHIFF OF ROGUE OR HOSTILE SKRULLS, WE'D NEED A SECRET CALL-AND-RESPONSE CHALLENGE WITH EACH OTHER TO PROVE WE HADN'T BEEN REPLACED.
ONE YOU JUST FAILED.
YOU'RE A $&@%#& SKRULL, "NICK."

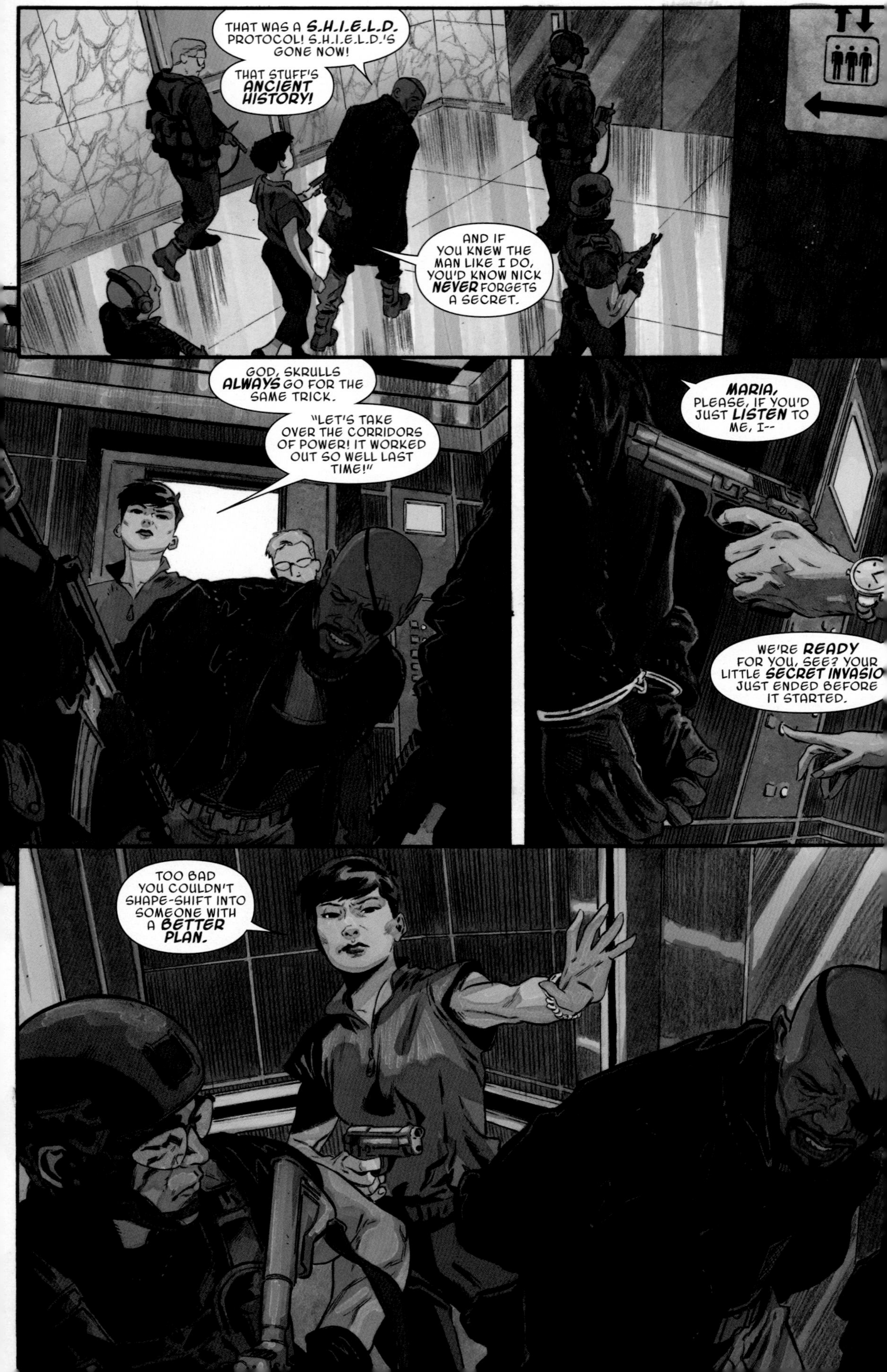
THAT WAS A **S.H.I.E.L.D.** PROTOCOL! S.H.I.E.L.D.'S GONE NOW!
THAT STUFF'S **ANCIENT HISTORY!**
AND IF YOU KNEW THE MAN LIKE I DO, YOU'D KNOW NICK **NEVER** FORGETS A SECRET.
GOD, SKRULLS **ALWAYS** GO FOR THE SAME TRICK.
"LET'S TAKE OVER THE CORRIDORS OF POWER! IT WORKED OUT SO WELL LAST TIME!"
MARIA, PLEASE, IF YOU'D JUST **LISTEN** TO ME, I--
WE'RE **READY** FOR YOU, SEE? YOUR LITTLE **SECRET INVASIO** JUST ENDED BEFORE IT STARTED.
TOO BAD YOU COULDN'T SHAPE-SHIFT INTO SOMEONE WITH A **BETTER PLAN.**

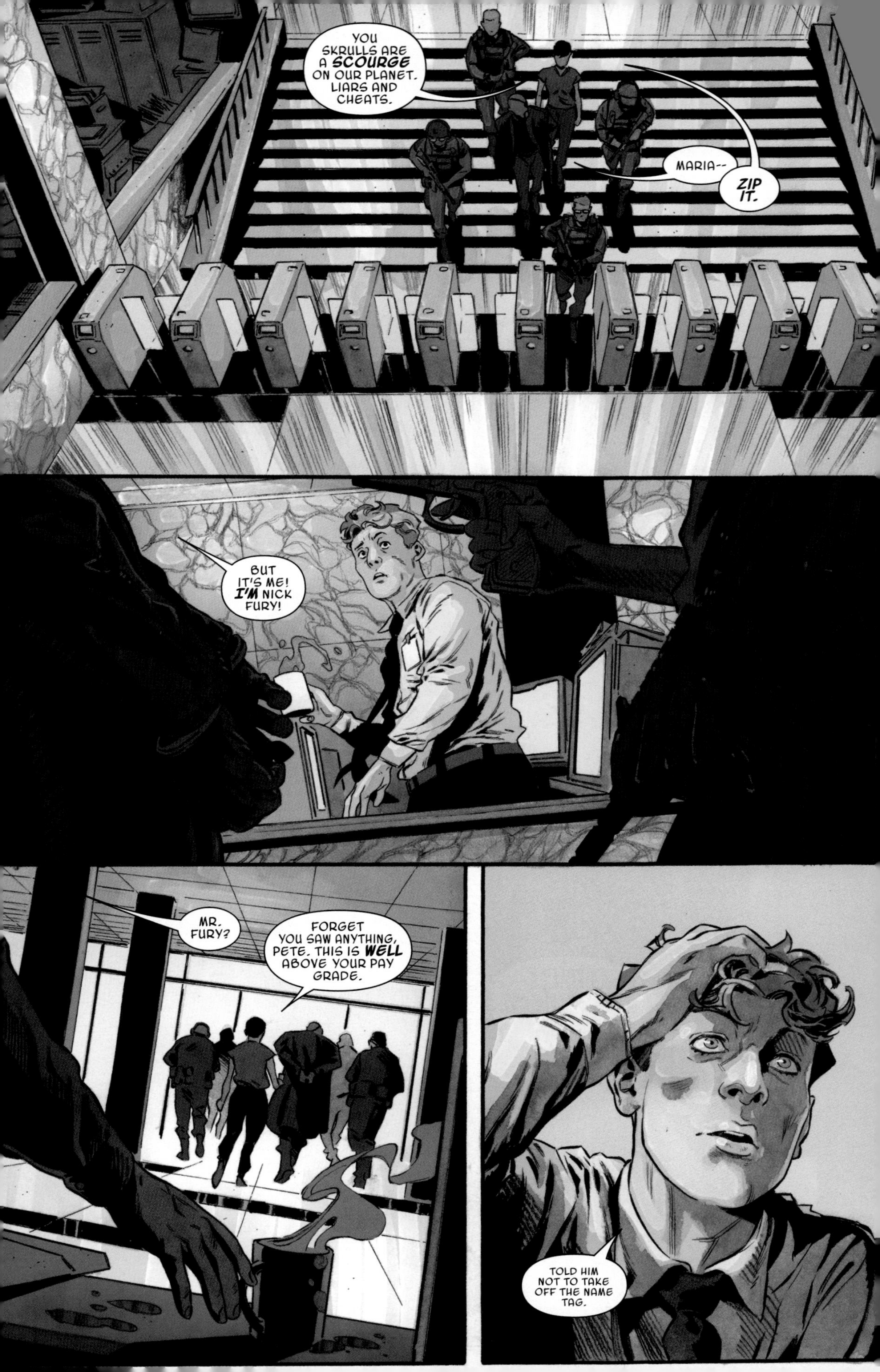
YOU SKRULLS ARE A SCOURGE ON OUR PLANET. LIARS AND CHEATS.
MARIA--
ZIP IT.
BUT IT'S ME! I'M NICK FURY!
MR. FURY?
FORGET YOU SAW ANYTHING, PETE. THIS IS WELL ABOVE YOUR PAY GRADE.
TOLD HIM NOT TO TAKE OFF THE NAME TAG.

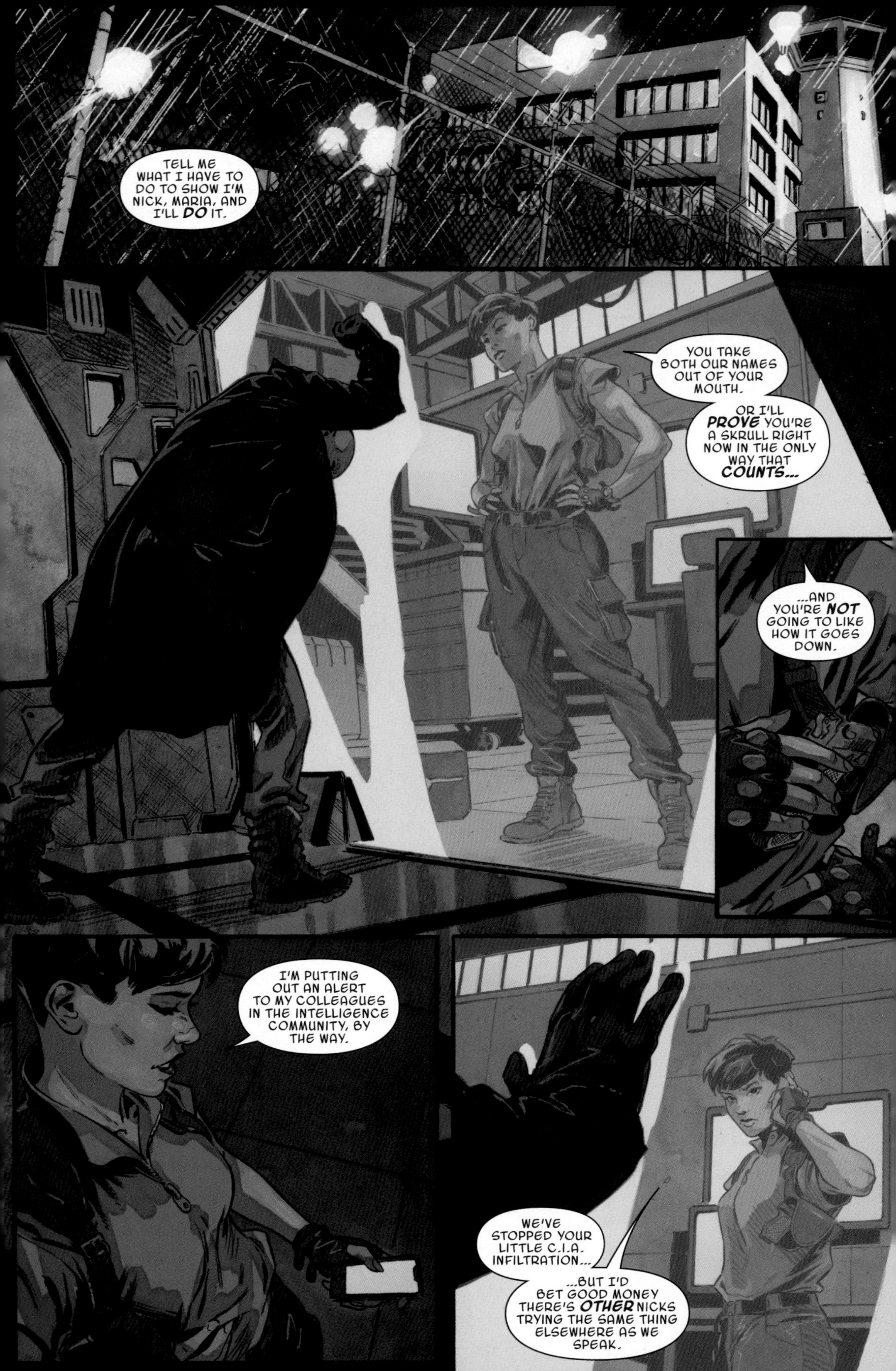
TELL ME WHAT I HAVE TO DO TO SHOW I'M NICK, MARIA, AND I'LL **DO** IT.
YOU TAKE BOTH OUR NAMES OUT OF YOUR MOUTH.
OR I'LL **PROVE** YOU'RE A SKRULL RIGHT NOW IN THE ONLY WAY THAT **COUNTS...**
...AND YOU'RE **NOT** GOING TO LIKE HOW IT GOES DOWN.
I'M PUTTING OUT AN ALERT TO MY COLLEAGUES IN THE INTELLIGENCE COMMUNITY, BY THE WAY.
WE'VE STOPPED YOUR LITTLE C.I.A. INFILTRATION...
...BUT I'D BET GOOD MONEY THERE'S **OTHER** NICKS TRYING THE SAME THING ELSEWHERE AS WE SPEAK.

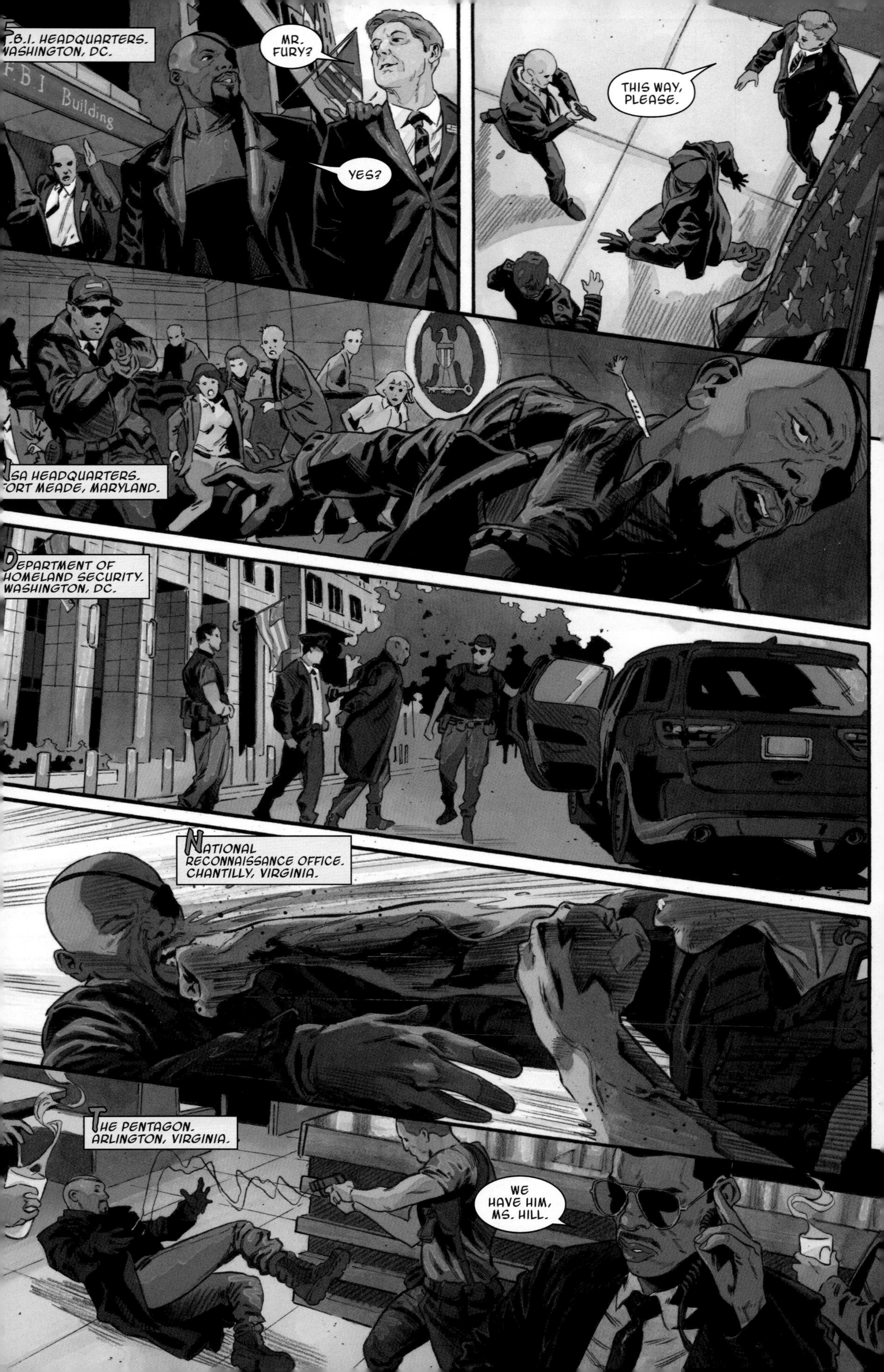
F.B.I. HEADQUARTERS. WASHINGTON, DC.
MR. FURY?
YES?
F.B.I Building
THIS WAY, PLEASE.
NSA HEADQUARTERS. FORT MEADE, MARYLAND.
DEPARTMENT OF HOMELAND SECURITY. WASHINGTON, DC.
NATIONAL RECONNAISSANCE OFFICE. CHANTILLY, VIRGINIA.
THE PENTAGON. ARLINGTON, VIRGINIA.
WE HAVE HIM, MS. HILL.

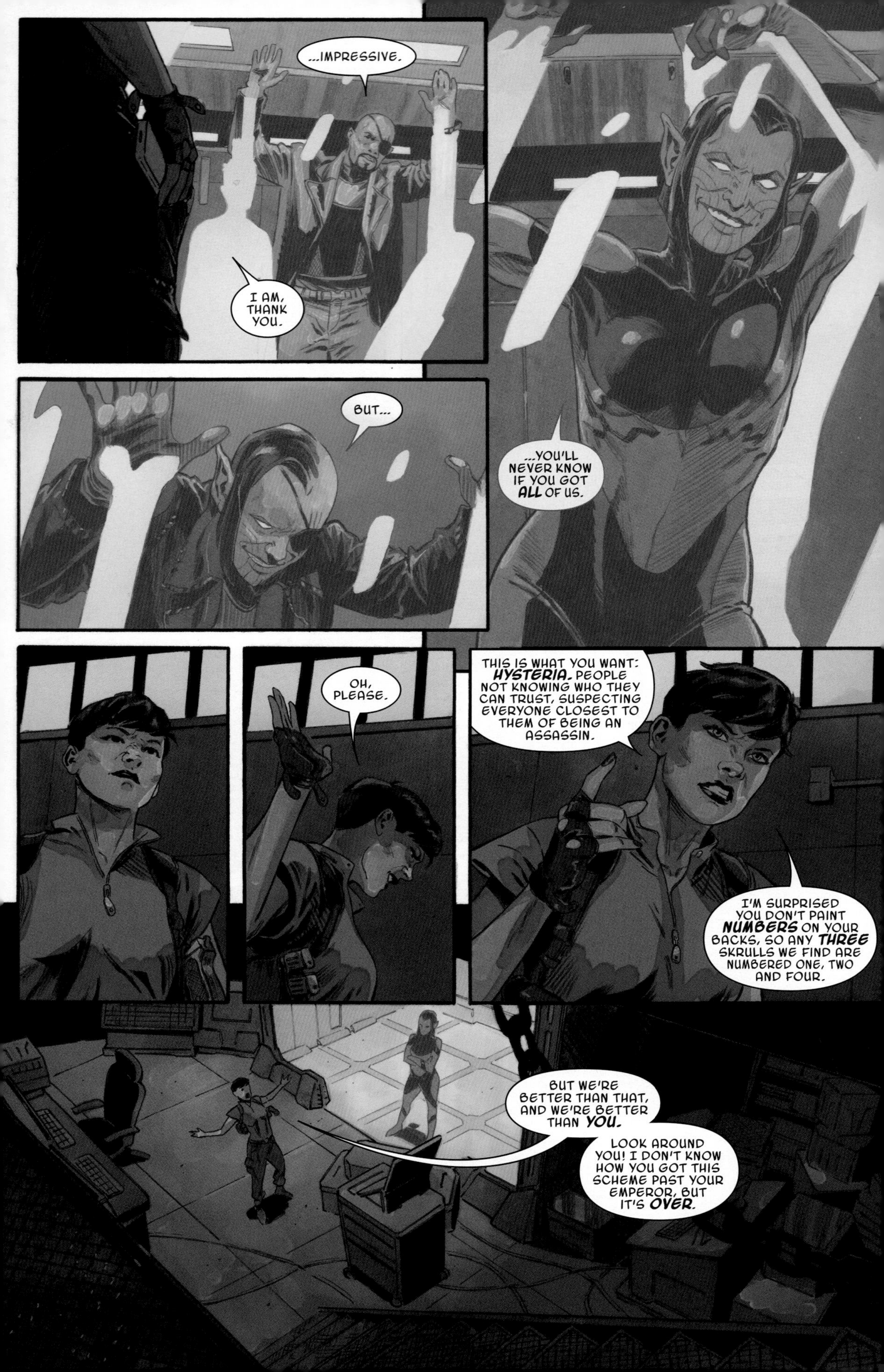
...IMPRESSIVE.
I AM, THANK YOU.
BUT...
...YOU'LL NEVER KNOW IF YOU GOT ALL OF US.
OH, PLEASE.
THIS IS WHAT YOU WANT: HYSTERIA. PEOPLE NOT KNOWING WHO THEY CAN TRUST, SUSPECTING EVERYONE CLOSEST TO THEM OF BEING AN ASSASSIN.
I'M SURPRISED YOU DON'T PAINT NUMBERS ON YOUR BACKS, SO ANY THREE SKRULLS WE FIND ARE NUMBERED ONE, TWO AND FOUR.
BUT WE'RE BETTER THAN THAT, AND WE'RE BETTER THAN YOU.
LOOK AROUND YOU! I DON'T KNOW HOW YOU GOT THIS SCHEME PAST YOUR EMPEROR, BUT IT'S OVER.

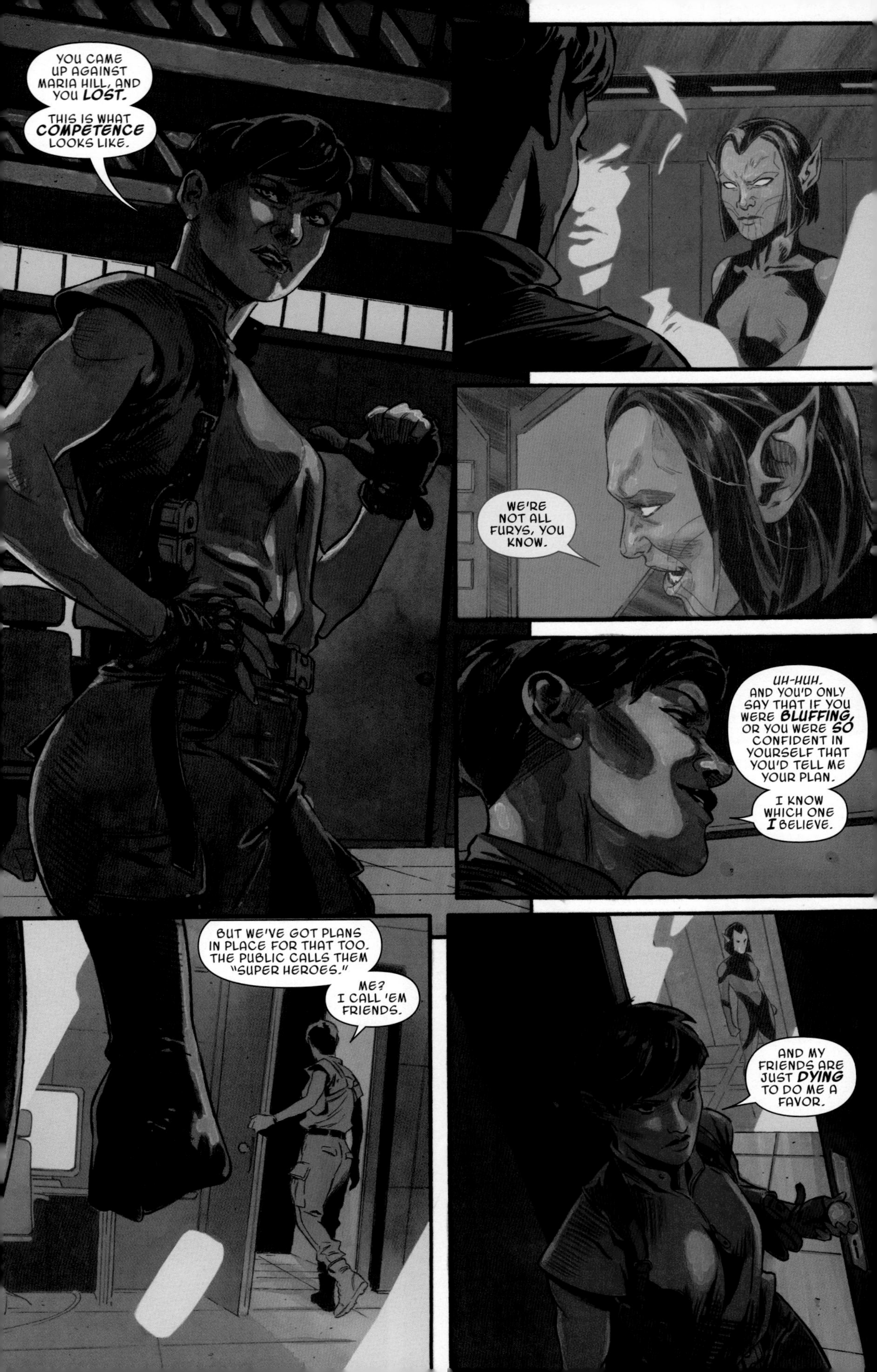
YOU CAME UP AGAINST MARIA HILL, AND YOU LOST.
THIS IS WHAT COMPETENCE LOOKS LIKE.
WE'RE NOT ALL FURYS, YOU KNOW.
UH-HUH. AND YOU'D ONLY SAY THAT IF YOU WERE BLUFFING, OR YOU WERE SO CONFIDENT IN YOURSELF THAT YOU'D TELL ME YOUR PLAN.
I KNOW WHICH ONE I BELIEVE.
BUT WE'VE GOT PLANS IN PLACE FOR THAT TOO. THE PUBLIC CALLS THEM "SUPER HEROES."
ME? I CALL 'EM FRIENDS.
AND MY FRIENDS ARE JUST DYING TO DO ME A FAVOR.

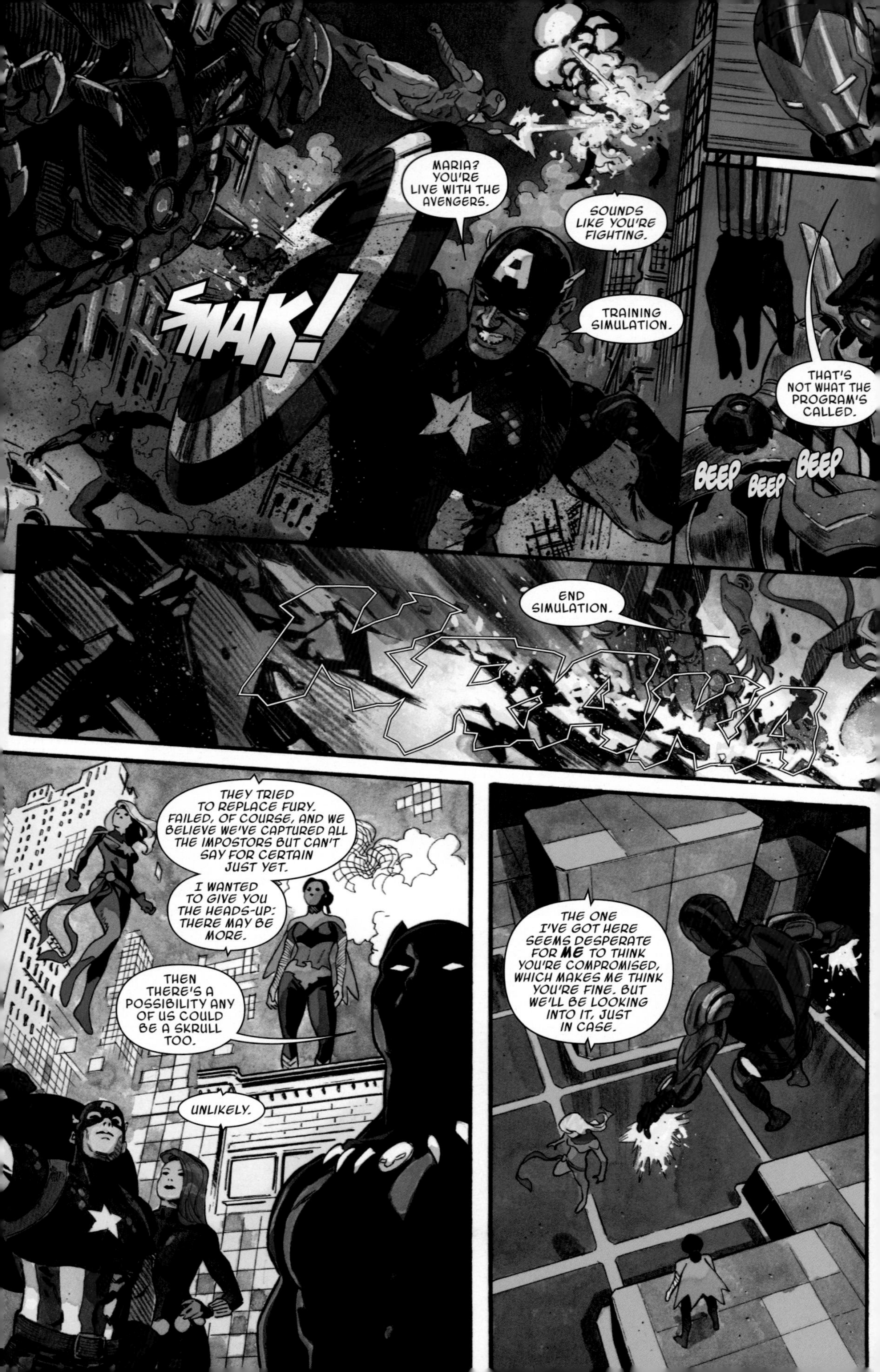
MARIA? YOU'RE LIVE WITH THE AVENGERS.
SOUNDS LIKE YOU'RE FIGHTING.
SMAK!
TRAINING SIMULATION.
THAT'S NOT WHAT THE PROGRAM'S CALLED.
BEEP BEEP BEEP
END SIMULATION.
THEY TRIED TO REPLACE FURY. FAILED, OF COURSE, AND WE BELIEVE WE'VE CAPTURED ALL THE IMPOSTORS BUT CAN'T SAY FOR CERTAIN JUST YET.
I WANTED TO GIVE YOU THE HEADS-UP: THERE MAY BE MORE.
THEN THERE'S A POSSIBILITY ANY OF US COULD BE A SKRULL TOO.
UNLIKELY.
THE ONE I'VE GOT HERE SEEMS DESPERATE FOR ME TO THINK YOU'RE COMPROMISED, WHICH MAKES ME THINK YOU'RE FINE. BUT WE'LL BE LOOKING INTO IT, JUST IN CASE.

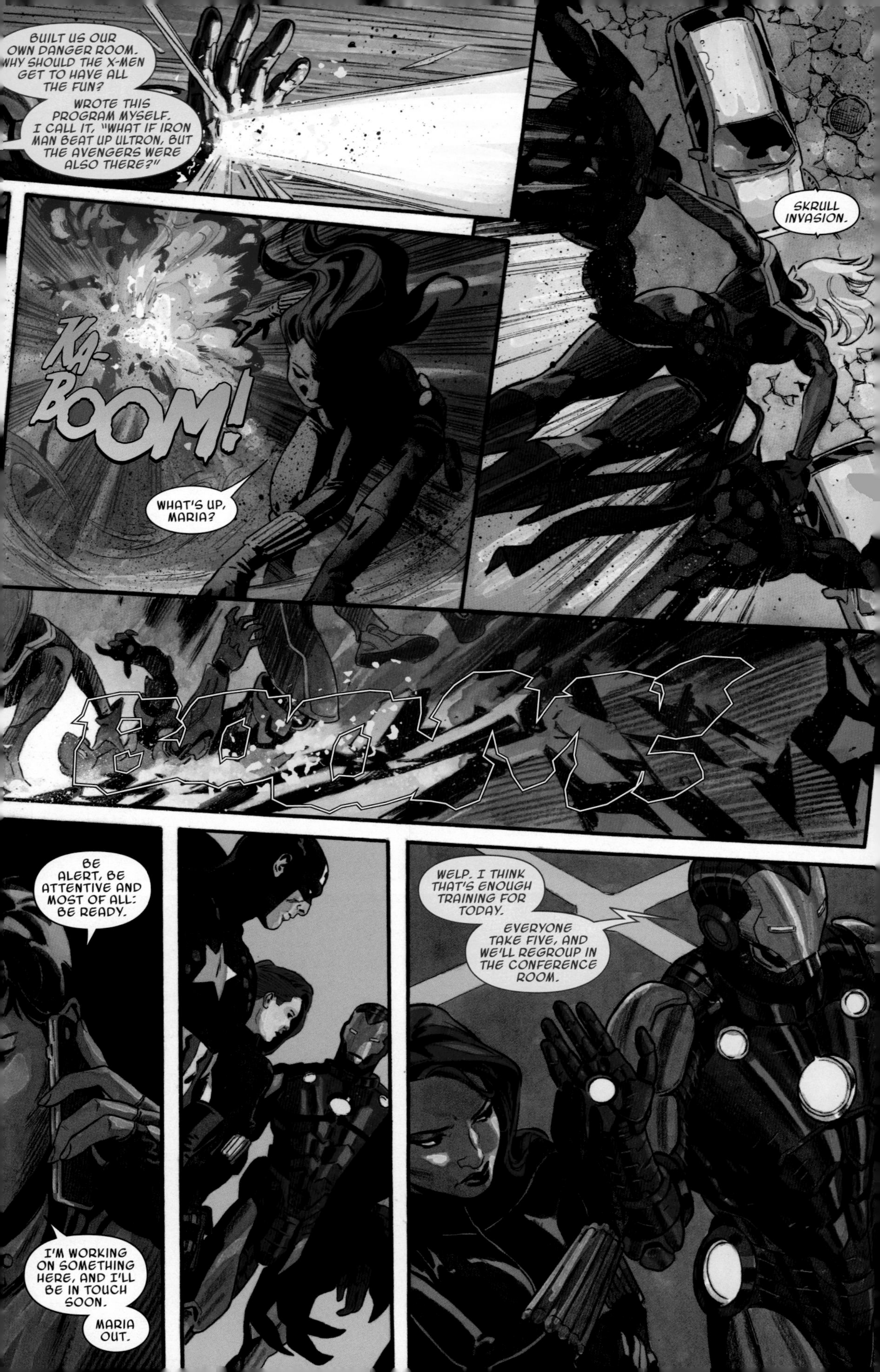
BUILT US OUR OWN DANGER ROOM. WHY SHOULD THE X-MEN GET TO HAVE ALL THE FUN?
WROTE THIS PROGRAM MYSELF. I CALL IT, "WHAT IF IRON MAN BEAT UP ULTRON, BUT THE AVENGERS WERE ALSO THERE?"
KA-BOOM!
WHAT'S UP, MARIA?
SKRULL INVASION.
BE ALERT, BE ATTENTIVE AND MOST OF ALL: BE READY.
WELP. I THINK THAT'S ENOUGH TRAINING FOR TODAY.
EVERYONE TAKE FIVE, AND WE'LL REGROUP IN THE CONFERENCE ROOM.
I'M WORKING ON SOMETHING HERE, AND I'LL BE IN TOUCH SOON.
MARIA OUT.

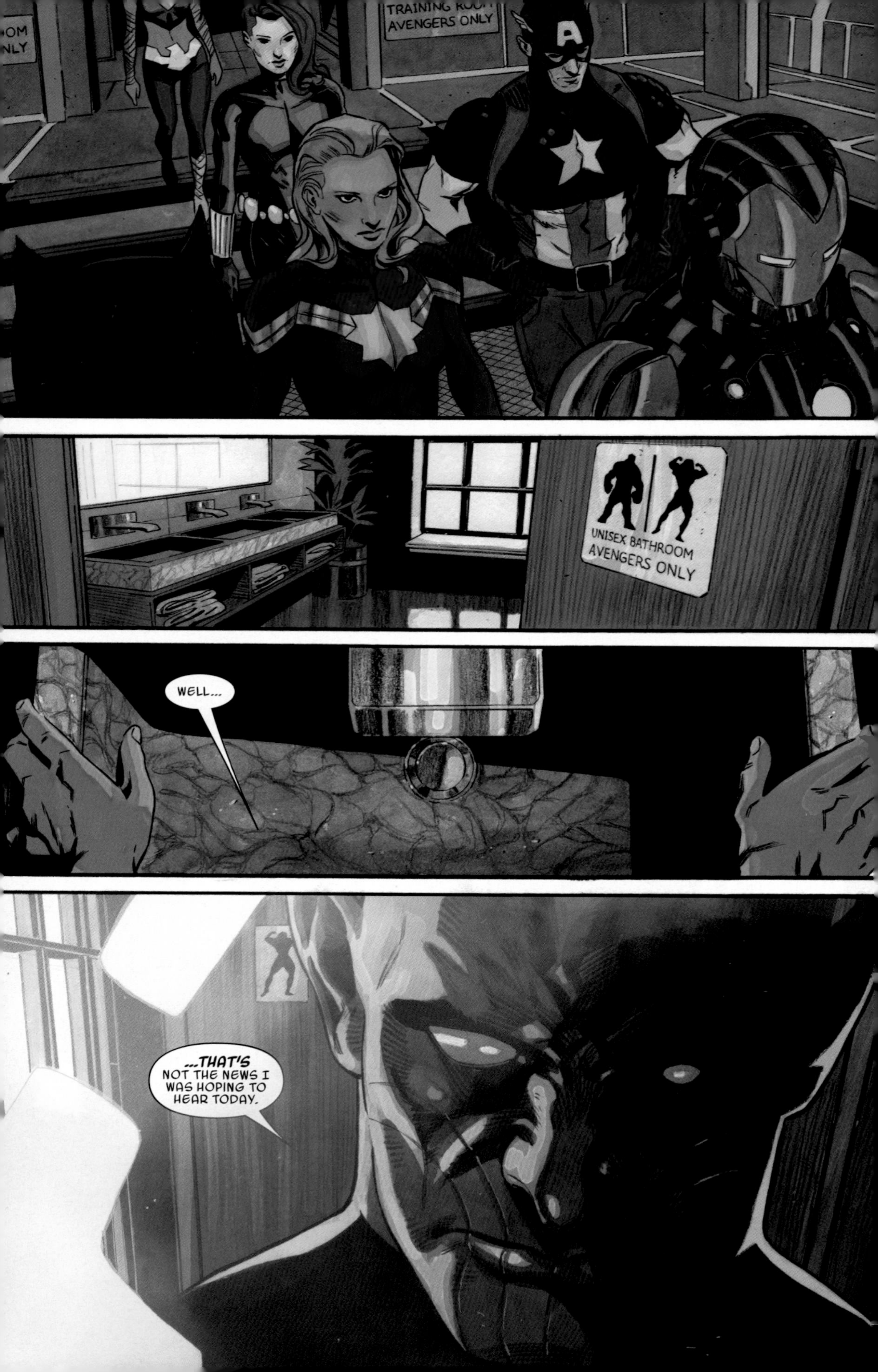
TRAINING ROOM
AVENGERS ONLY
UNISEX BATHROOM
AVENGERS ONLY
WELL...
...THAT'S NOT THE NEWS I WAS HOPING TO HEAR TODAY.

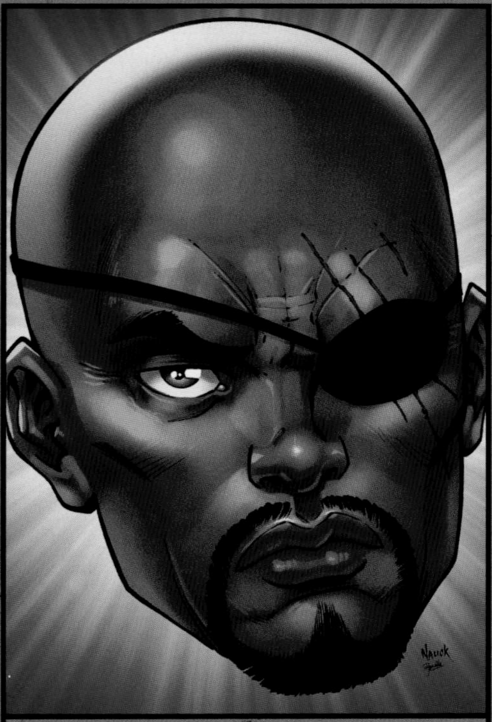

#1 Headshot variant by
Todd Nauck & Rachelle Rosenberg

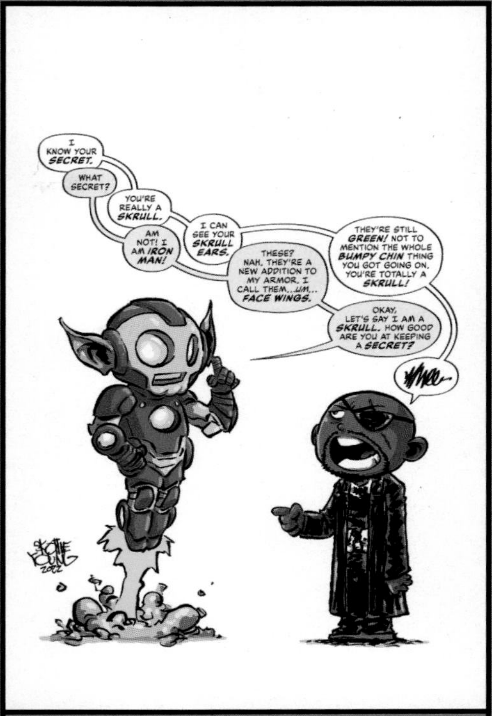
I KNOW YOUR SECRET.
WHAT SECRET?
YOU'RE REALLY A SKRULL.
AM NOT! I AM IRON MAN!
I CAN SEE YOUR SKRULL EARS.
THESE? NAH, THEY'RE A NEW ADDITION TO MY ARMOR. I CALL THEM...UM... FACE WINGS.
THEY'RE STILL GREEN! NOT TO MENTION THE WHOLE BUMPY CHIN THING YOU GOT GOING ON. YOU'RE TOTALLY A SKRULL!
OKAY, LET'S SAY I AM A SKRULL. HOW GOOD ARE YOU AT KEEPING A SECRET?

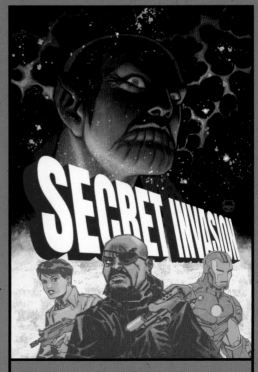

#1 variant by
Skottie Young

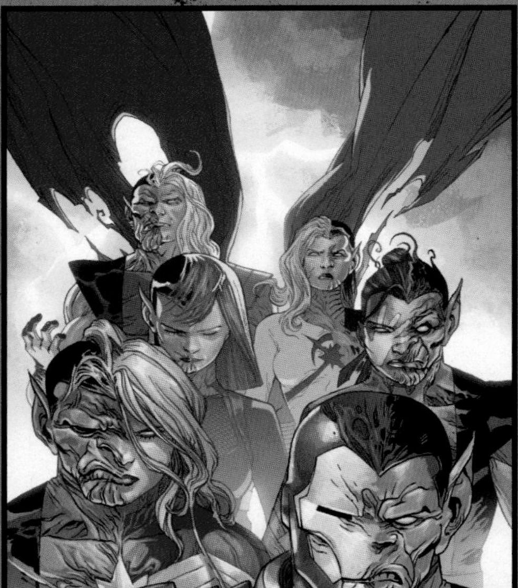

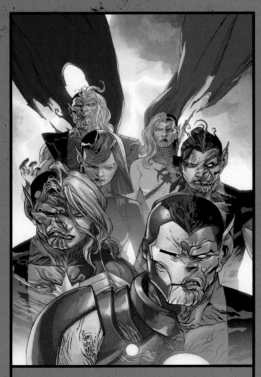

#1 variant by
Giuseppe Camuncoli & Matthew Wilson

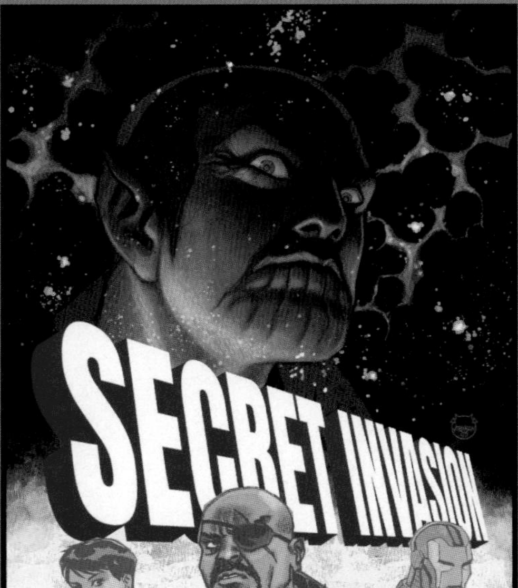
SECRET INVASION

#2 variant by
Dave Johnson

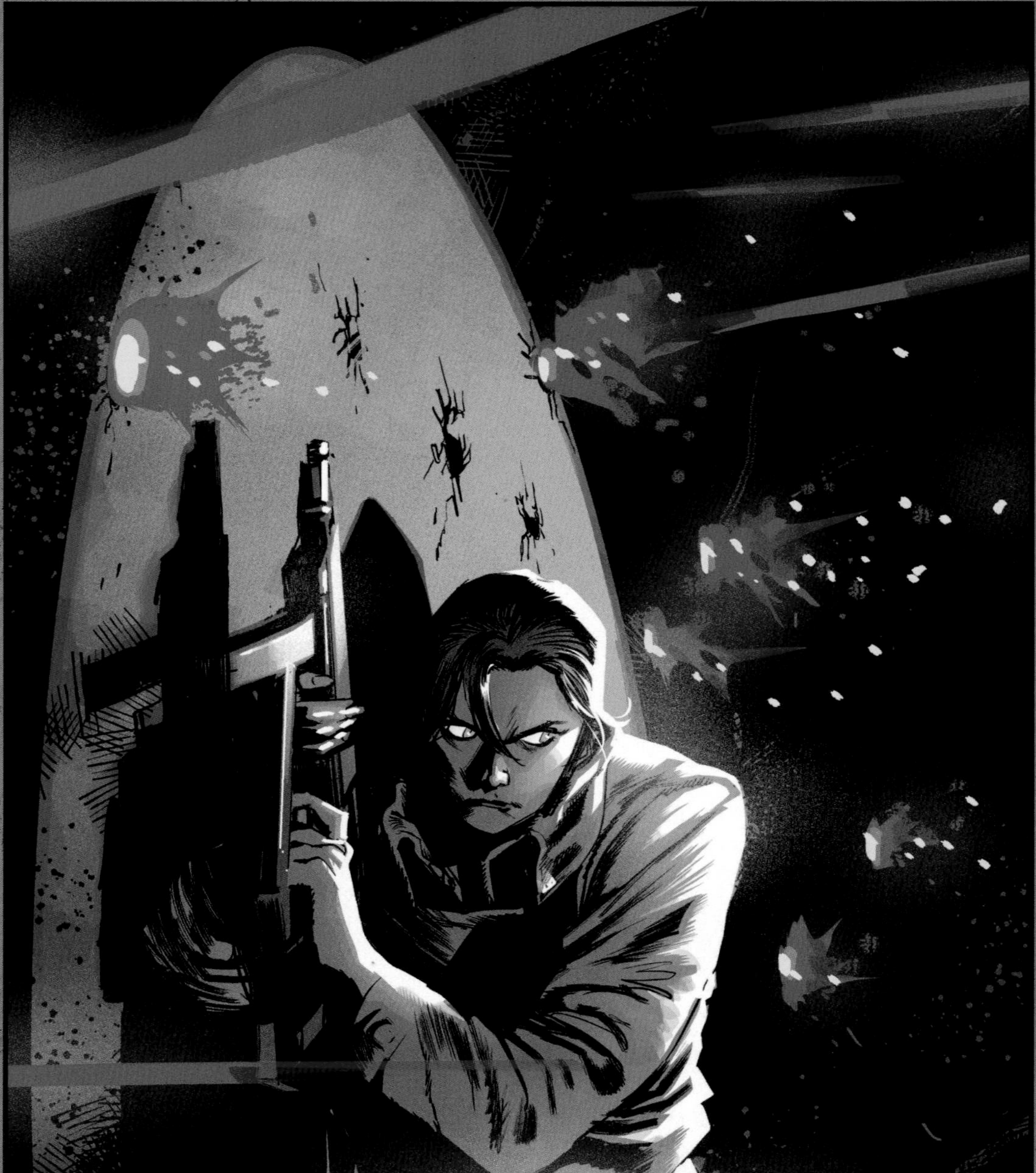

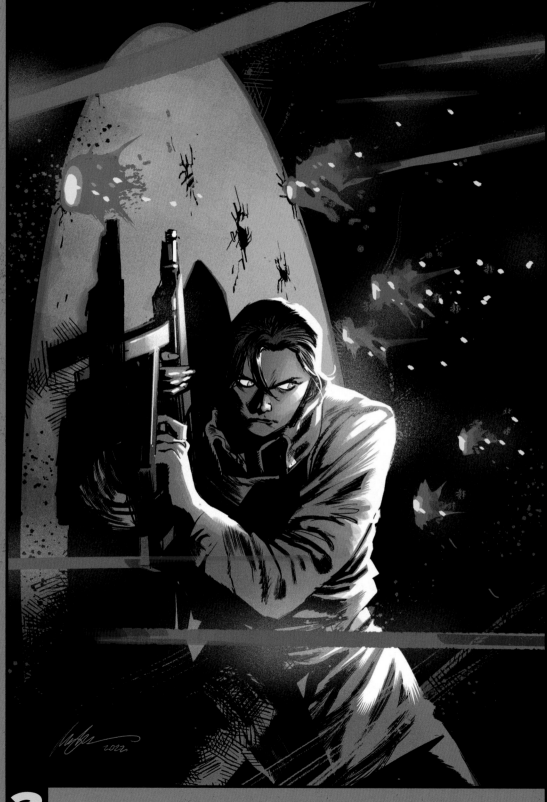

2

"All I Need To Do Is Kill It"

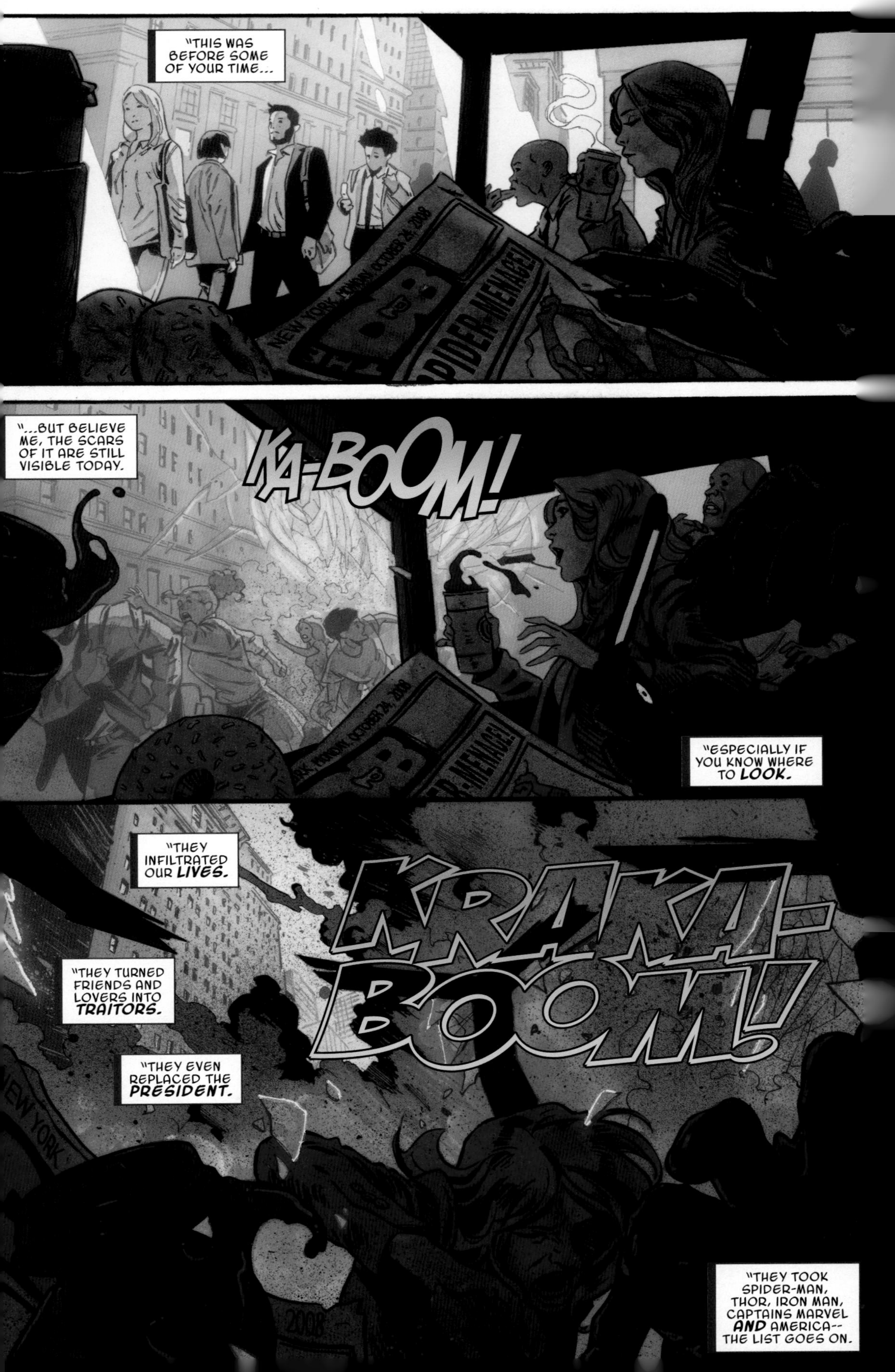
"THIS WAS BEFORE SOME OF YOUR TIME...
NEW YORK, MONDAY, OCTOBER 24, 2008
SPIDER-MENACE!
"...BUT BELIEVE ME, THE SCARS OF IT ARE STILL VISIBLE TODAY.
KA-BOOM!
"ESPECIALLY IF YOU KNOW WHERE TO LOOK.
"THEY INFILTRATED OUR LIVES.
KRAKA-BOOM!
"THEY TURNED FRIENDS AND LOVERS INTO TRAITORS.
"THEY EVEN REPLACED THE PRESIDENT.
"THEY TOOK SPIDER-MAN, THOR, IRON MAN, CAPTAINS MARVEL AND AMERICA-- THE LIST GOES ON.

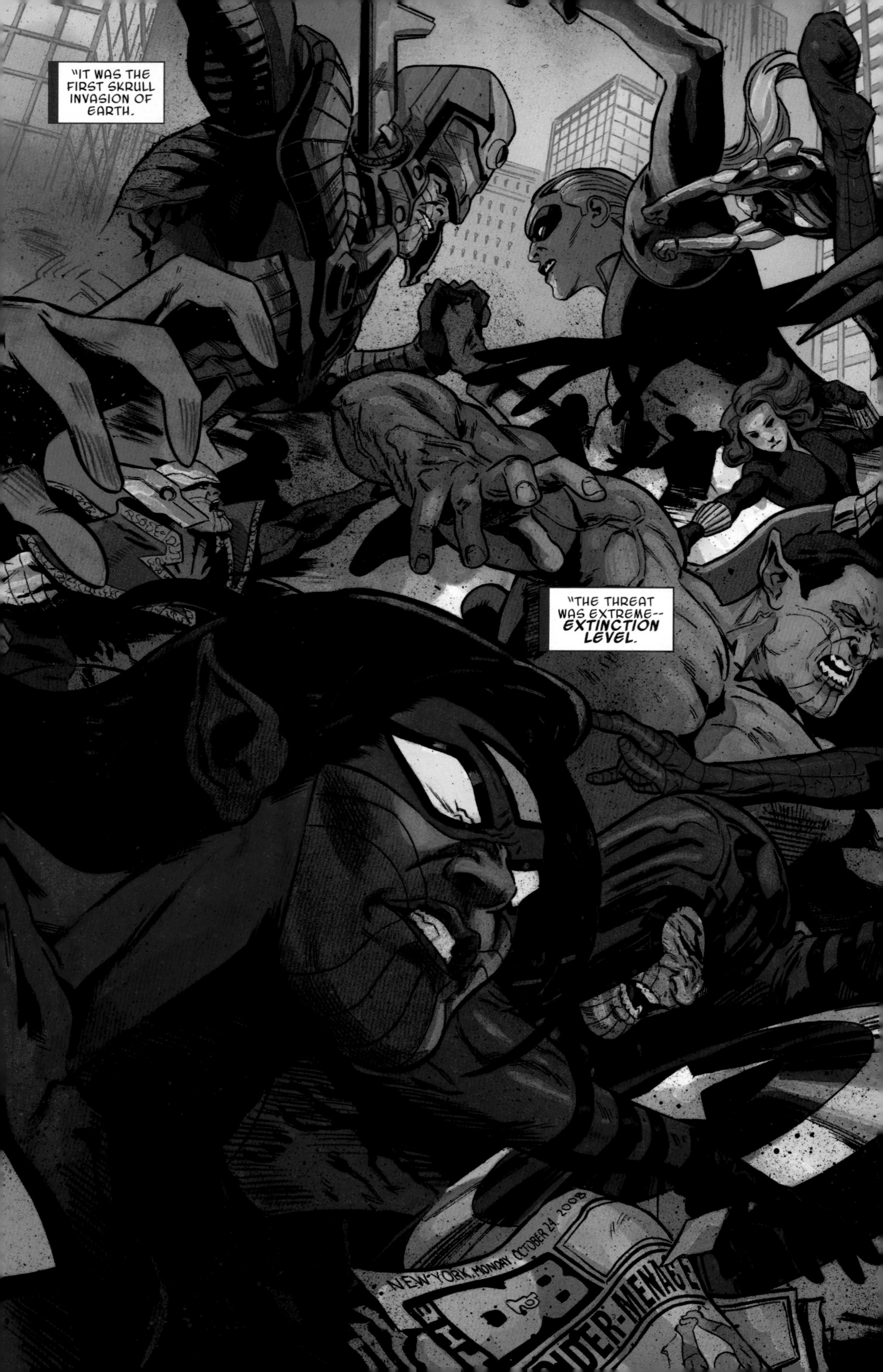
"IT WAS THE FIRST SKRULL INVASION OF EARTH.
"THE THREAT WAS EXTREME--EXTINCTION LEVEL.
NEW YORK, MONDAY, OCTOBER 24, 2008
IDER-MENACE

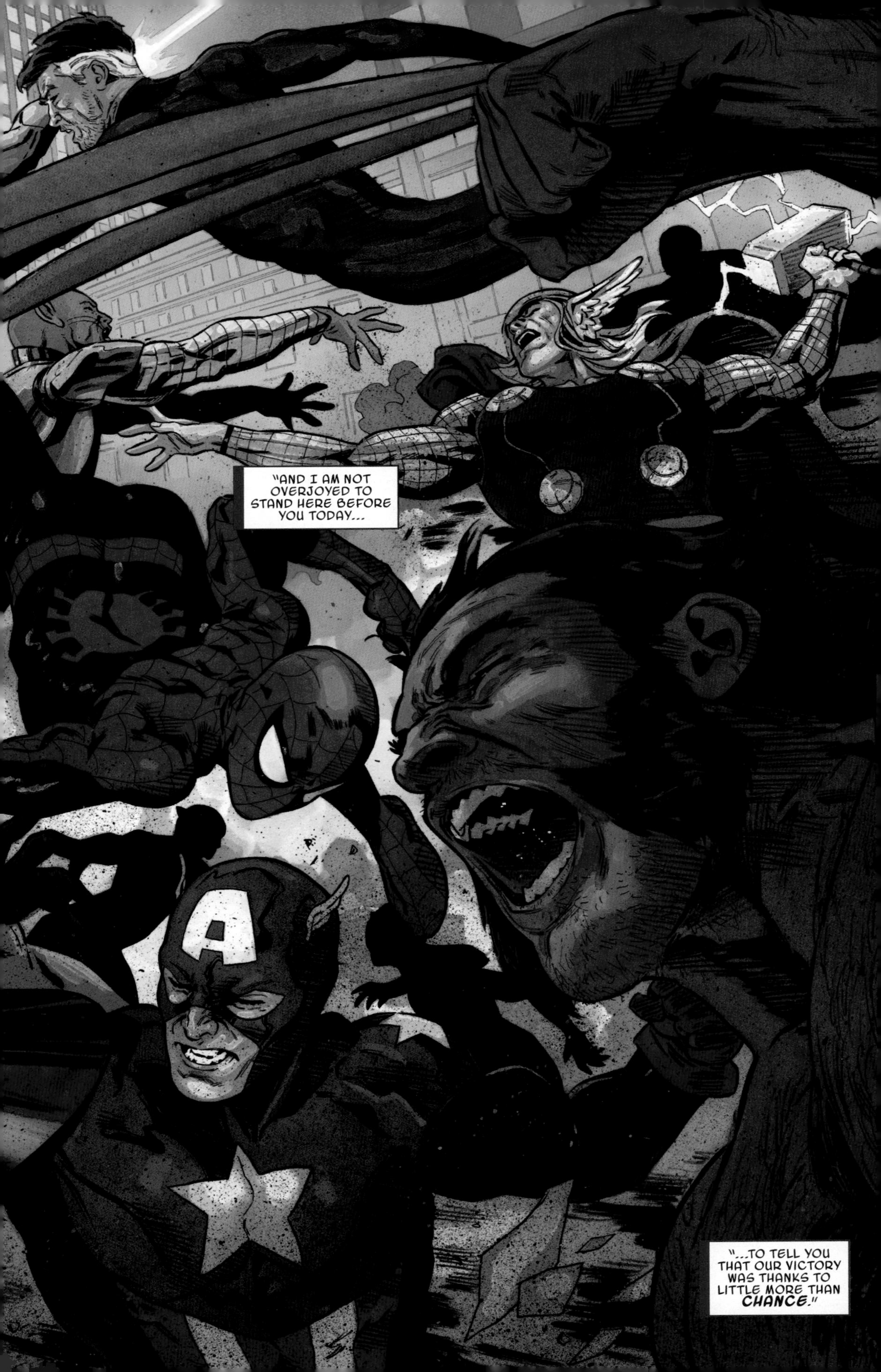
"AND I AM NOT OVERJOYED TO STAND HERE BEFORE YOU TODAY...
"...TO TELL YOU THAT OUR VICTORY WAS THANKS TO LITTLE MORE THAN ***CHANCE***."

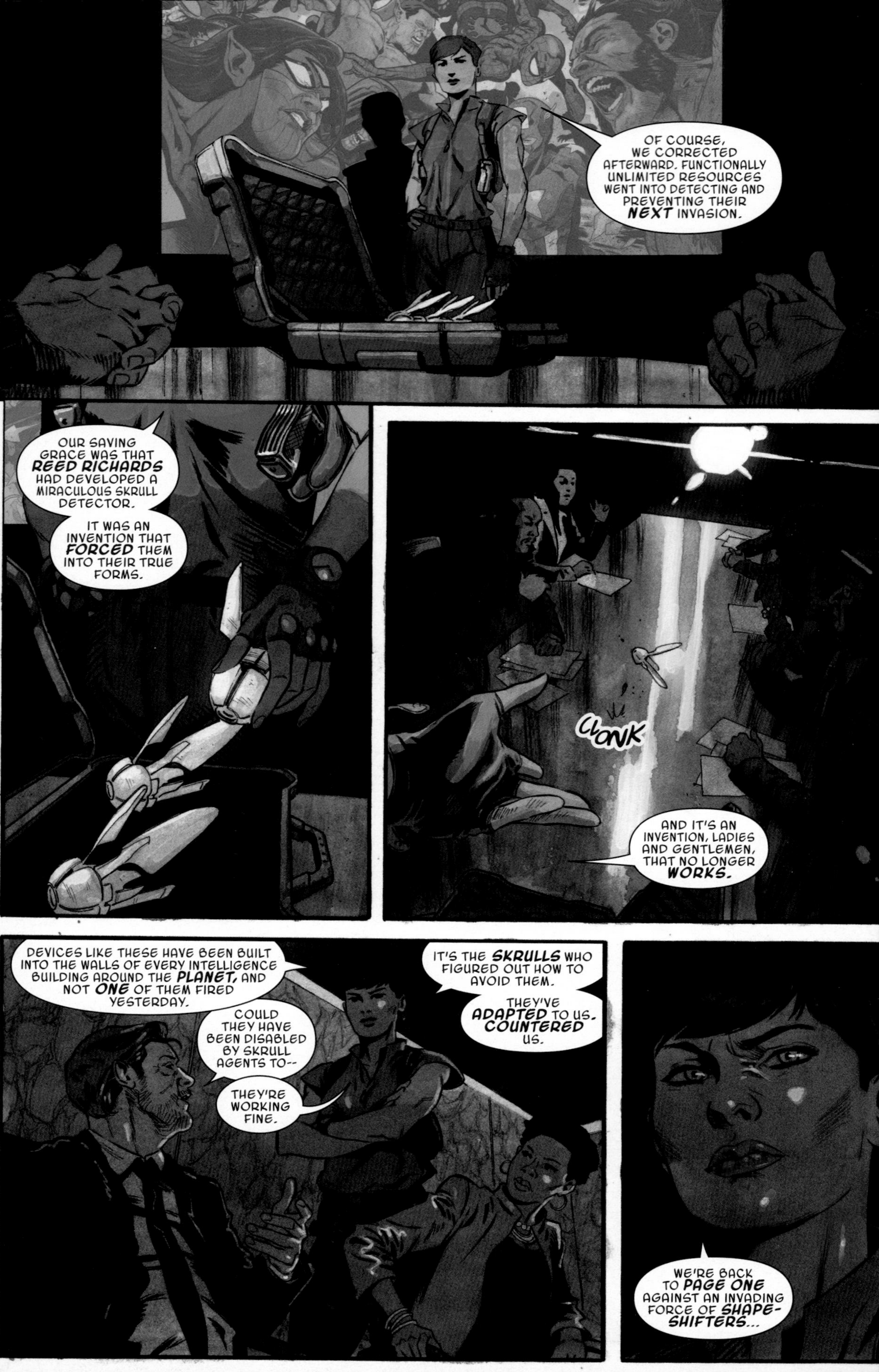
OF COURSE, WE CORRECTED AFTERWARD. FUNCTIONALLY UNLIMITED RESOURCES WENT INTO DETECTING AND PREVENTING THEIR NEXT INVASION.
OUR SAVING GRACE WAS THAT REED RICHARDS HAD DEVELOPED A MIRACULOUS SKRULL DETECTOR.
IT WAS AN INVENTION THAT FORCED THEM INTO THEIR TRUE FORMS.
CLONK
AND IT'S AN INVENTION, LADIES AND GENTLEMEN, THAT NO LONGER WORKS.
DEVICES LIKE THESE HAVE BEEN BUILT INTO THE WALLS OF EVERY INTELLIGENCE BUILDING AROUND THE PLANET, AND NOT ONE OF THEM FIRED YESTERDAY.
COULD THEY HAVE BEEN DISABLED BY SKRULL AGENTS TO--
THEY'RE WORKING FINE.
IT'S THE SKRULLS WHO FIGURED OUT HOW TO AVOID THEM.
THEY'VE ADAPTED TO US. COUNTERED US.
WE'RE BACK TO PAGE ONE AGAINST AN INVADING FORCE OF SHAPE-SHIFTERS...

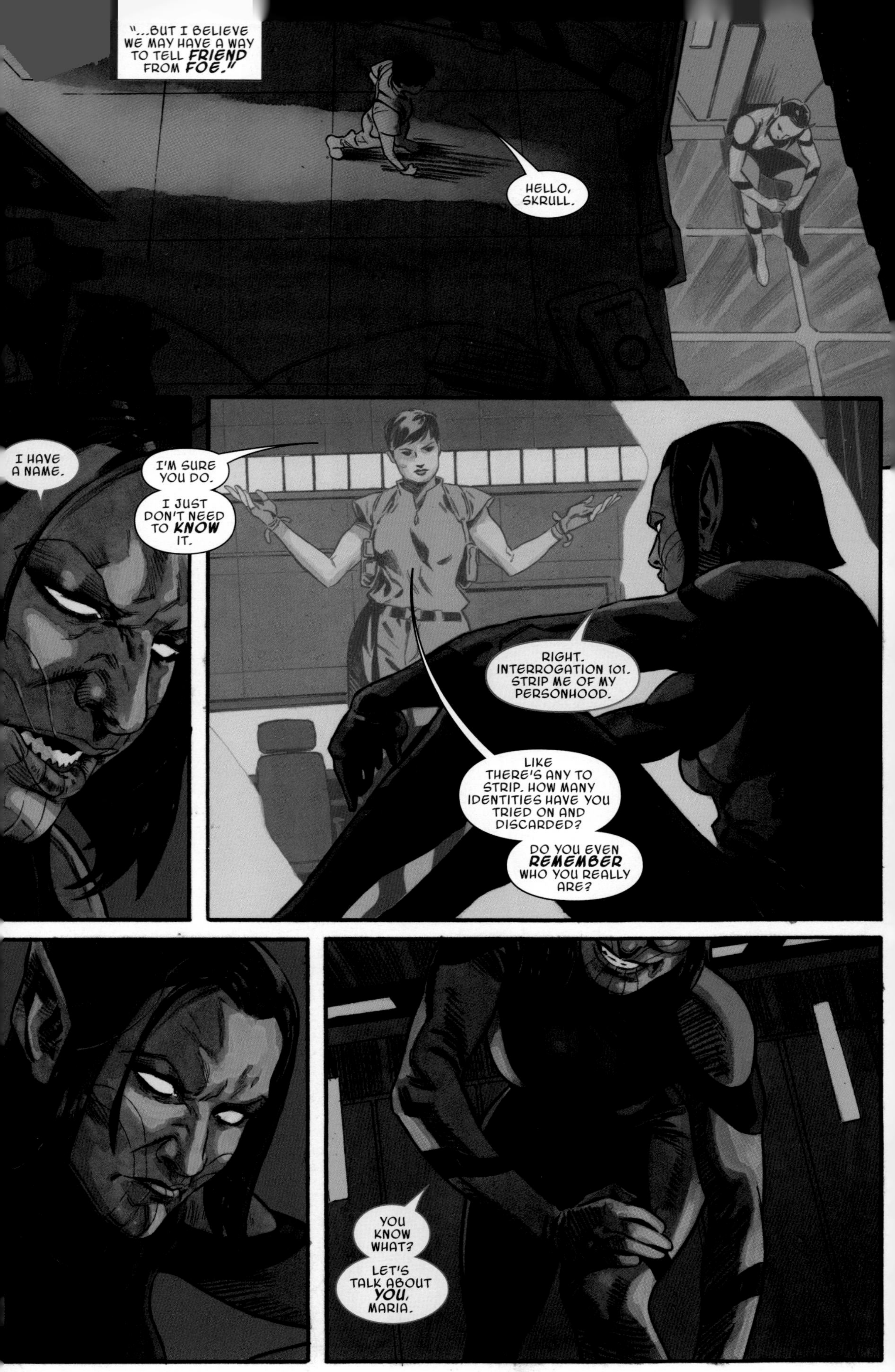
"...BUT I BELIEVE WE MAY HAVE A WAY TO TELL FRIEND FROM FOE."
HELLO, SKRULL.
I HAVE A NAME.
I'M SURE YOU DO.
I JUST DON'T NEED TO KNOW IT.
RIGHT. INTERROGATION 101. STRIP ME OF MY PERSONHOOD.
LIKE THERE'S ANY TO STRIP. HOW MANY IDENTITIES HAVE YOU TRIED ON AND DISCARDED?
DO YOU EVEN REMEMBER WHO YOU REALLY ARE?
YOU KNOW WHAT?
LET'S TALK ABOUT YOU, MARIA.

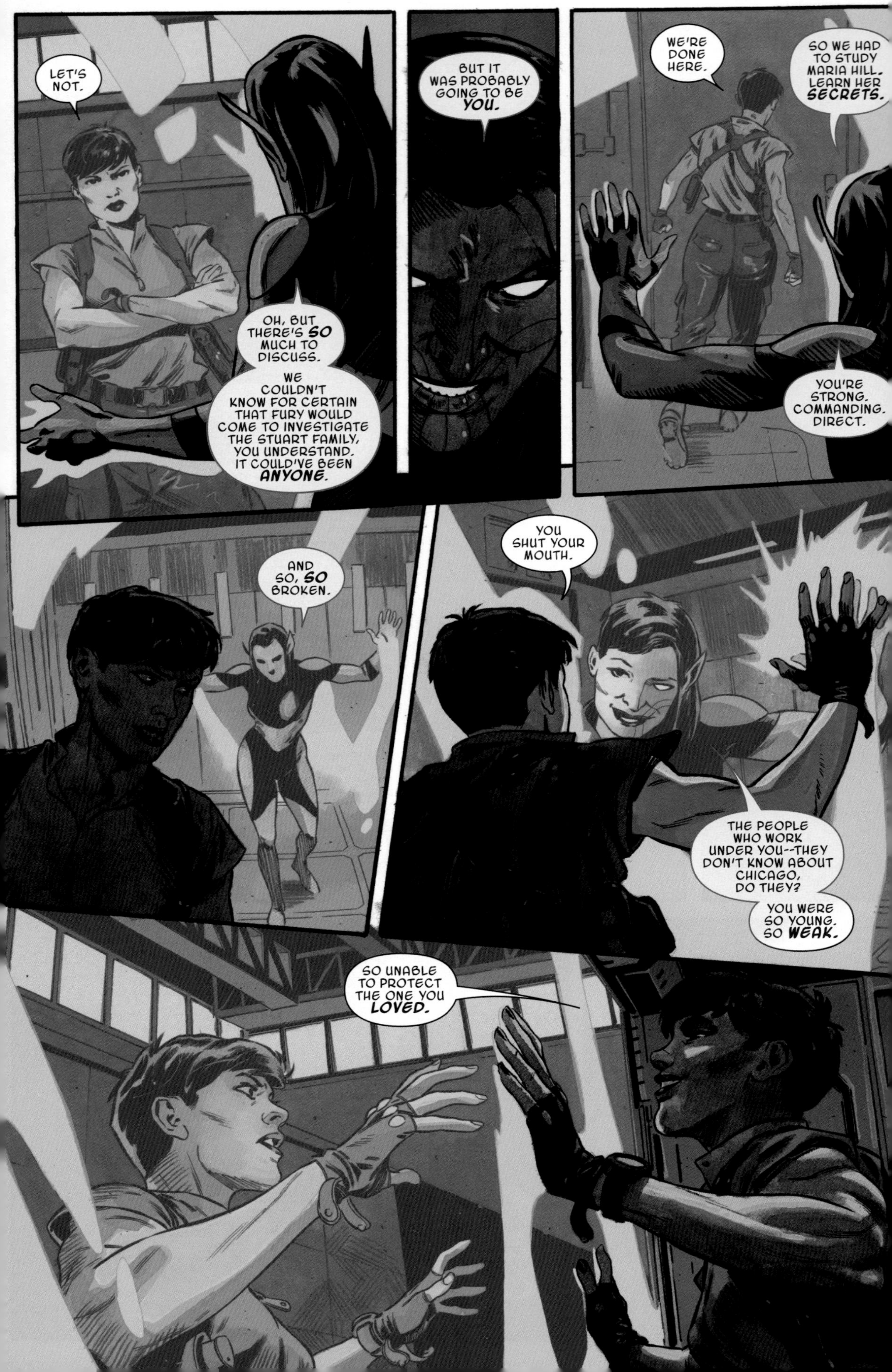
LET'S NOT.
OH, BUT THERE'S SO MUCH TO DISCUSS.
WE COULDN'T KNOW FOR CERTAIN THAT FURY WOULD COME TO INVESTIGATE THE STUART FAMILY, YOU UNDERSTAND. IT COULD'VE BEEN ANYONE.
BUT IT WAS PROBABLY GOING TO BE YOU.
WE'RE DONE HERE.
SO WE HAD TO STUDY MARIA HILL. LEARN HER SECRETS.
YOU'RE STRONG. COMMANDING. DIRECT.
AND SO, SO BROKEN.
YOU SHUT YOUR MOUTH.
THE PEOPLE WHO WORK UNDER YOU--THEY DON'T KNOW ABOUT CHICAGO, DO THEY?
YOU WERE SO YOUNG. SO WEAK.
SO UNABLE TO PROTECT THE ONE YOU LOVED.

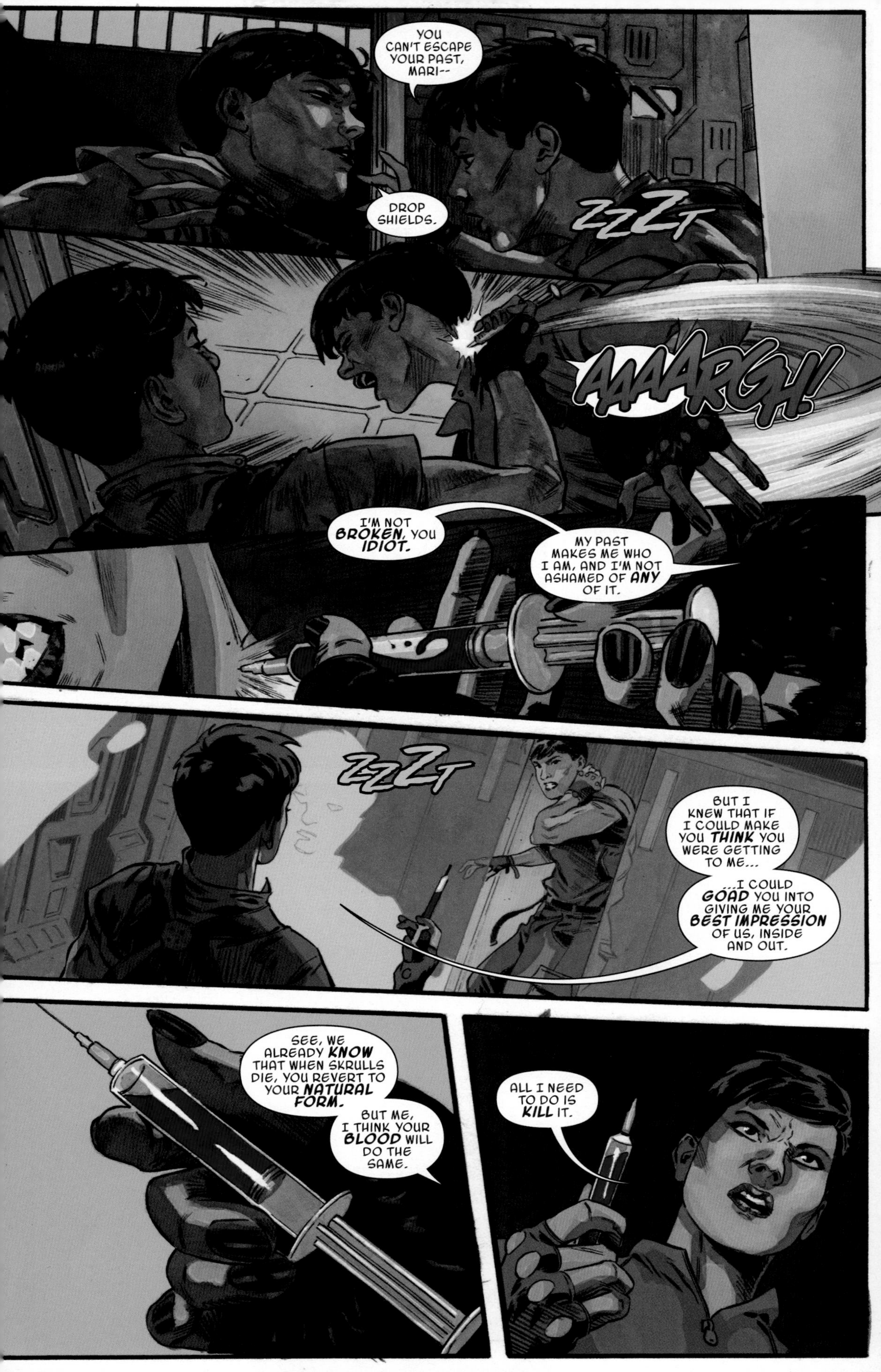
YOU CAN'T ESCAPE YOUR PAST, MARI--
DROP SHIELDS.
ZZZT
AAAARGH!
I'M NOT BROKEN, YOU IDIOT.
MY PAST MAKES ME WHO I AM, AND I'M NOT ASHAMED OF ANY OF IT.
ZZZT
BUT I KNEW THAT IF I COULD MAKE YOU THINK YOU WERE GETTING TO ME...
...I COULD GOAD YOU INTO GIVING ME YOUR BEST IMPRESSION OF US, INSIDE AND OUT.
SEE, WE ALREADY KNOW THAT WHEN SKRULLS DIE, YOU REVERT TO YOUR NATURAL FORM.
BUT ME, I THINK YOUR BLOOD WILL DO THE SAME.
ALL I NEED TO DO IS KILL IT.

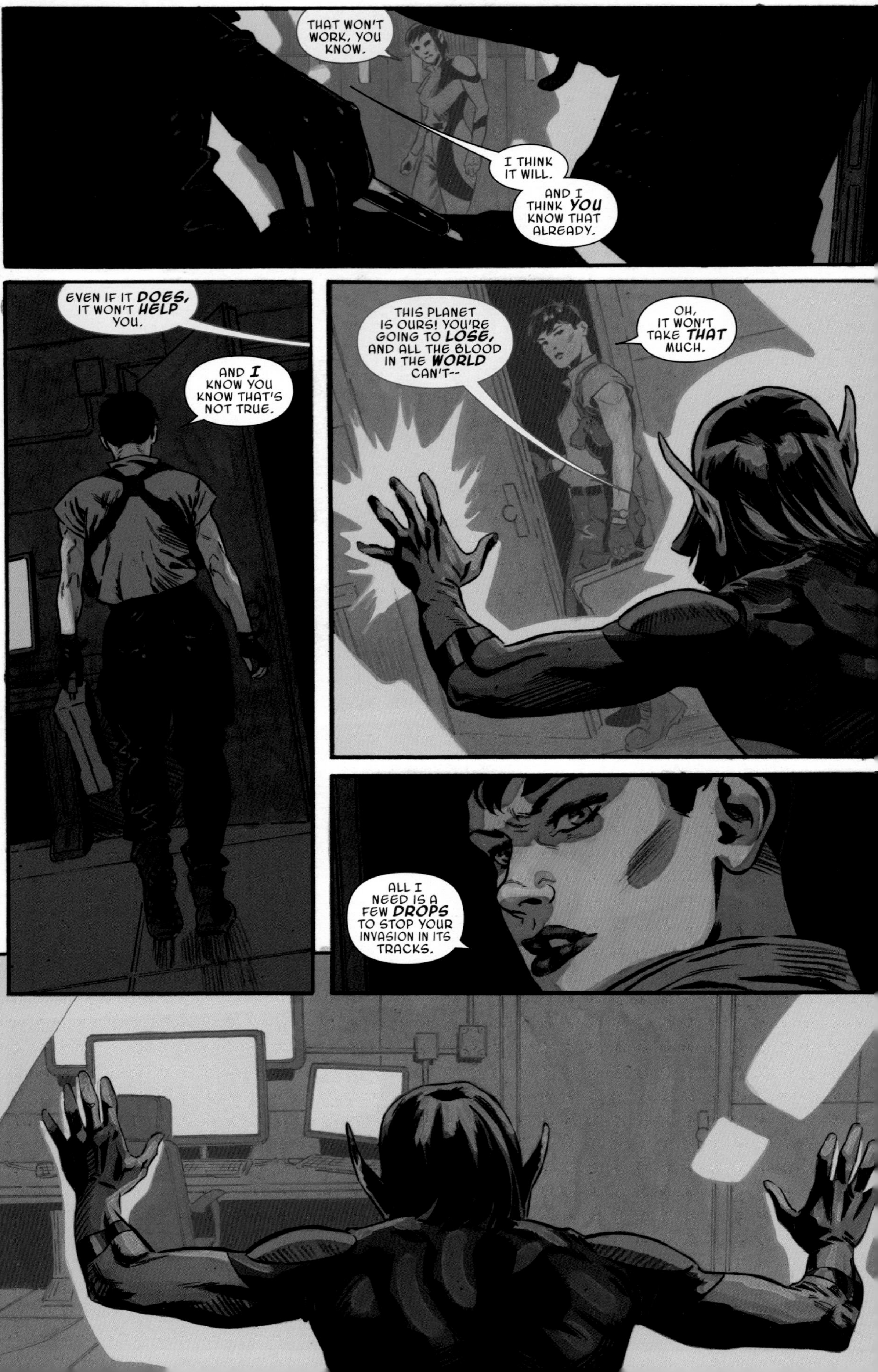
THAT WON'T WORK, YOU KNOW.
I THINK IT WILL.
AND I THINK YOU KNOW THAT ALREADY.
EVEN IF IT DOES, IT WON'T HELP YOU.
AND I KNOW YOU KNOW THAT'S NOT TRUE.
THIS PLANET IS OURS! YOU'RE GOING TO LOSE, AND ALL THE BLOOD IN THE WORLD CAN'T--
OH, IT WON'T TAKE THAT MUCH.
ALL I NEED IS A FEW DROPS TO STOP YOUR INVASION IN ITS TRACKS.

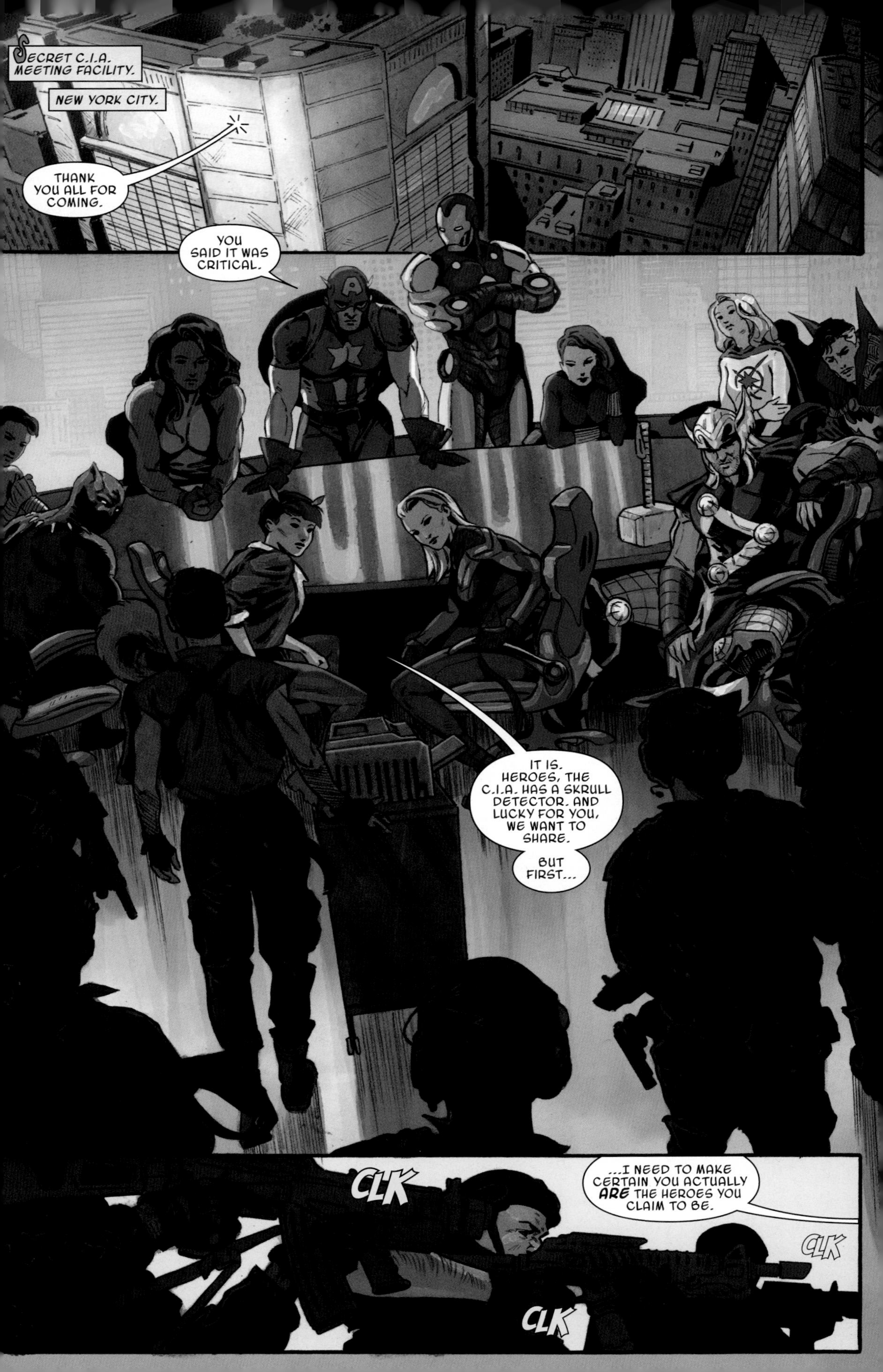
SECRET C.I.A. MEETING FACILITY.
NEW YORK CITY.
THANK YOU ALL FOR COMING.
YOU SAID IT WAS CRITICAL.
IT IS. HEROES, THE C.I.A. HAS A SKRULL DETECTOR. AND LUCKY FOR YOU, WE WANT TO SHARE.
BUT FIRST...
CLK
...I NEED TO MAKE CERTAIN YOU ACTUALLY ARE THE HEROES YOU CLAIM TO BE.
CLK
CLK

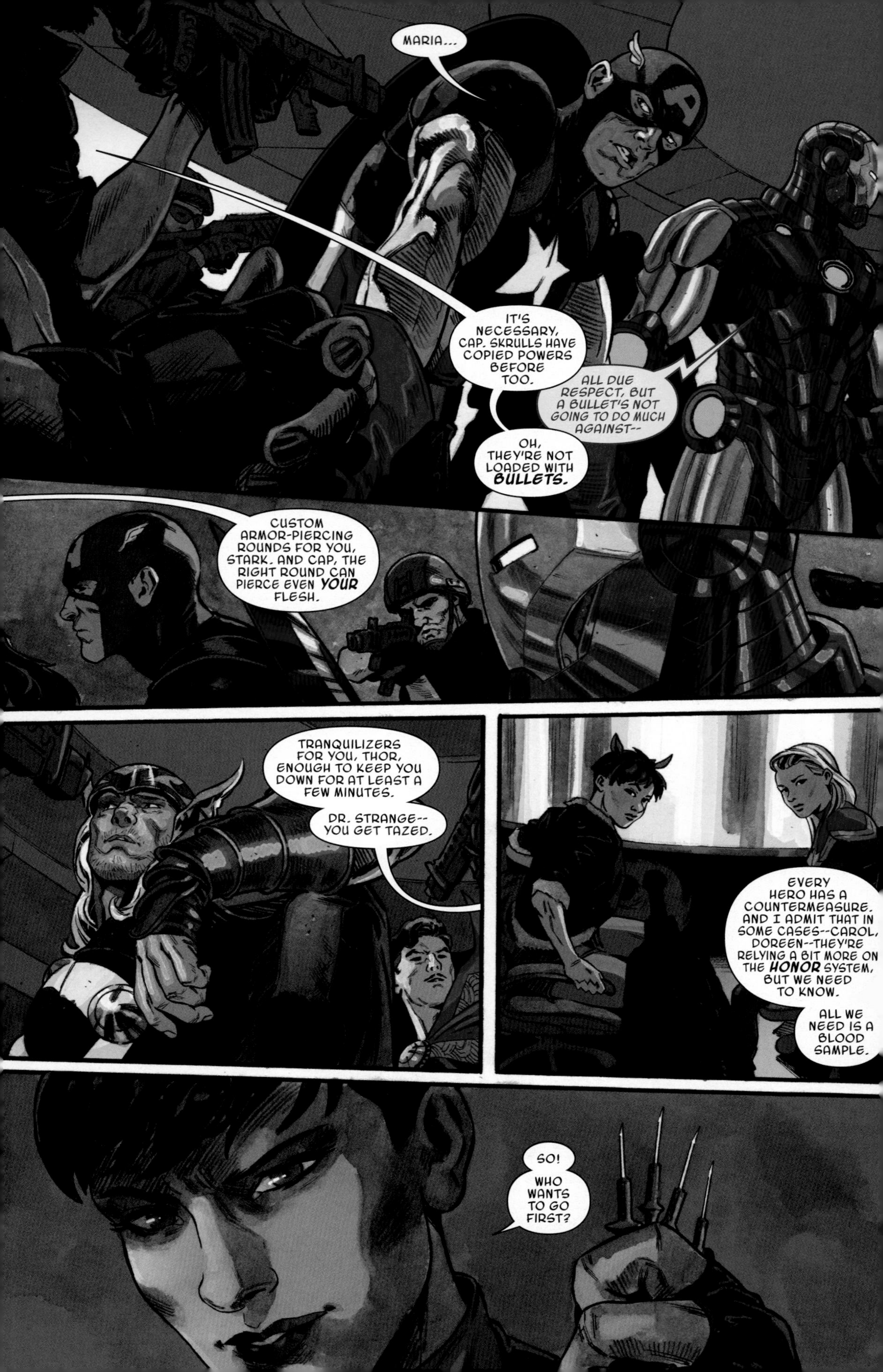
MARIA...
IT'S NECESSARY, CAP. SKRULLS HAVE COPIED POWERS BEFORE TOO.
ALL DUE RESPECT, BUT A BULLET'S NOT GOING TO DO MUCH AGAINST--
OH, THEY'RE NOT LOADED WITH BULLETS.
CUSTOM ARMOR-PIERCING ROUNDS FOR YOU, STARK. AND CAP, THE RIGHT ROUND CAN PIERCE EVEN YOUR FLESH.
TRANQUILIZERS FOR YOU, THOR, ENOUGH TO KEEP YOU DOWN FOR AT LEAST A FEW MINUTES.
DR. STRANGE-- YOU GET TAZED.
EVERY HERO HAS A COUNTERMEASURE. AND I ADMIT THAT IN SOME CASES--CAROL, DOREEN--THEY'RE RELYING A BIT MORE ON THE HONOR SYSTEM, BUT WE NEED TO KNOW.
ALL WE NEED IS A BLOOD SAMPLE.
SO!
WHO WANTS TO GO FIRST?

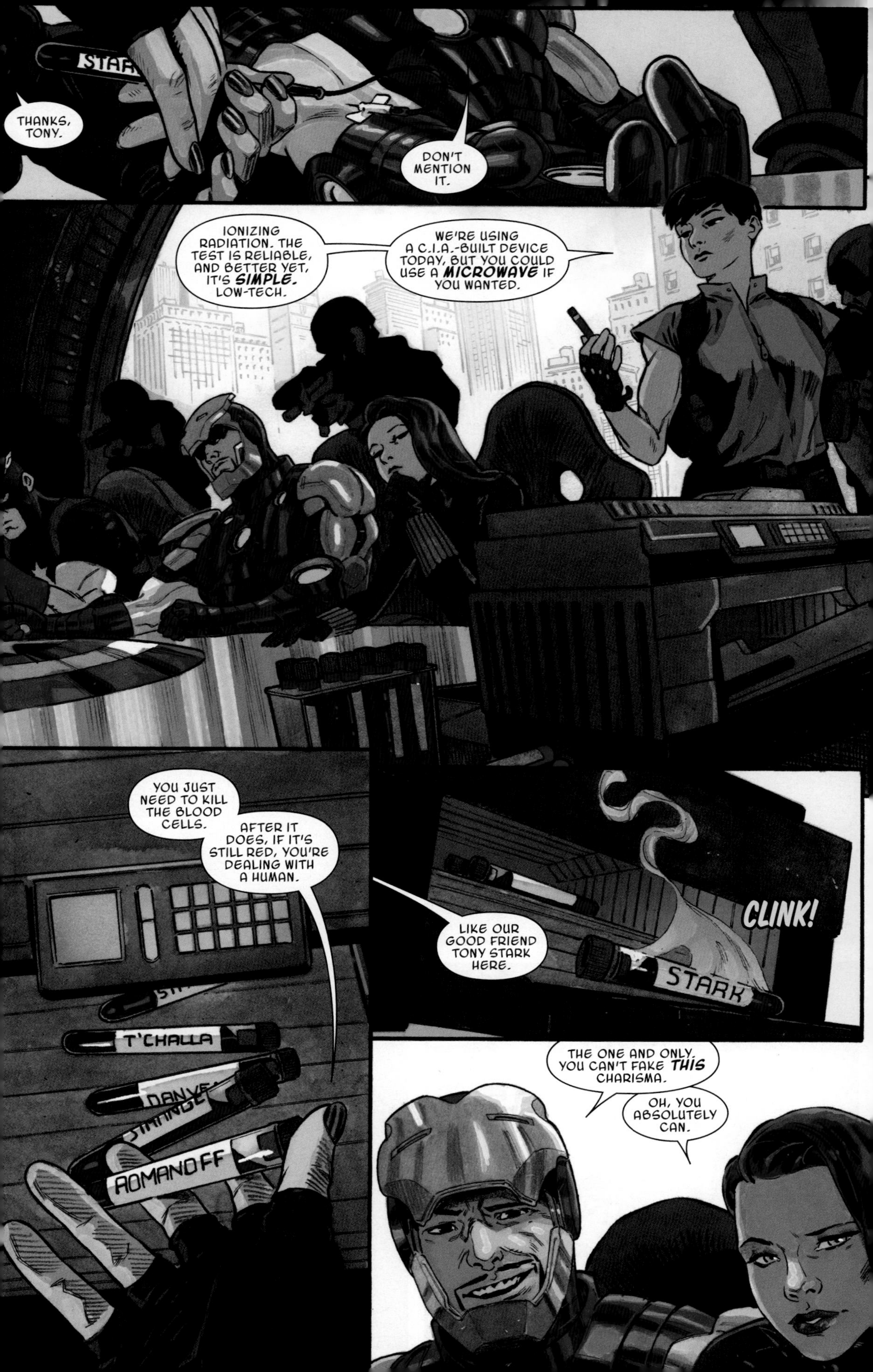
STARK
THANKS, TONY.
DON'T MENTION IT.
IONIZING RADIATION. THE TEST IS RELIABLE, AND BETTER YET, IT'S SIMPLE. LOW-TECH.
WE'RE USING A C.I.A.-BUILT DEVICE TODAY, BUT YOU COULD USE A MICROWAVE IF YOU WANTED.
YOU JUST NEED TO KILL THE BLOOD CELLS.
AFTER IT DOES, IF IT'S STILL RED, YOU'RE DEALING WITH A HUMAN.
T'CHALLA
ROMANOFF
LIKE OUR GOOD FRIEND TONY STARK HERE.
CLINK!
STARK
THE ONE AND ONLY. YOU CAN'T FAKE THIS CHARISMA.
OH, YOU ABSOLUTELY CAN.

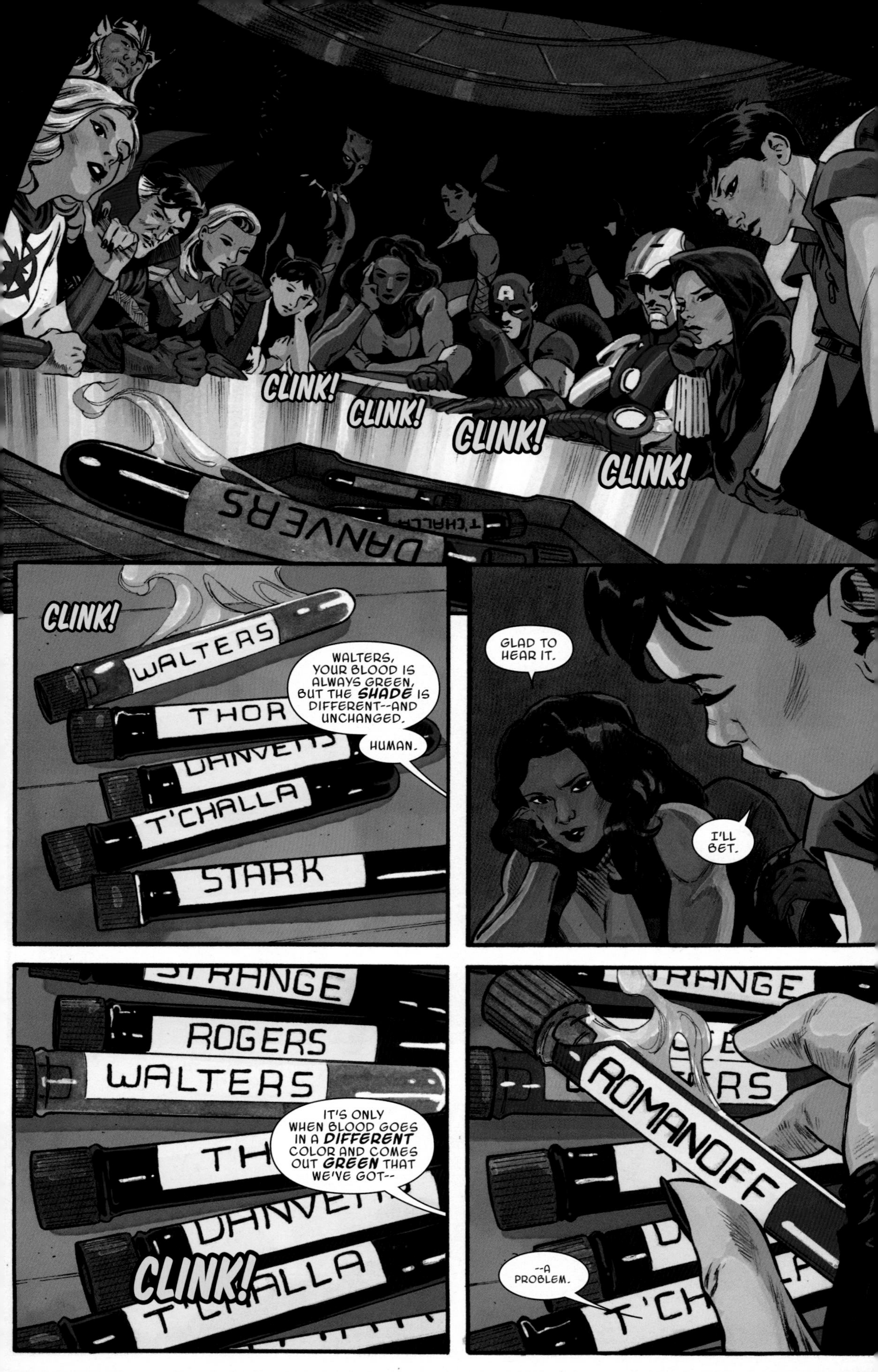
CLINK!
CLINK!
CLINK!
CLINK!
DANVERS
T'CHALLA
CLINK!
WALTERS
THOR
T'CHALLA
STARK
WALTERS, YOUR BLOOD IS ALWAYS GREEN, BUT THE SHADE IS DIFFERENT--AND UNCHANGED.
HUMAN.
GLAD TO HEAR IT.
I'LL BET.
RANGE
ROGERS
WALTERS
IT'S ONLY WHEN BLOOD GOES IN A DIFFERENT COLOR AND COMES OUT GREEN THAT WE'VE GOT--
CLINK!
ROMANOFF
--A PROBLEM.

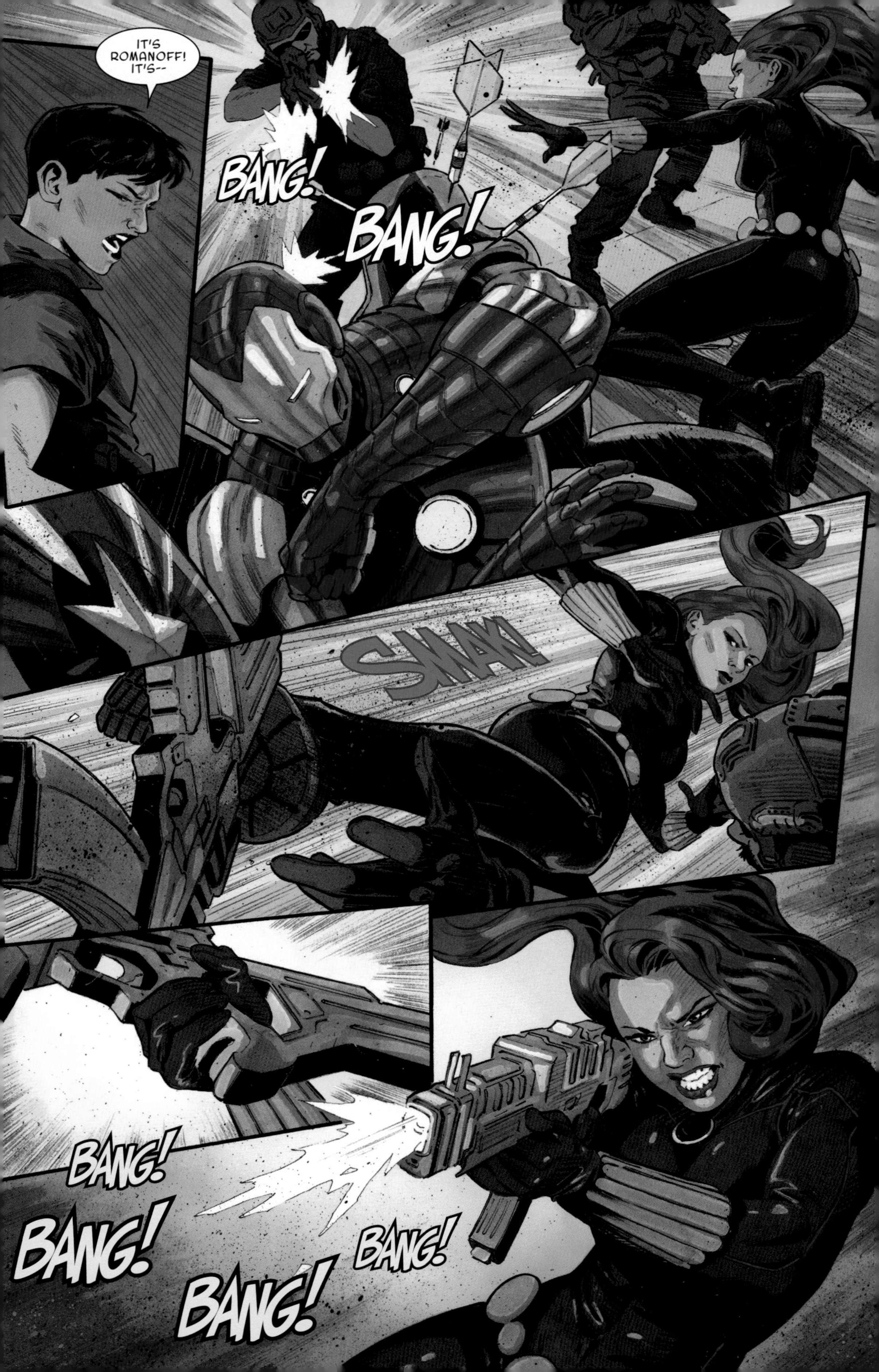

IT'S ROMANOFF! IT'S--
BANG!
BANG!
SMAK!
BANG!
BANG!
BANG!
BANG!

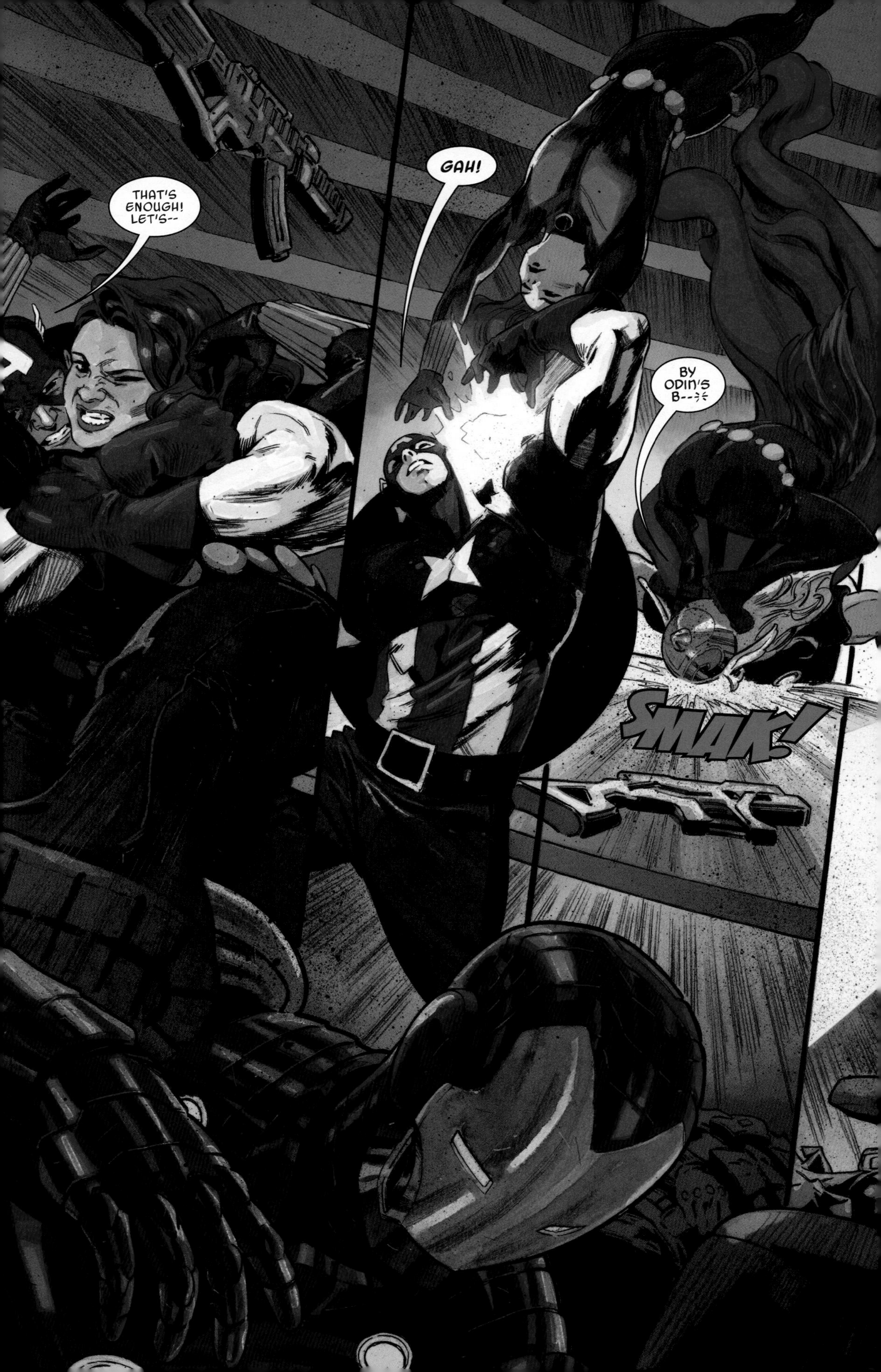
THAT'S ENOUGH! LET'S--
GAH!
BY ODIN'S B--
SMAK!

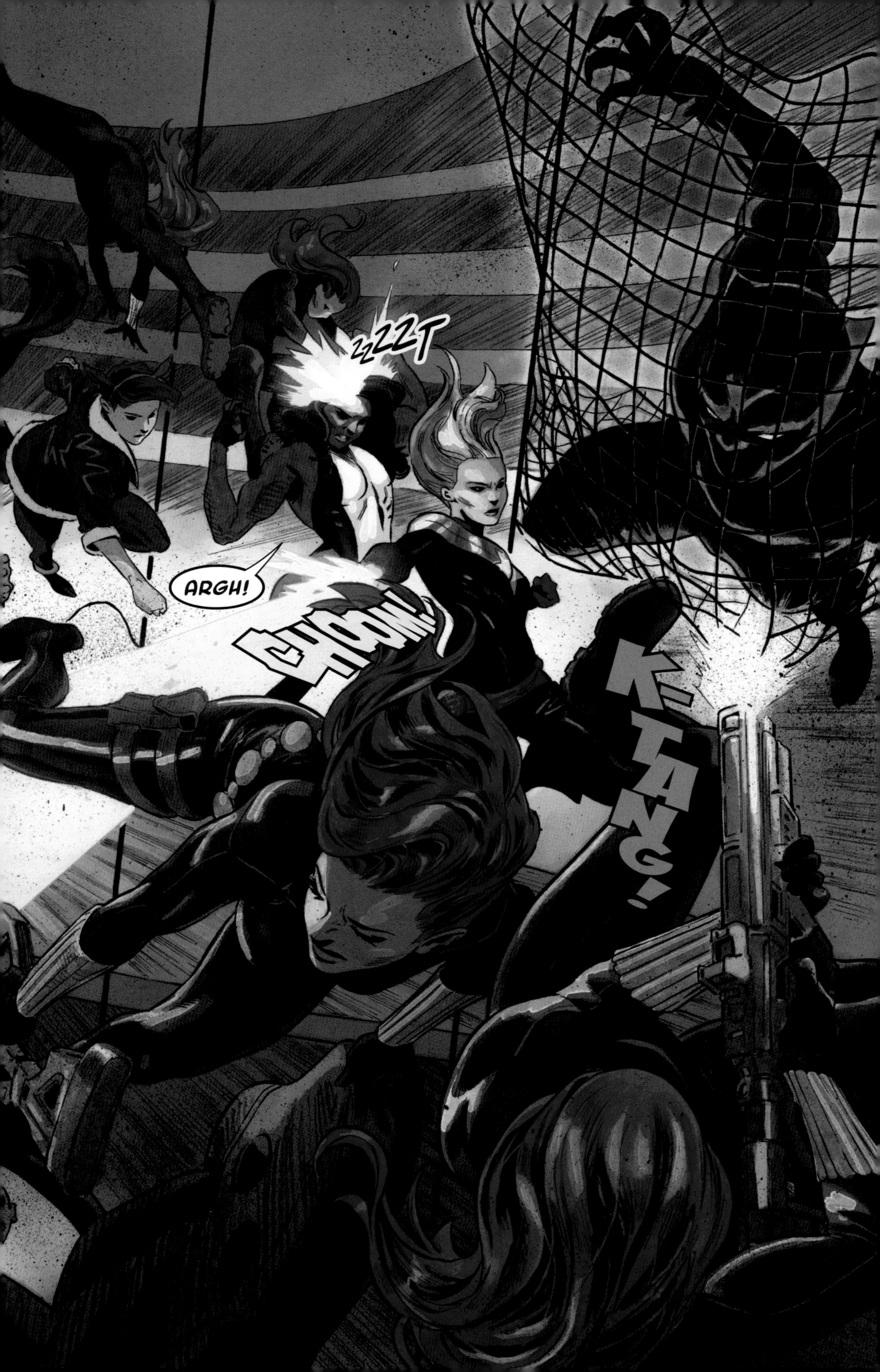

zzZZT
ARGH!
K-TANG!

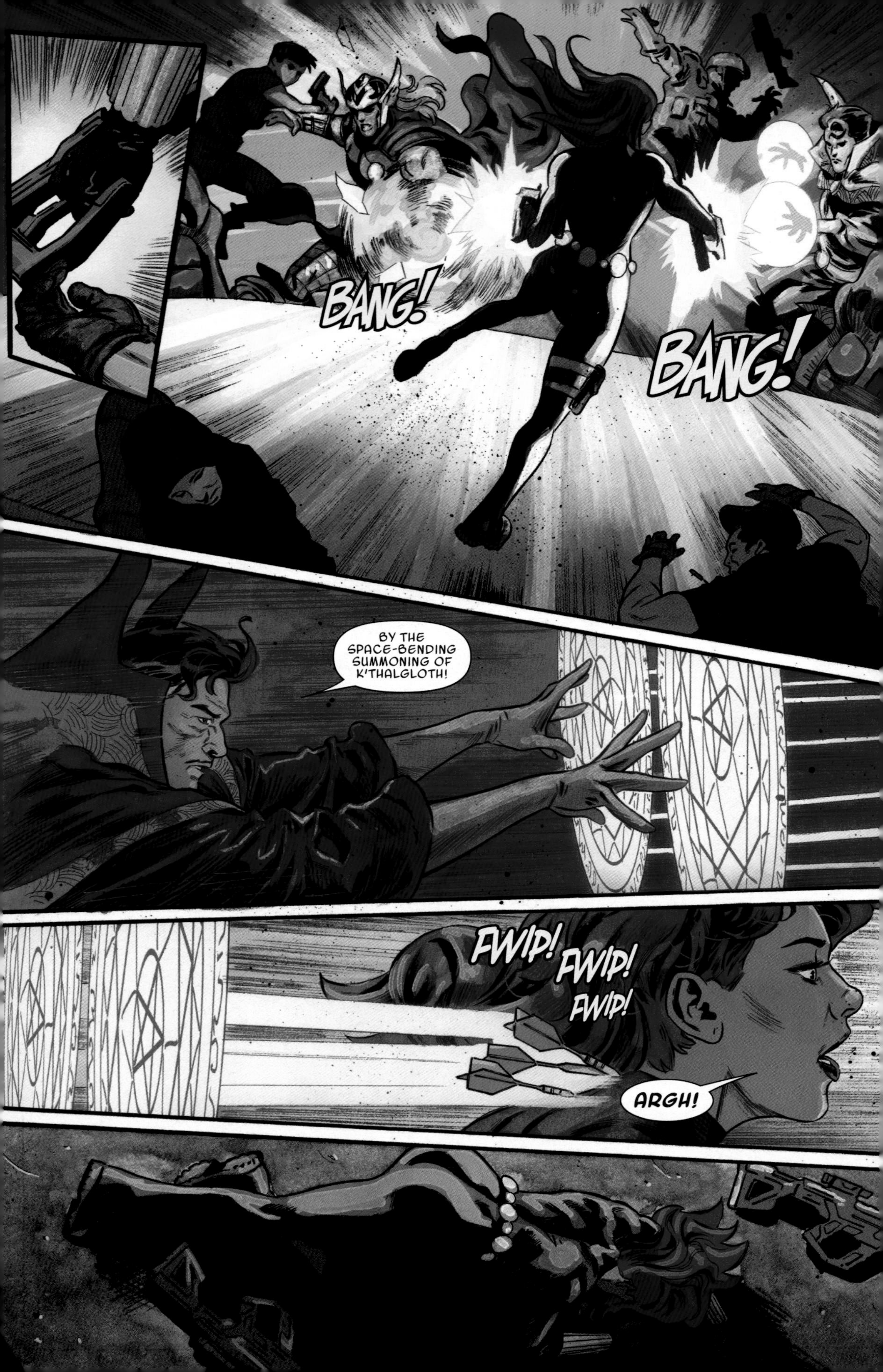
BANG!
BANG!
BY THE SPACE-BENDING SUMMONING OF K'THALGLOTH!
FWIP!
FWIP!
FWIP!
ARGH!

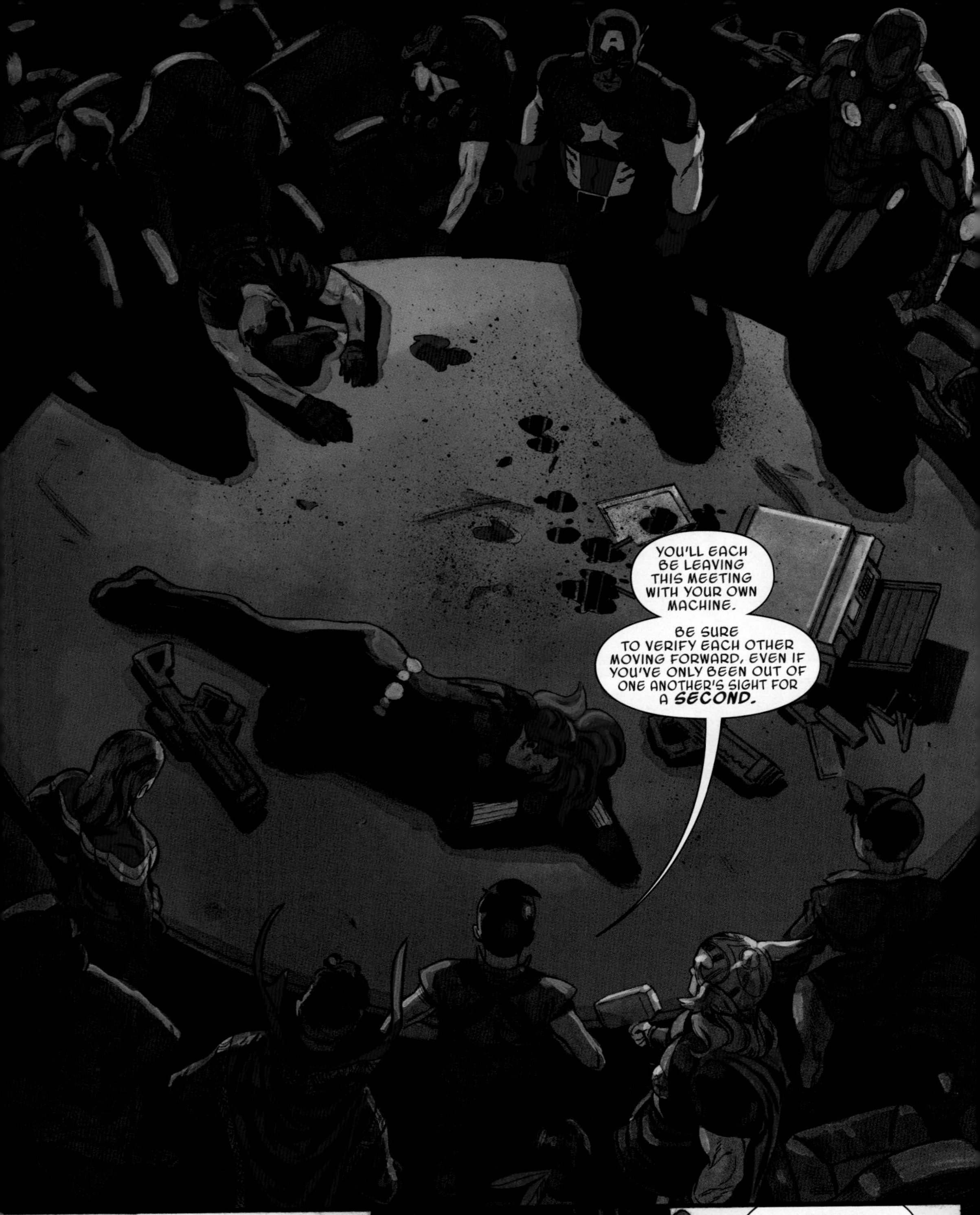
YOU'LL EACH BE LEAVING THIS MEETING WITH YOUR OWN MACHINE.
BE SURE TO VERIFY EACH OTHER MOVING FORWARD, EVEN IF YOU'VE ONLY BEEN OUT OF ONE ANOTHER'S SIGHT FOR A **SECOND.**

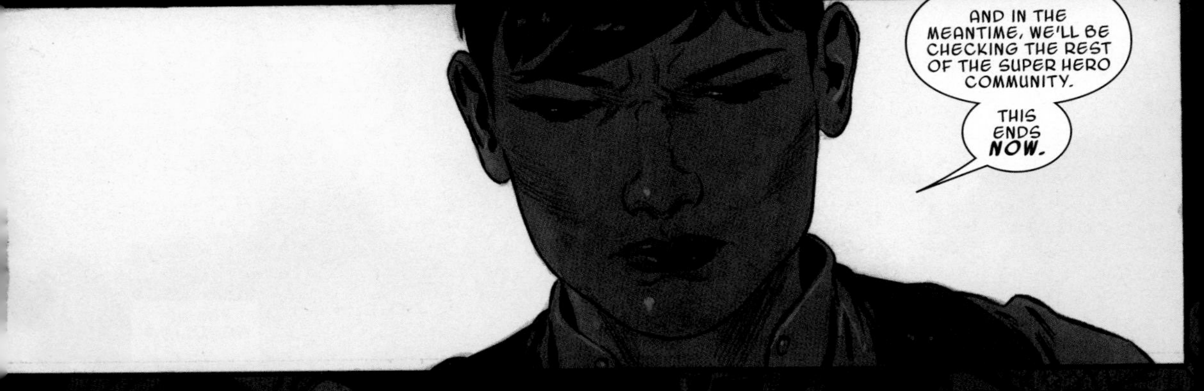
AND IN THE MEANTIME, WE'LL BE CHECKING THE REST OF THE SUPER HERO COMMUNITY.
THIS ENDS **NOW.**

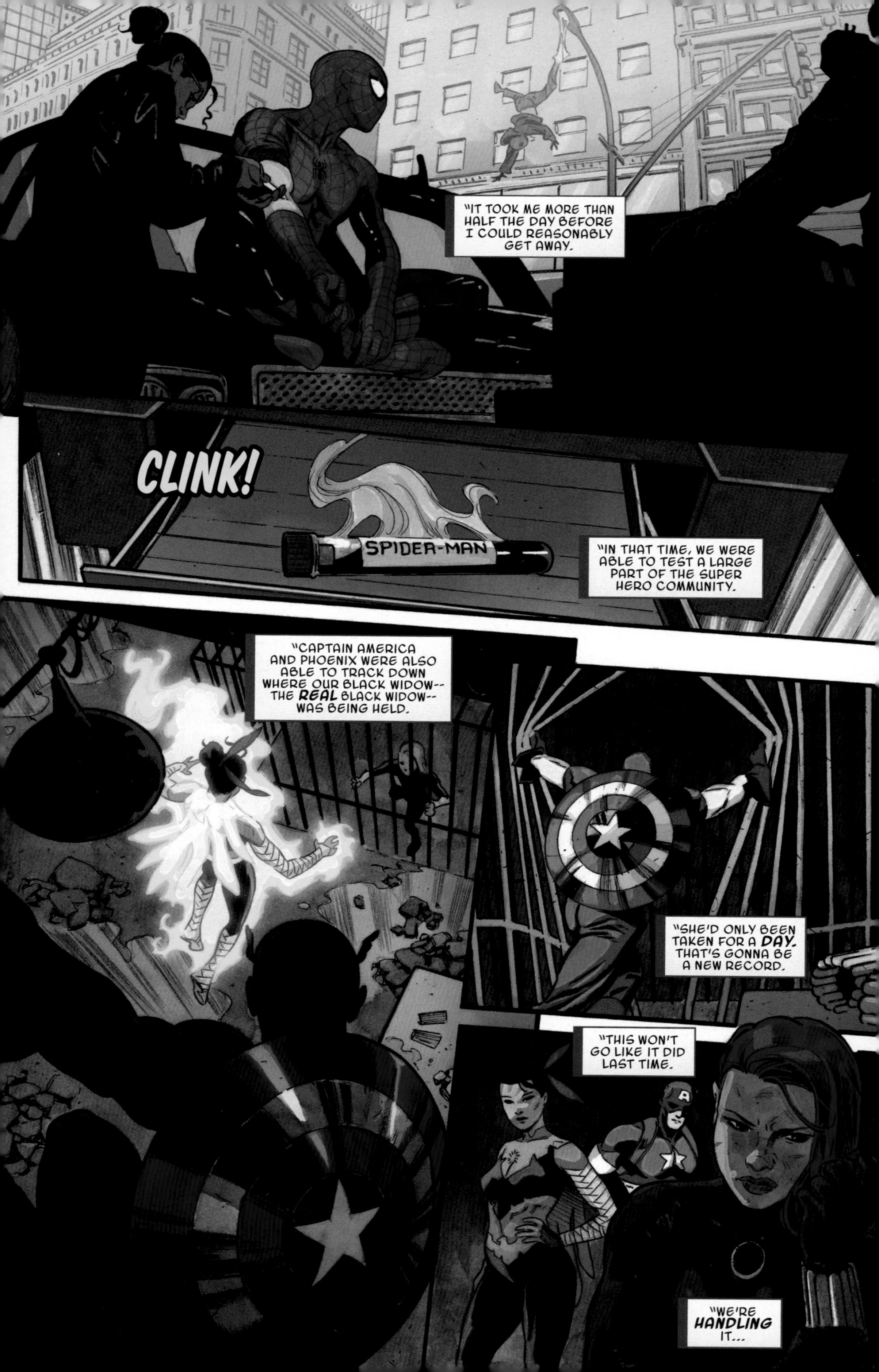
"IT TOOK ME MORE THAN HALF THE DAY BEFORE I COULD REASONABLY GET AWAY.
CLINK!
SPIDER-MAN
"IN THAT TIME, WE WERE ABLE TO TEST A LARGE PART OF THE SUPER HERO COMMUNITY.
"CAPTAIN AMERICA AND PHOENIX WERE ALSO ABLE TO TRACK DOWN WHERE OUR BLACK WIDOW-- THE REAL BLACK WIDOW-- WAS BEING HELD.
"SHE'D ONLY BEEN TAKEN FOR A DAY. THAT'S GONNA BE A NEW RECORD.
"THIS WON'T GO LIKE IT DID LAST TIME.
"WE'RE HANDLING IT...

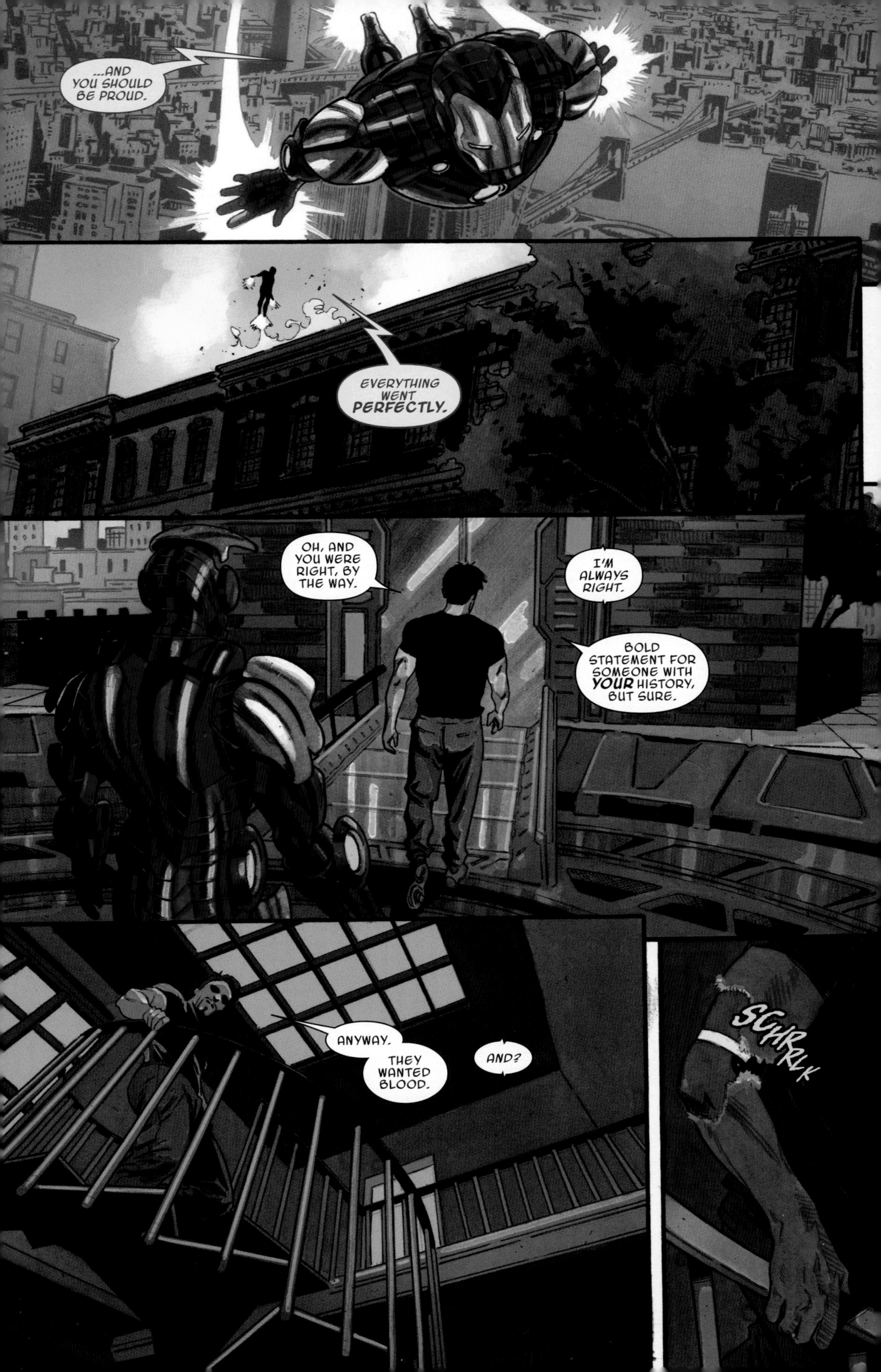
...AND YOU SHOULD BE PROUD.
EVERYTHING WENT PERFECTLY.
OH, AND YOU WERE RIGHT, BY THE WAY.
I'M ALWAYS RIGHT.
BOLD STATEMENT FOR SOMEONE WITH YOUR HISTORY, BUT SURE.
ANYWAY.
THEY WANTED BLOOD.
AND?
SCHRRLK

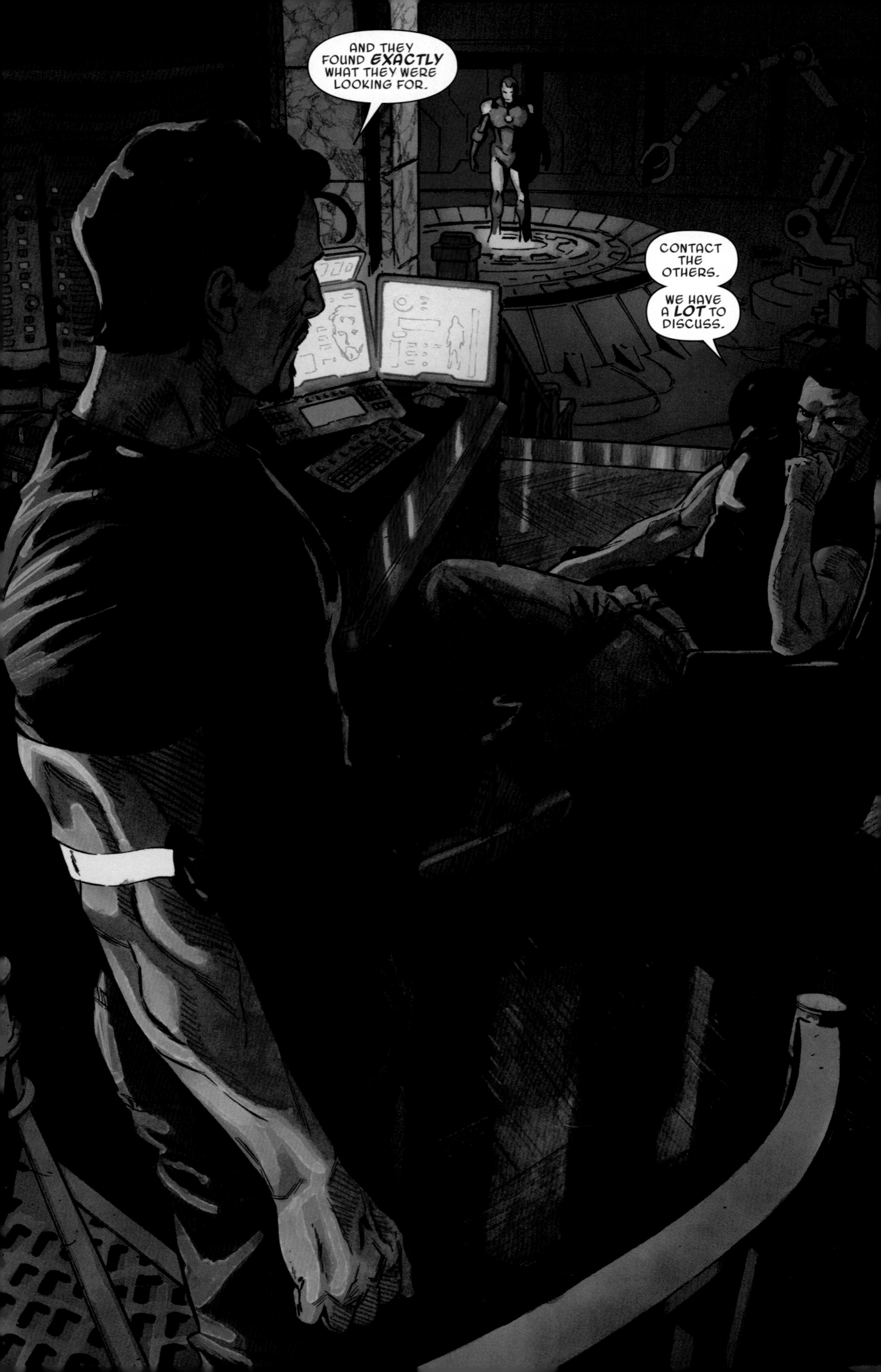
AND THEY FOUND EXACTLY WHAT THEY WERE LOOKING FOR.
CONTACT THE OTHERS.
WE HAVE A LOT TO DISCUSS.

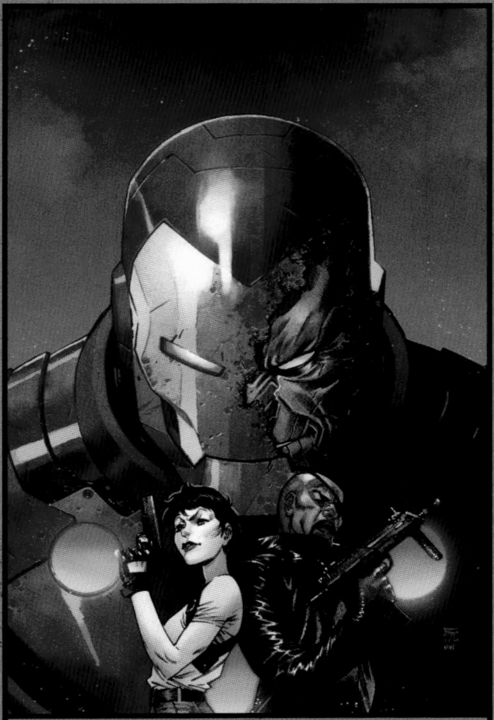

#2 variant by
Dike Ruan & Matthew Wilson

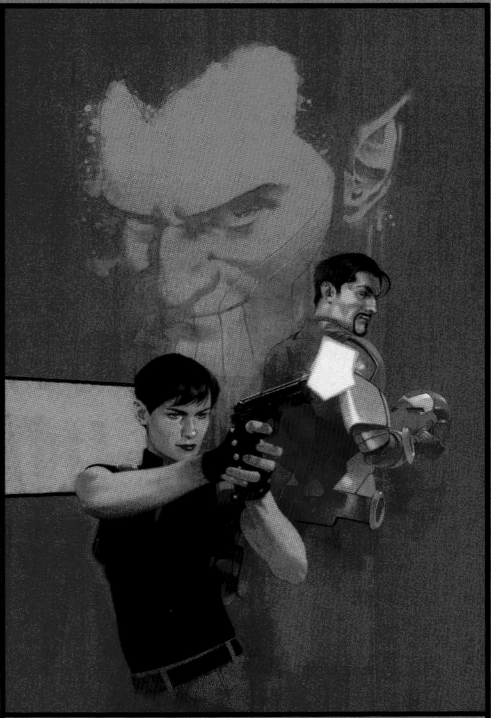

#3 variant by
Marc Aspinall

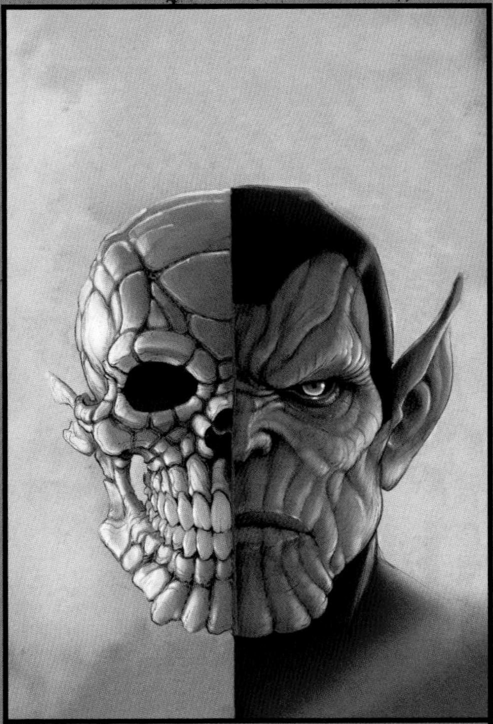

#3 Marvel Anatomy
variant by Jonah Lobe

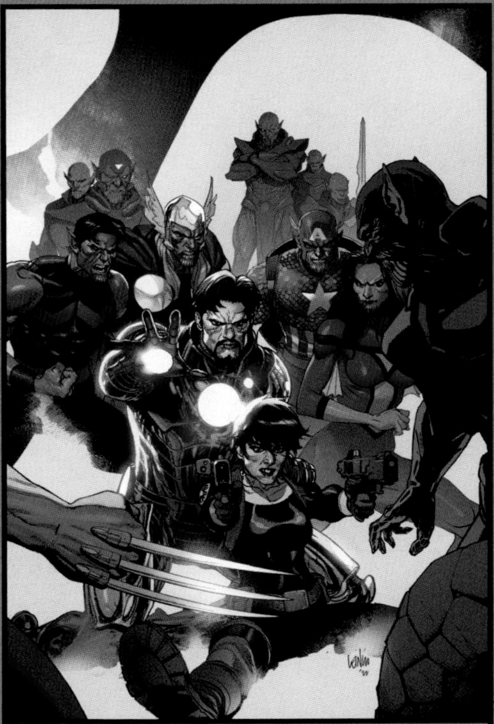

#4 variant by
Leinil Francis Yu & Sunny Gho

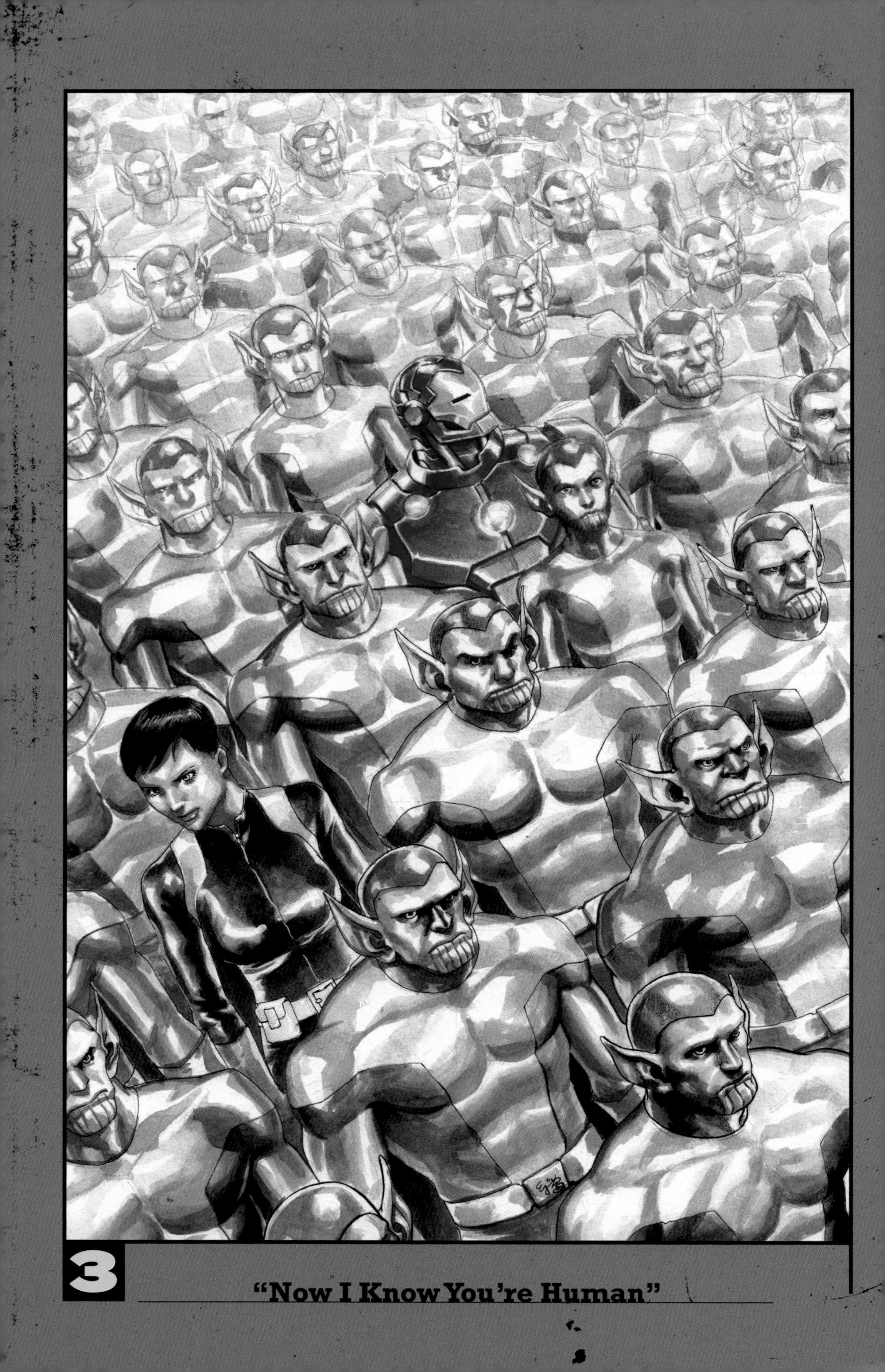

3

"Now I Know You're Human"

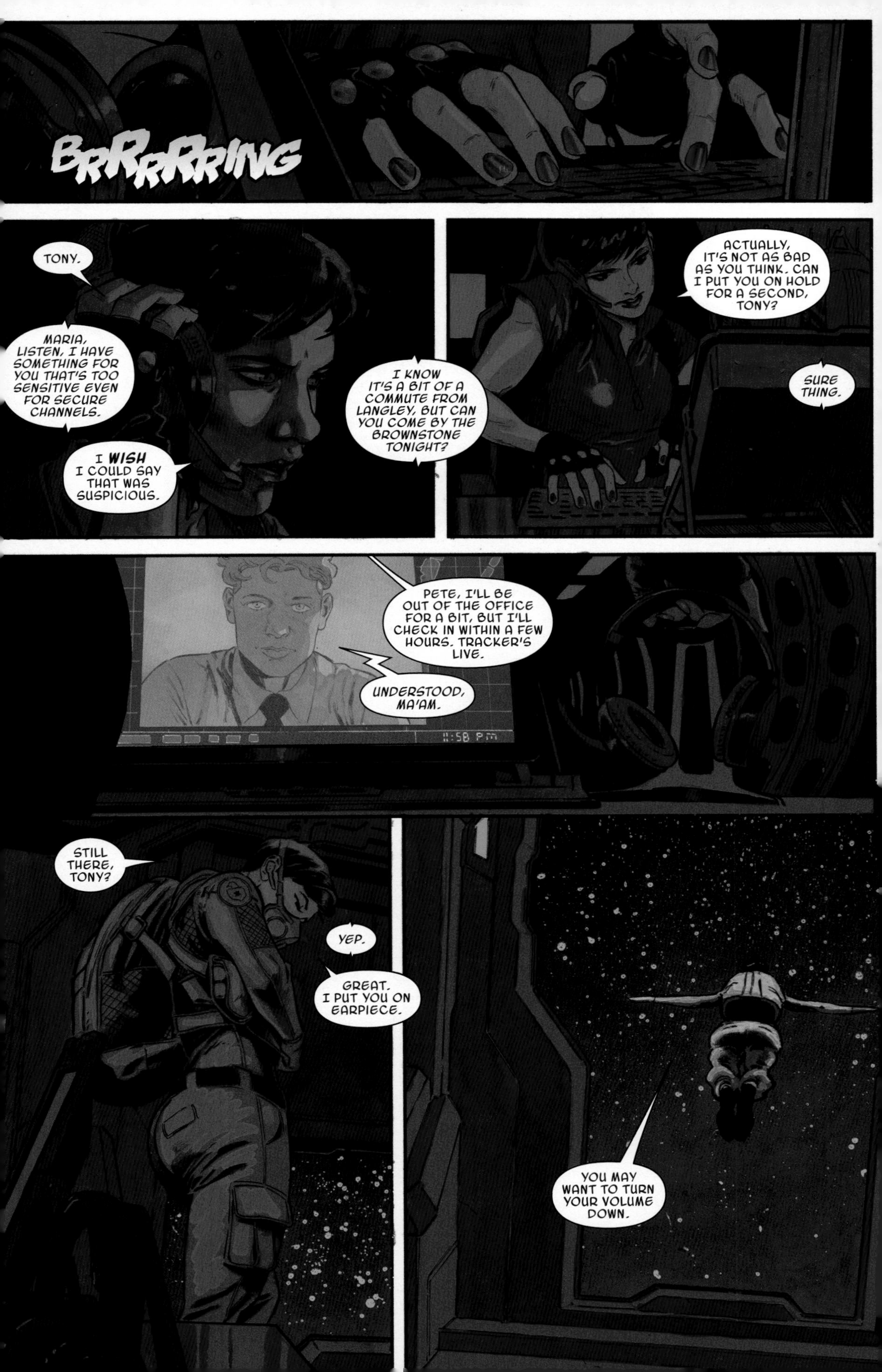
BRRRRRRING
TONY.
MARIA, LISTEN, I HAVE SOMETHING FOR YOU THAT'S TOO SENSITIVE EVEN FOR SECURE CHANNELS.
I WISH I COULD SAY THAT WAS SUSPICIOUS.
I KNOW IT'S A BIT OF A COMMUTE FROM LANGLEY, BUT CAN YOU COME BY THE BROWNSTONE TONIGHT?
ACTUALLY, IT'S NOT AS BAD AS YOU THINK. CAN I PUT YOU ON HOLD FOR A SECOND, TONY?
SURE THING.
PETE, I'LL BE OUT OF THE OFFICE FOR A BIT, BUT I'LL CHECK IN WITHIN A FEW HOURS. TRACKER'S LIVE.
UNDERSTOOD, MA'AM.
11:58 PM
STILL THERE, TONY?
YEP.
GREAT. I PUT YOU ON EARPIECE.
YOU MAY WANT TO TURN YOUR VOLUME DOWN.

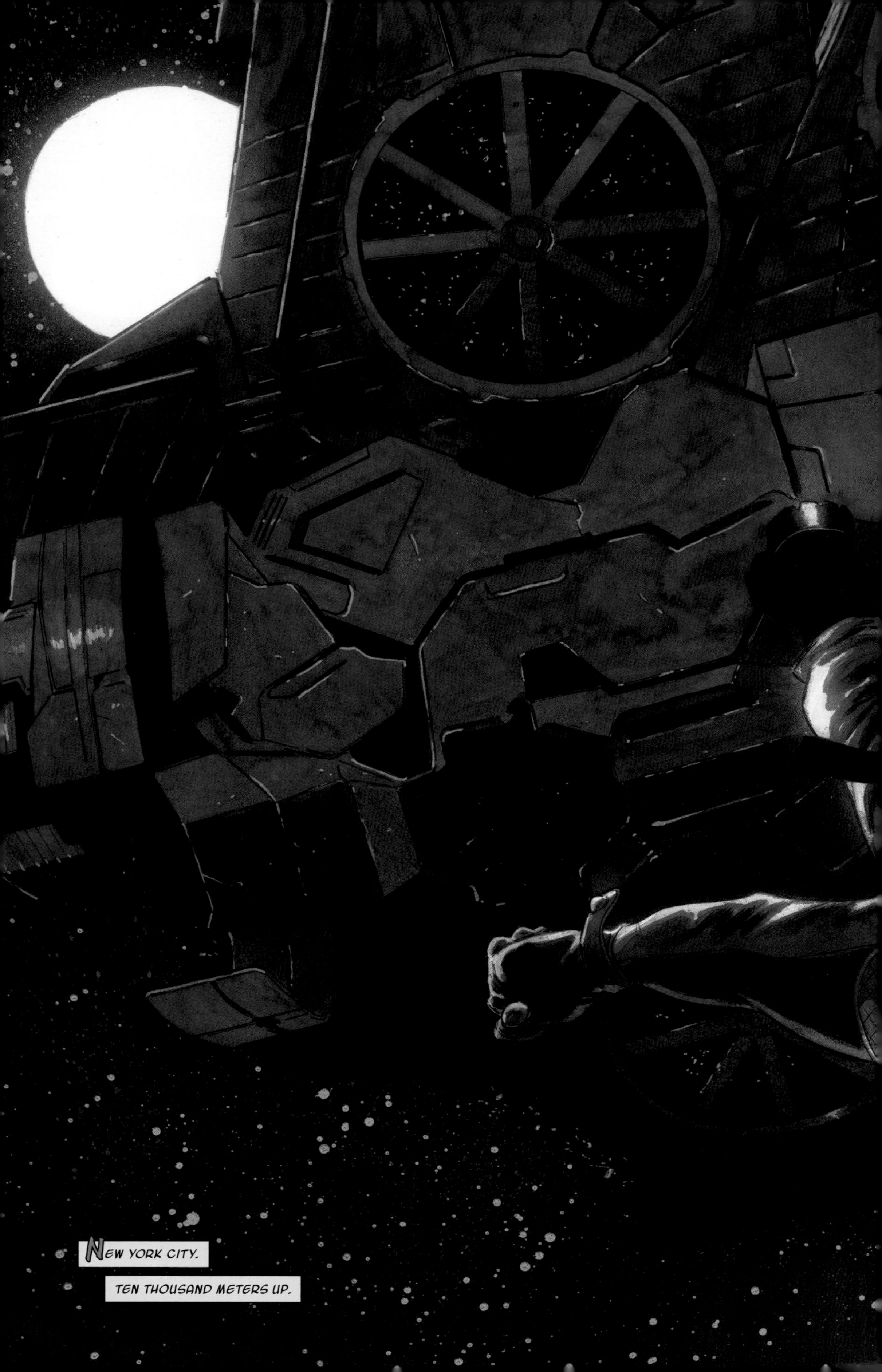
NEW YORK CITY.
TEN THOUSAND METERS UP.

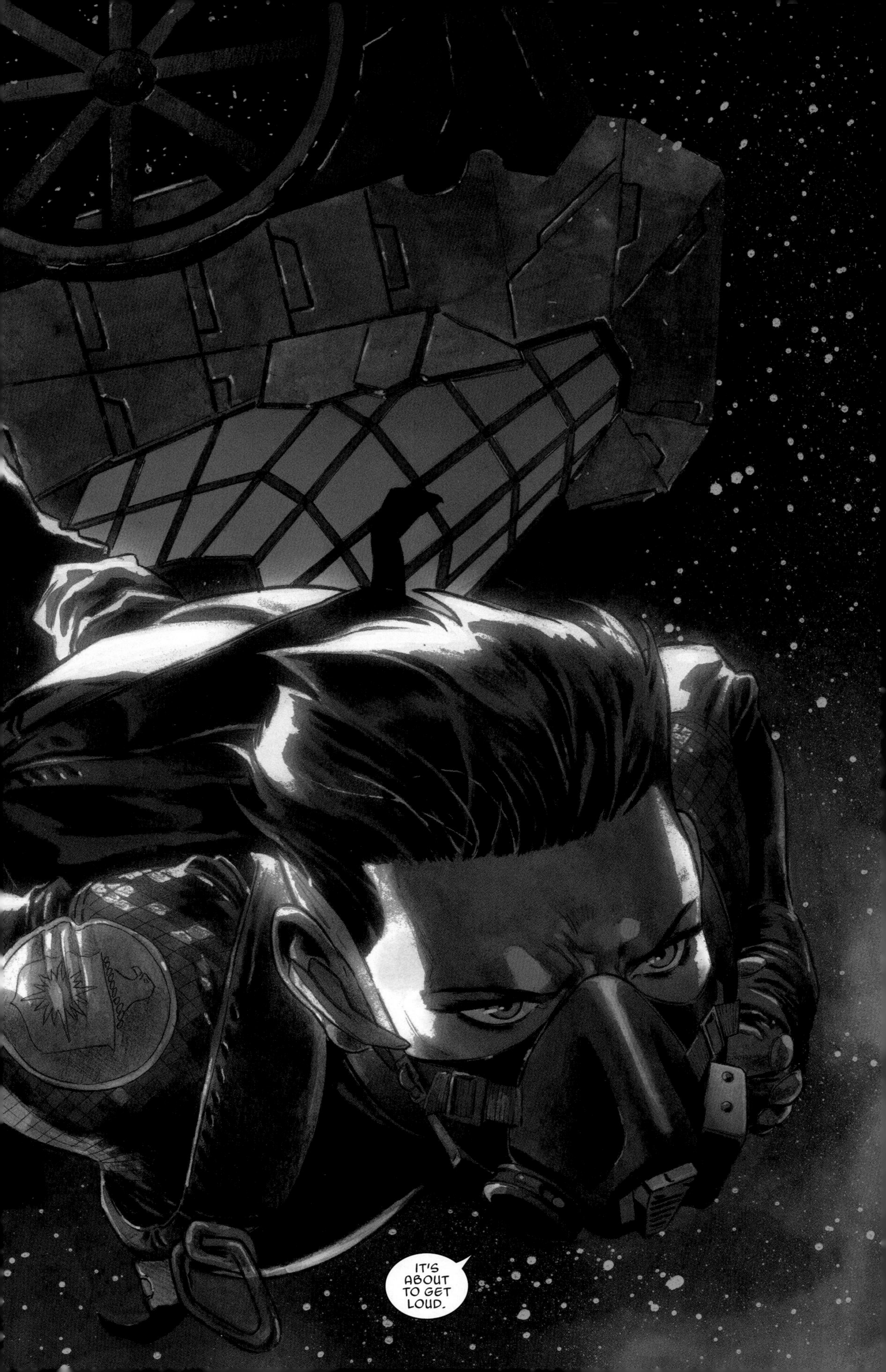
IT'S ABOUT TO GET LOUD.

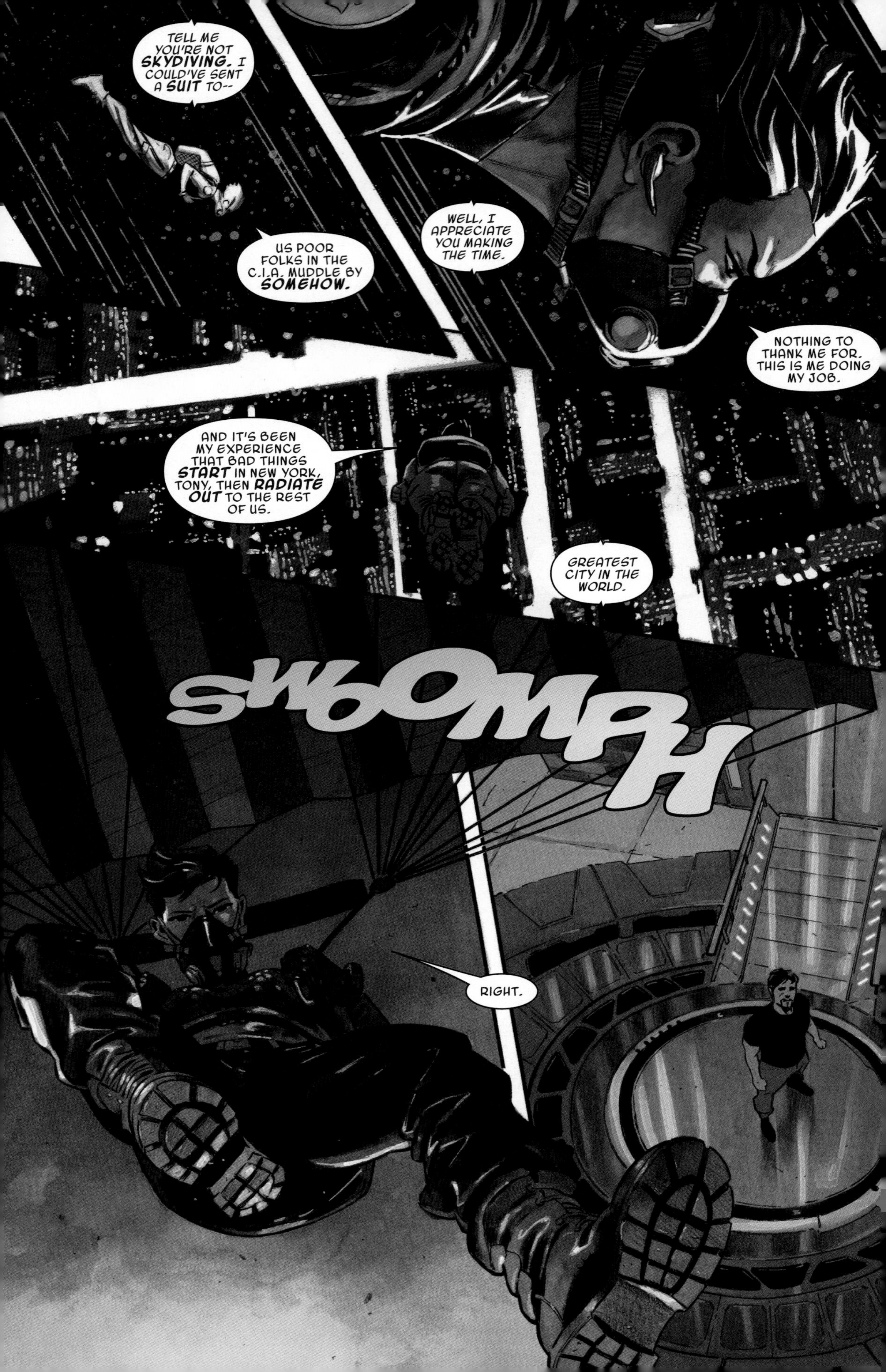
TELL ME YOU'RE NOT SKYDIVING. I COULD'VE SENT A SUIT TO--
US POOR FOLKS IN THE C.I.A. MUDDLE BY SOMEHOW.
WELL, I APPRECIATE YOU MAKING THE TIME.
NOTHING TO THANK ME FOR. THIS IS ME DOING MY JOB.
AND IT'S BEEN MY EXPERIENCE THAT BAD THINGS START IN NEW YORK, TONY, THEN RADIATE OUT TO THE REST OF US.
GREATEST CITY IN THE WORLD.
SWOOMPH
RIGHT.

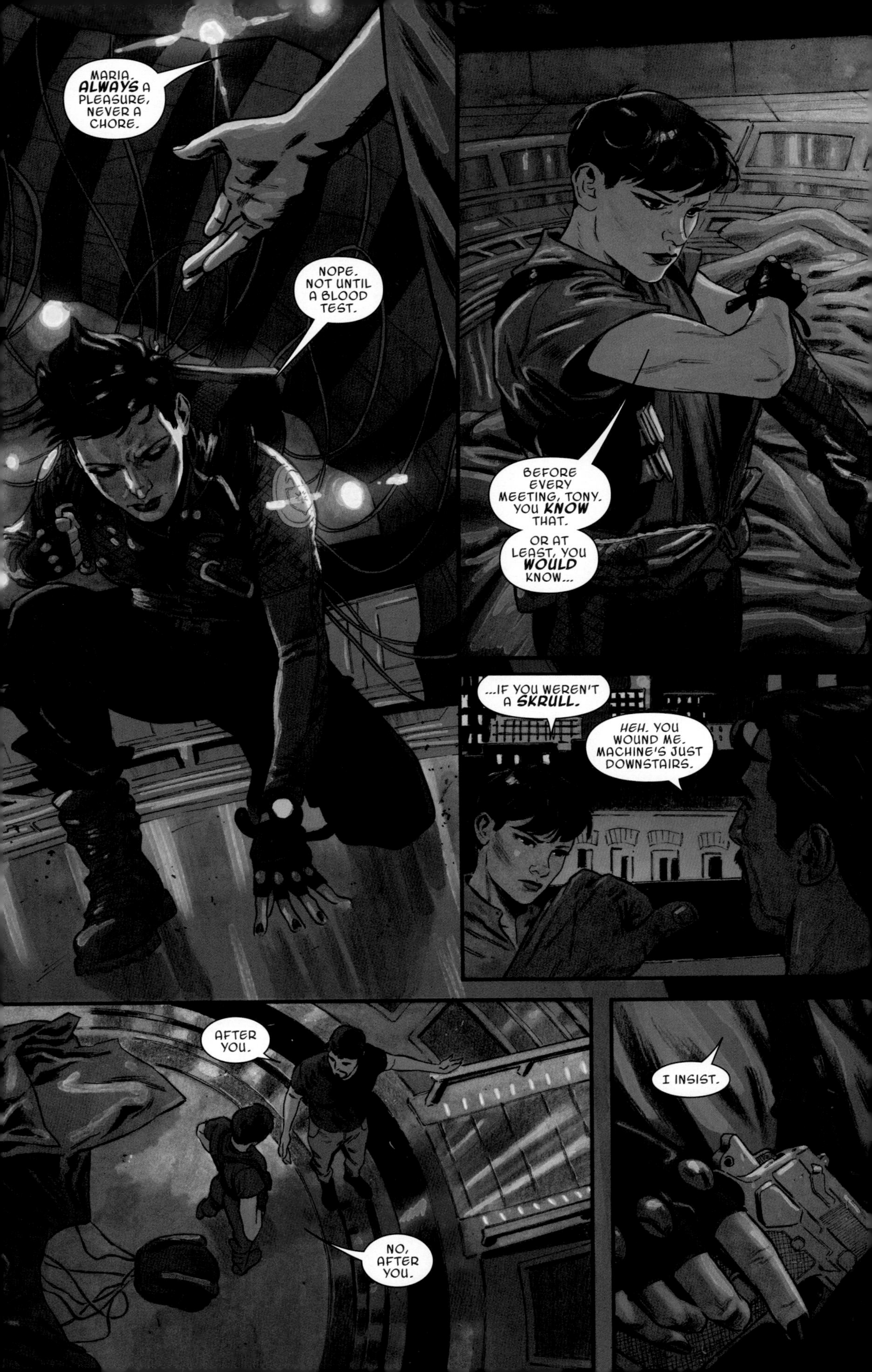
MARIA. **ALWAYS** A PLEASURE, NEVER A CHORE.
NOPE. NOT UNTIL A BLOOD TEST.
BEFORE EVERY MEETING, TONY. YOU **KNOW** THAT.
OR AT LEAST, YOU **WOULD** KNOW...
...IF YOU WEREN'T A **SKRULL.**
HEH. YOU WOUND ME. MACHINE'S JUST DOWNSTAIRS.
AFTER YOU.
NO, AFTER YOU.
I INSIST.

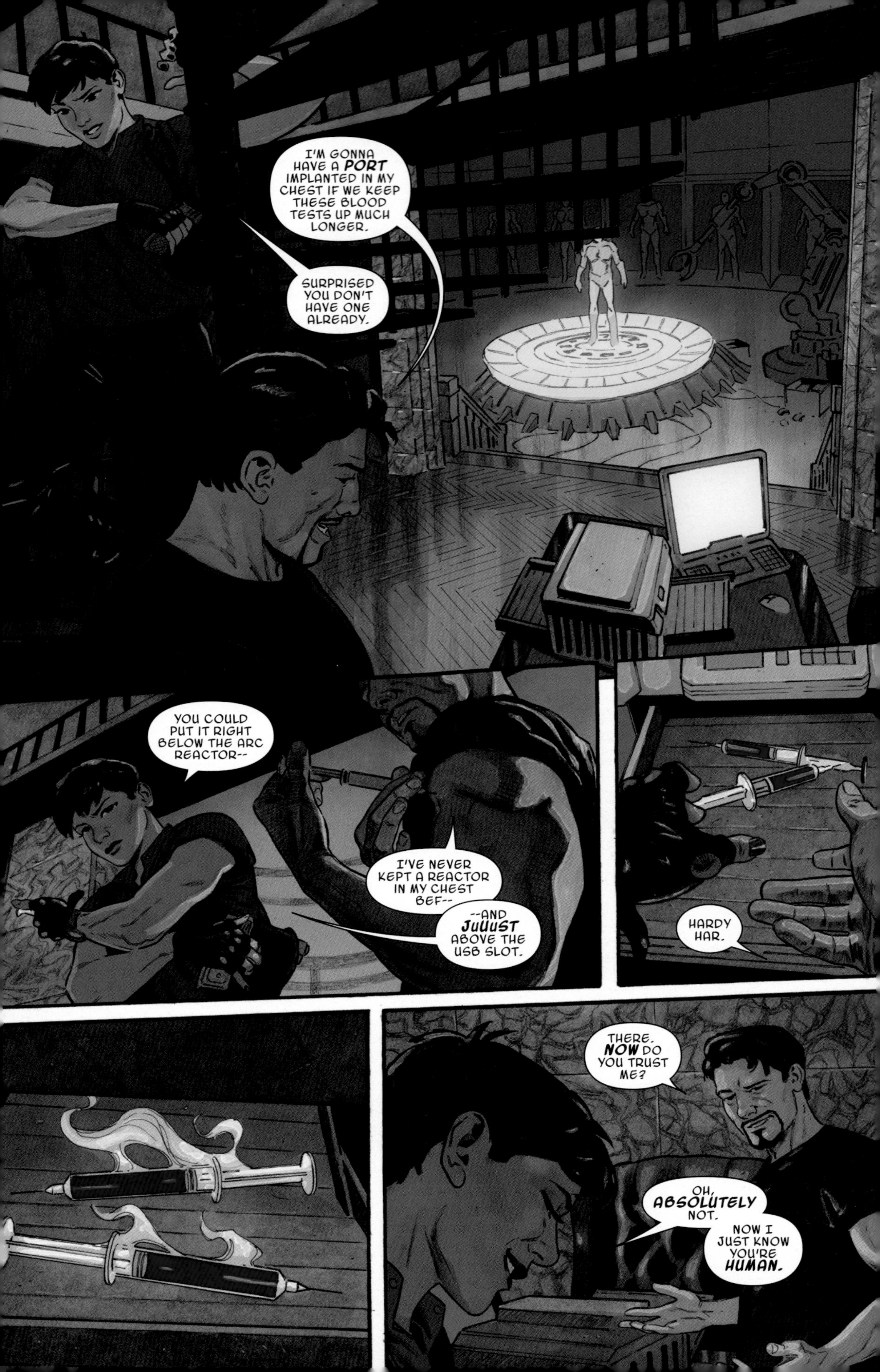
I'M GONNA HAVE A **PORT** IMPLANTED IN MY CHEST IF WE KEEP THESE BLOOD TESTS UP MUCH LONGER.
SURPRISED YOU DON'T HAVE ONE ALREADY.
YOU COULD PUT IT RIGHT BELOW THE ARC REACTOR--
I'VE NEVER KEPT A REACTOR IN MY CHEST BEF--
--AND ***JuUuST*** ABOVE THE USB SLOT.
HARDY HAR.
THERE. ***NOW*** DO YOU TRUST ME?
OH, ***ABSOLUTELY*** NOT.
NOW I JUST KNOW YOU'RE ***HUMAN.***

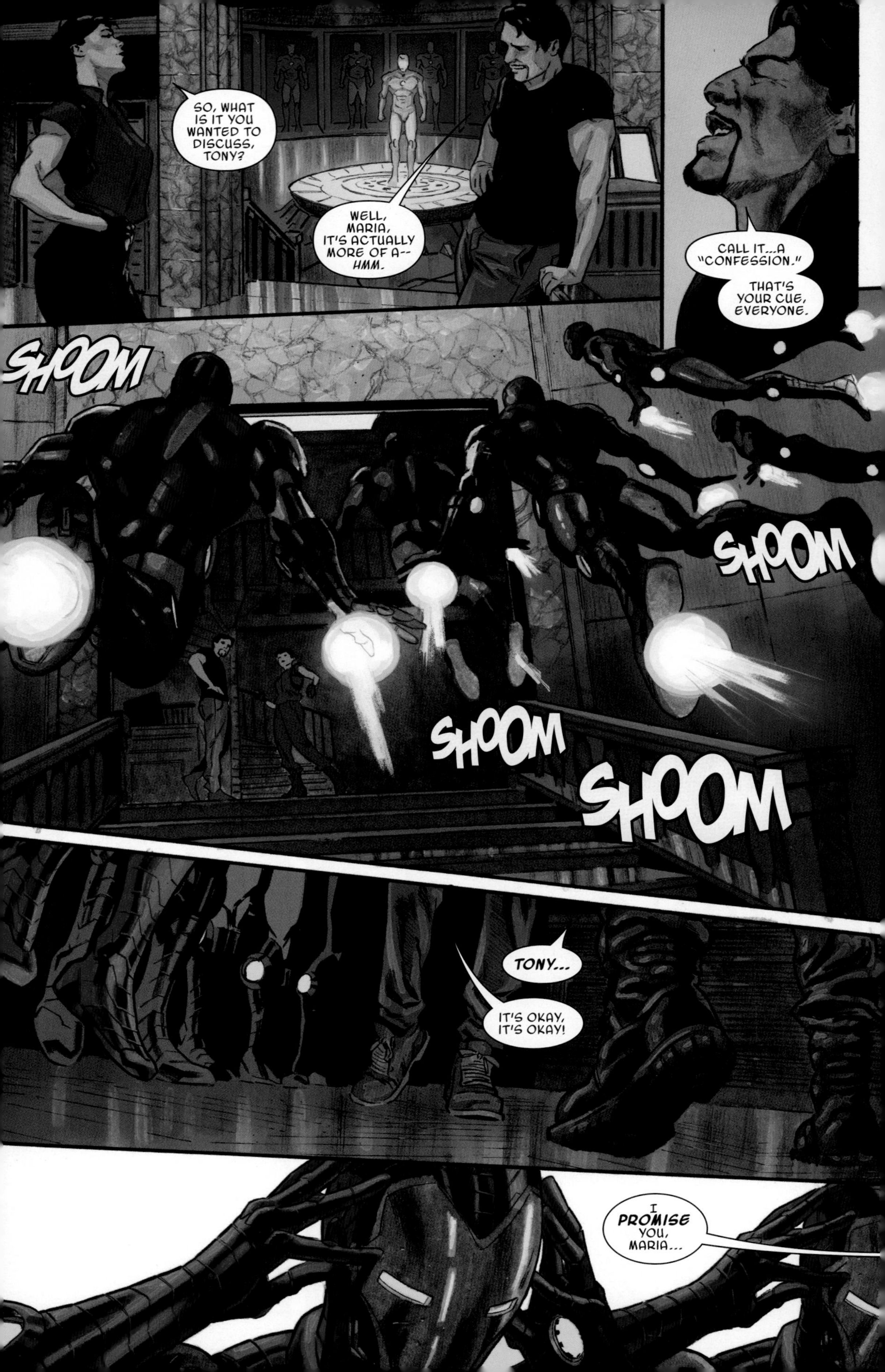

SO, WHAT IS IT YOU WANTED TO DISCUSS, TONY?
WELL, MARIA, IT'S ACTUALLY MORE OF A-- HMM.
CALL IT...A "CONFESSION."
THAT'S YOUR CUE, EVERYONE.
SHOOM
SHOOM
SHOOM
SHOOM
TONY...
IT'S OKAY, IT'S OKAY!
I PROMISE YOU, MARIA...

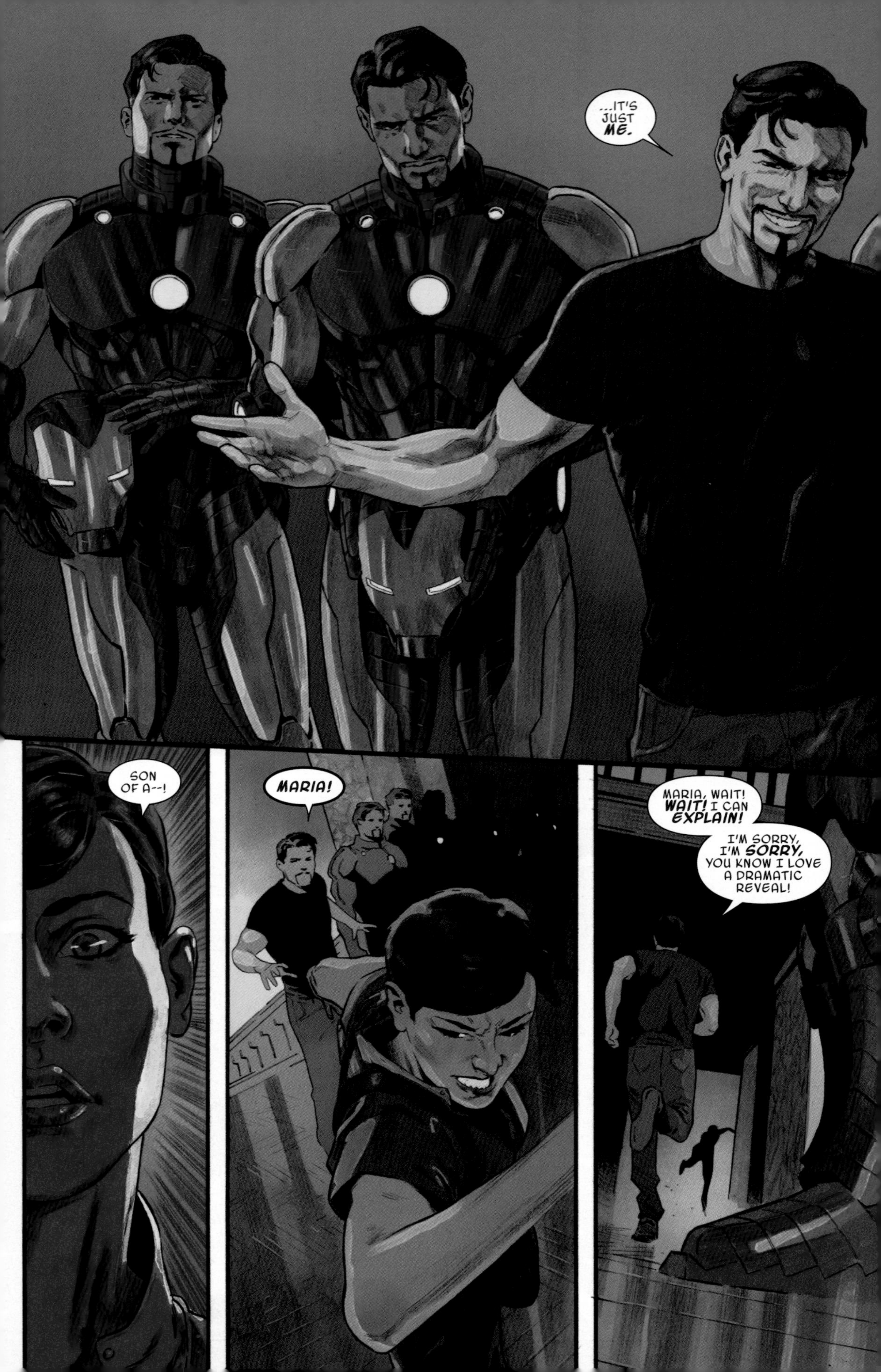
...IT'S JUST **ME.**
SON OF A--!
MARIA!
MARIA, WAIT! **WAIT!** I CAN **EXPLAIN!**
I'M SORRY, I'M **SORRY,** YOU KNOW I LOVE A DRAMATIC REVEAL!

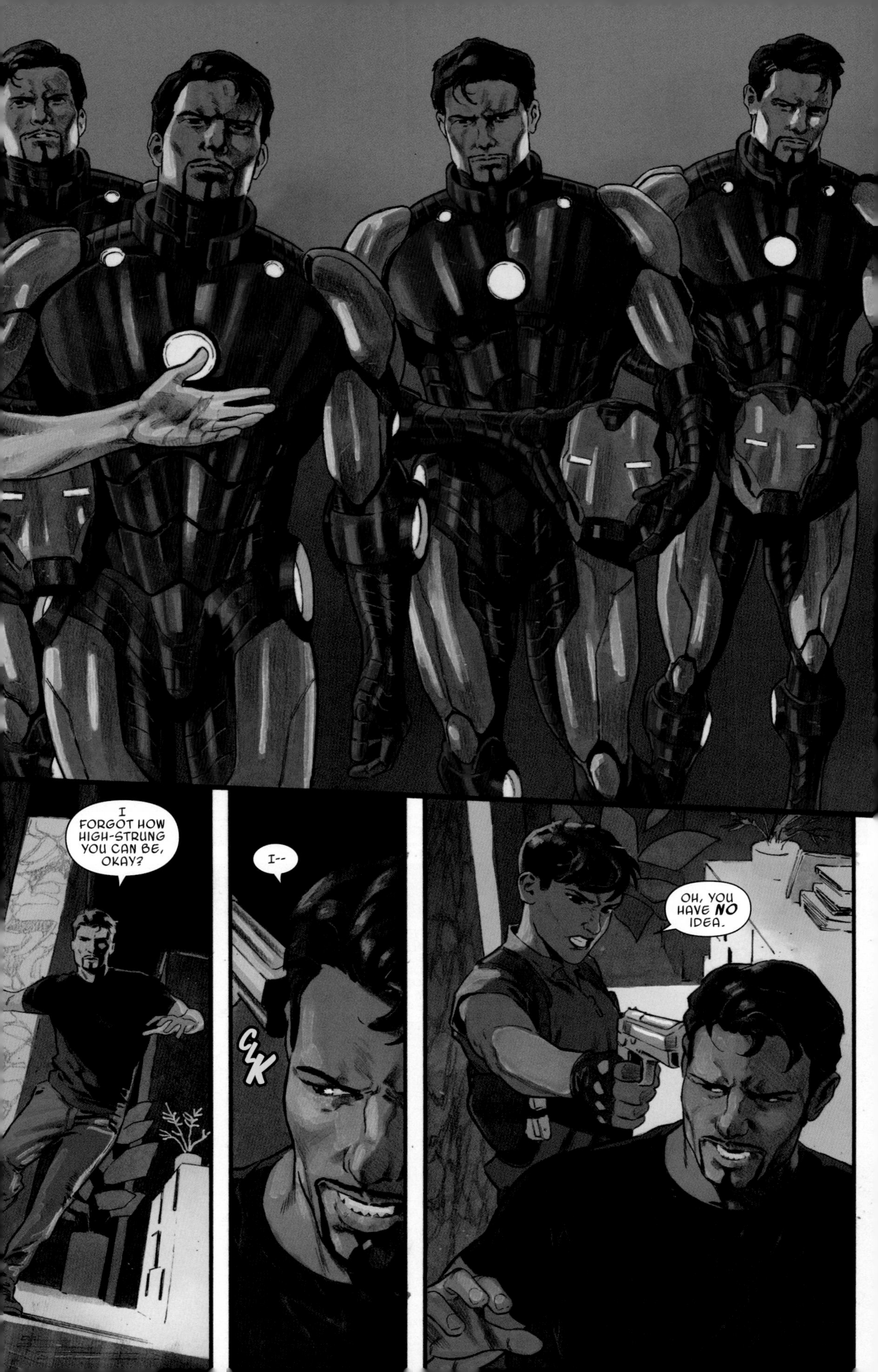
I FORGOT HOW HIGH-STRUNG YOU CAN BE, OKAY?
I--
CLK
OH, YOU HAVE NO IDEA.

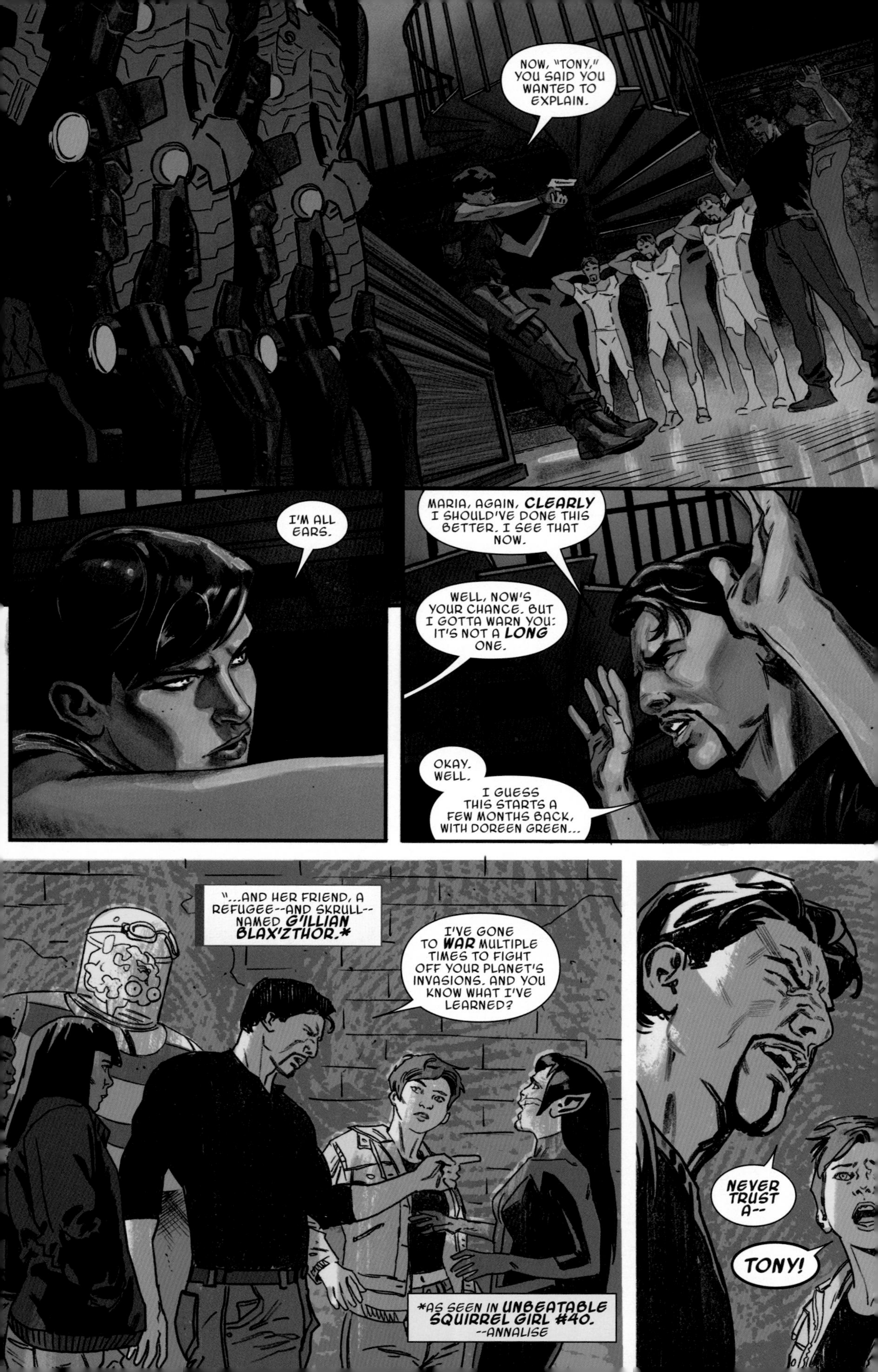
NOW, "TONY," YOU SAID YOU WANTED TO EXPLAIN.
I'M ALL EARS.
MARIA, AGAIN, CLEARLY I SHOULD'VE DONE THIS BETTER. I SEE THAT NOW.
WELL, NOW'S YOUR CHANCE. BUT I GOTTA WARN YOU: IT'S NOT A LONG ONE.
OKAY. WELL.
I GUESS THIS STARTS A FEW MONTHS BACK, WITH DOREEN GREEN...
"...AND HER FRIEND, A REFUGEE--AND SKRULL--NAMED G'ILLIAN BLAX'ZTHOR.*
I'VE GONE TO WAR MULTIPLE TIMES TO FIGHT OFF YOUR PLANET'S INVASIONS. AND YOU KNOW WHAT I'VE LEARNED?
*AS SEEN IN UNBEATABLE SQUIRREL GIRL #40. --ANNALISE
NEVER TRUST A--
TONY!

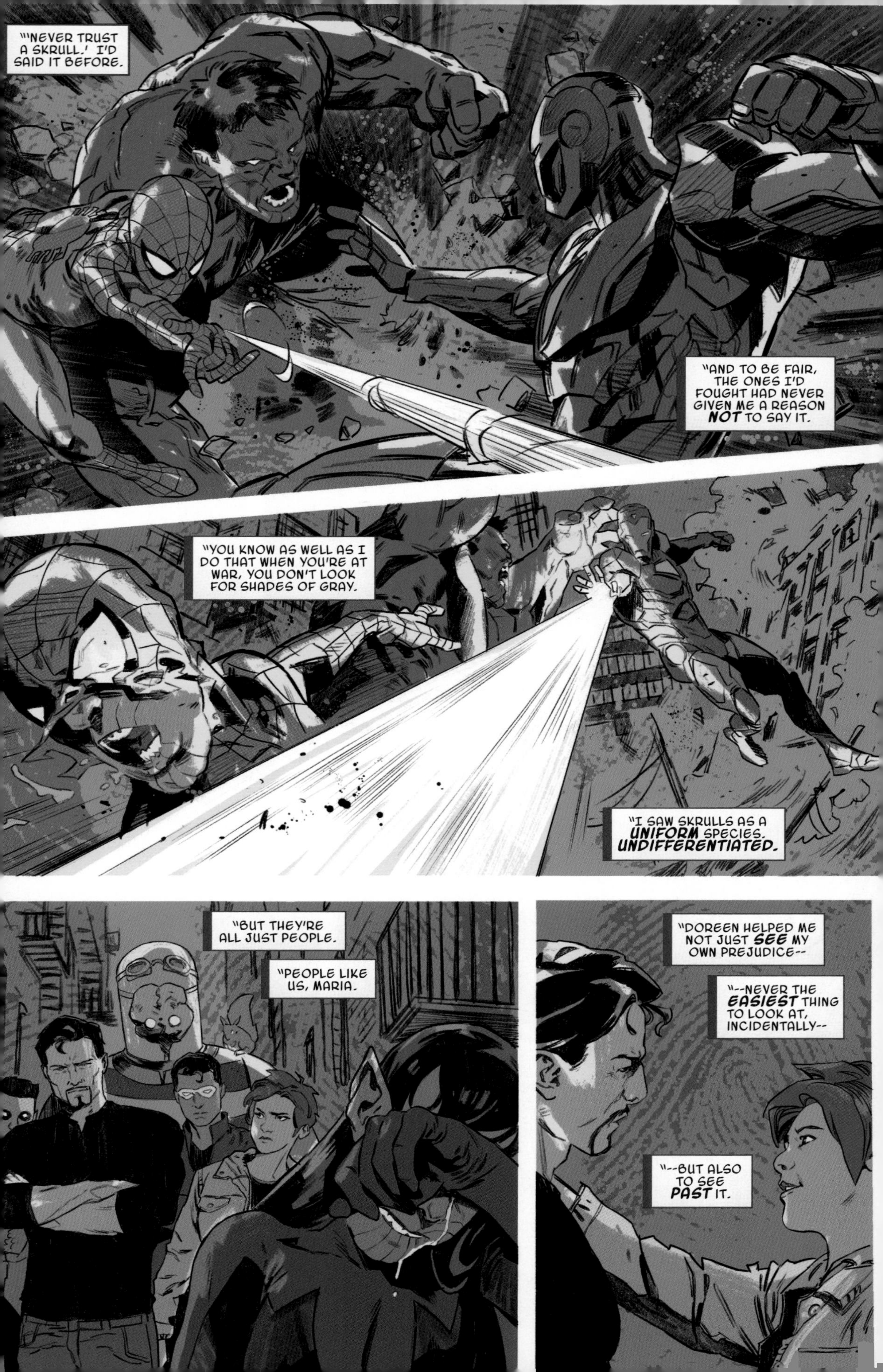

"'NEVER TRUST A SKRULL.' I'D SAID IT BEFORE.
"AND TO BE FAIR, THE ONES I'D FOUGHT HAD NEVER GIVEN ME A REASON **NOT** TO SAY IT.
"YOU KNOW AS WELL AS I DO THAT WHEN YOU'RE AT WAR, YOU DON'T LOOK FOR SHADES OF GRAY.
"I SAW SKRULLS AS A **UNIFORM** SPECIES. **UNDIFFERENTIATED.**
"BUT THEY'RE ALL JUST PEOPLE.
"PEOPLE LIKE US, MARIA.
"DOREEN HELPED ME NOT JUST **SEE** MY OWN PREJUDICE--
"--NEVER THE **EASIEST** THING TO LOOK AT, INCIDENTALLY--
"--BUT ALSO TO SEE **PAST** IT.

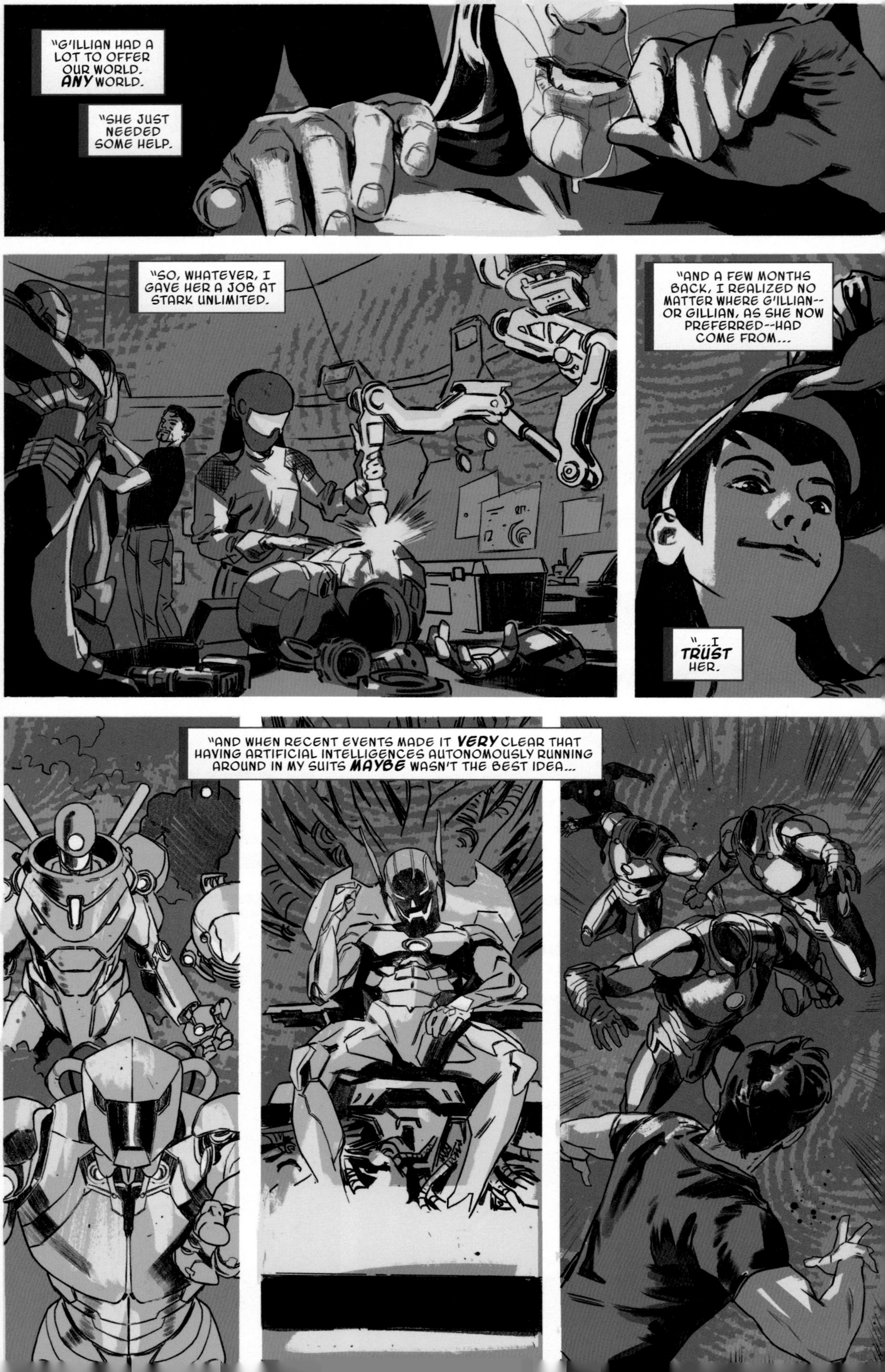
"G'ILLIAN HAD A LOT TO OFFER OUR WORLD. ANY WORLD.
"SHE JUST NEEDED SOME HELP.
"SO, WHATEVER, I GAVE HER A JOB AT STARK UNLIMITED.
"AND A FEW MONTHS BACK, I REALIZED NO MATTER WHERE G'ILLIAN--OR GILLIAN, AS SHE NOW PREFERRED--HAD COME FROM...
"...I TRUST HER.
"AND WHEN RECENT EVENTS MADE IT VERY CLEAR THAT HAVING ARTIFICIAL INTELLIGENCES AUTONOMOUSLY RUNNING AROUND IN MY SUITS MAYBE WASN'T THE BEST IDEA...

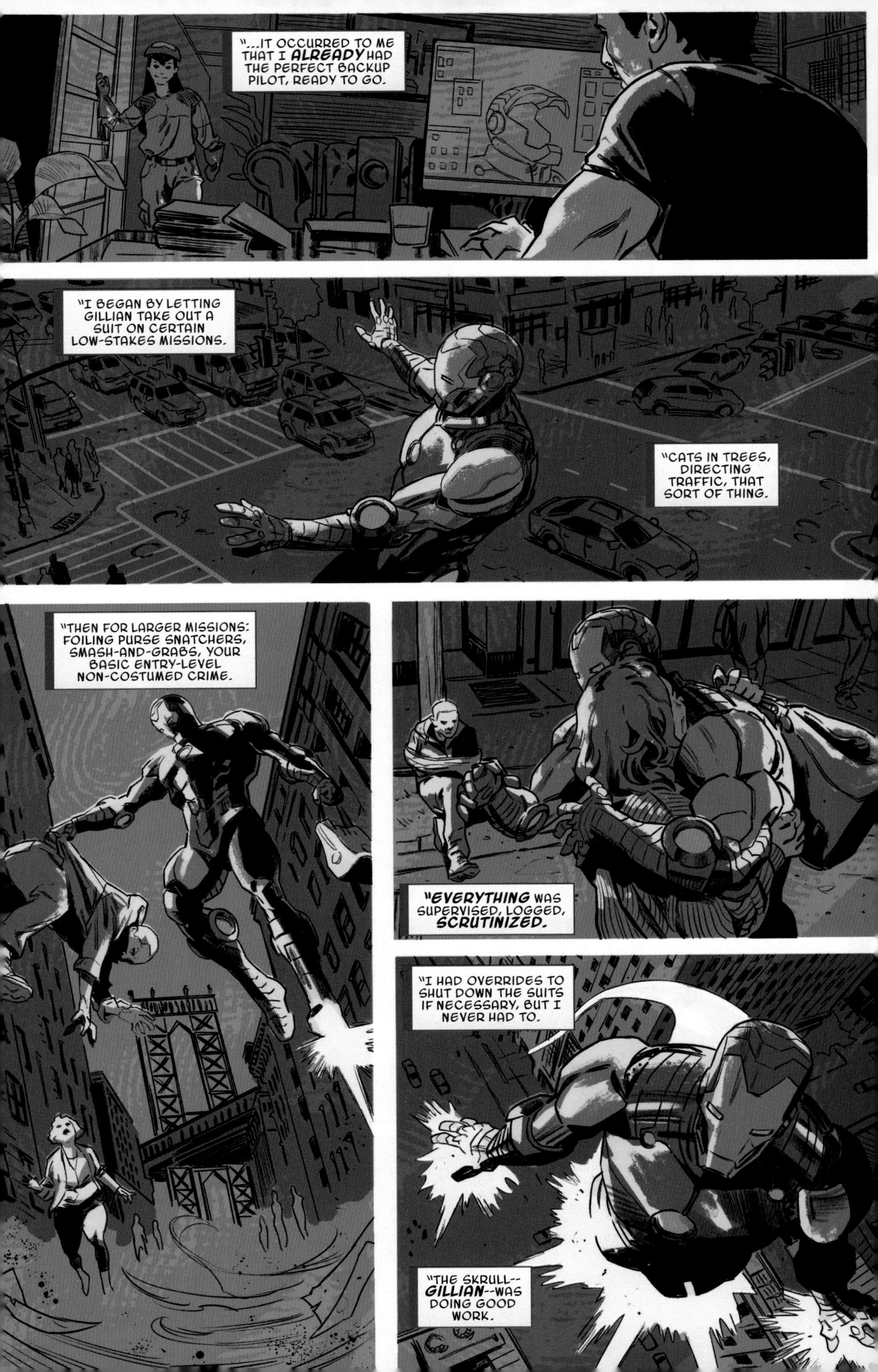
"...IT OCCURRED TO ME THAT I ALREADY HAD THE PERFECT BACKUP PILOT, READY TO GO.
"I BEGAN BY LETTING GILLIAN TAKE OUT A SUIT ON CERTAIN LOW-STAKES MISSIONS.
"CATS IN TREES, DIRECTING TRAFFIC, THAT SORT OF THING.
"THEN FOR LARGER MISSIONS: FOILING PURSE SNATCHERS, SMASH-AND-GRABS, YOUR BASIC ENTRY-LEVEL NON-COSTUMED CRIME.
"EVERYTHING WAS SUPERVISED, LOGGED, SCRUTINIZED.
"I HAD OVERRIDES TO SHUT DOWN THE SUITS IF NECESSARY, BUT I NEVER HAD TO.
"THE SKRULL--GILLIAN--WAS DOING GOOD WORK.

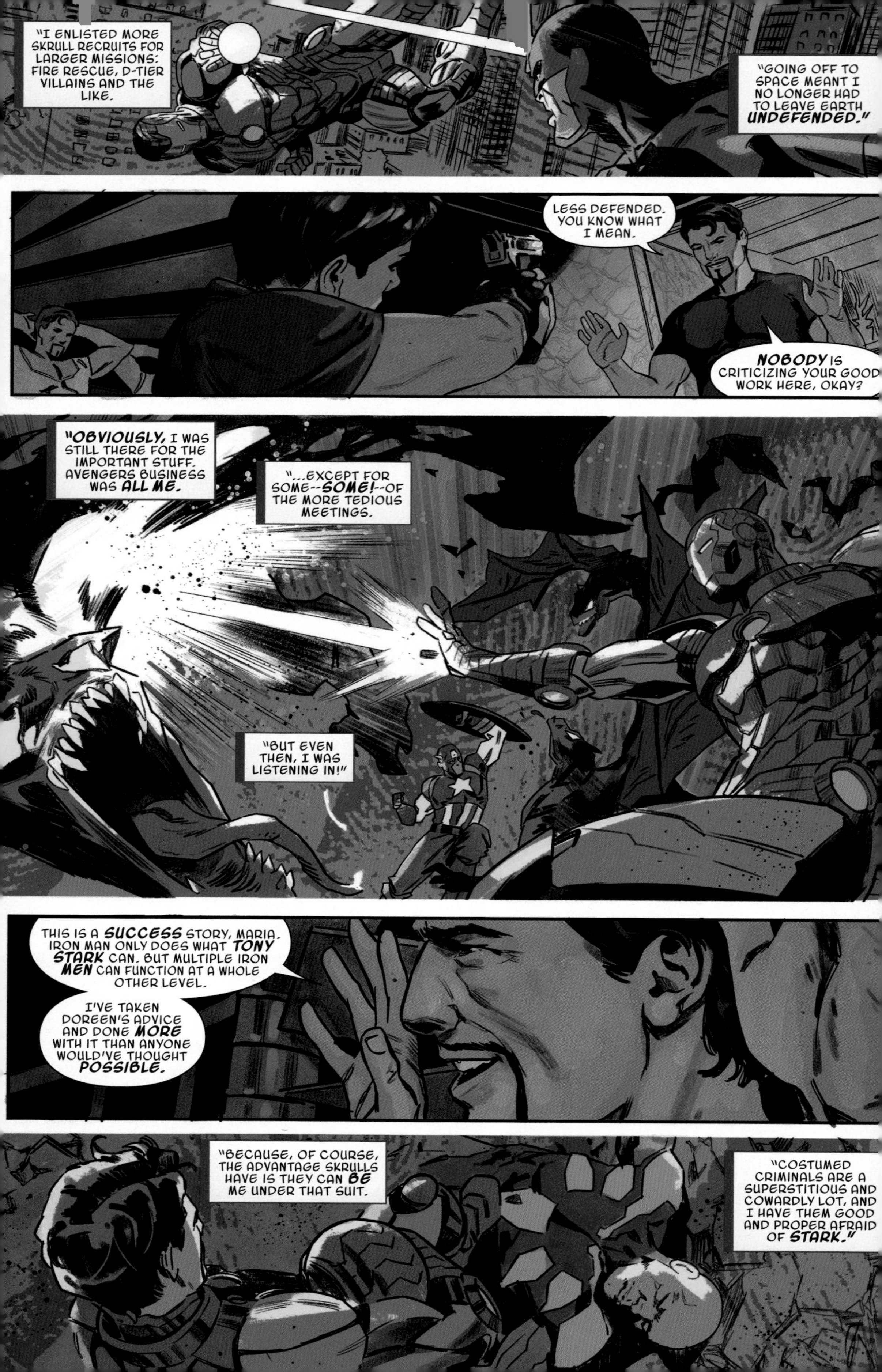
"I ENLISTED MORE SKRULL RECRUITS FOR LARGER MISSIONS: FIRE RESCUE, D-TIER VILLAINS AND THE LIKE.
"GOING OFF TO SPACE MEANT I NO LONGER HAD TO LEAVE EARTH UNDEFENDED."
LESS DEFENDED. YOU KNOW WHAT I MEAN.
NOBODY IS CRITICIZING YOUR GOOD WORK HERE, OKAY?
"OBVIOUSLY, I WAS STILL THERE FOR THE IMPORTANT STUFF. AVENGERS BUSINESS WAS ALL ME.
"...EXCEPT FOR SOME--SOME!--OF THE MORE TEDIOUS MEETINGS.
"BUT EVEN THEN, I WAS LISTENING IN!"
THIS IS A SUCCESS STORY, MARIA. IRON MAN ONLY DOES WHAT TONY STARK CAN. BUT MULTIPLE IRON MEN CAN FUNCTION AT A WHOLE OTHER LEVEL.
I'VE TAKEN DOREEN'S ADVICE AND DONE MORE WITH IT THAN ANYONE WOULD'VE THOUGHT POSSIBLE.
"BECAUSE, OF COURSE, THE ADVANTAGE SKRULLS HAVE IS THEY CAN BE ME UNDER THAT SUIT.
"COSTUMED CRIMINALS ARE A SUPERSTITIOUS AND COWARDLY LOT, AND I HAVE THEM GOOD AND PROPER AFRAID OF STARK."

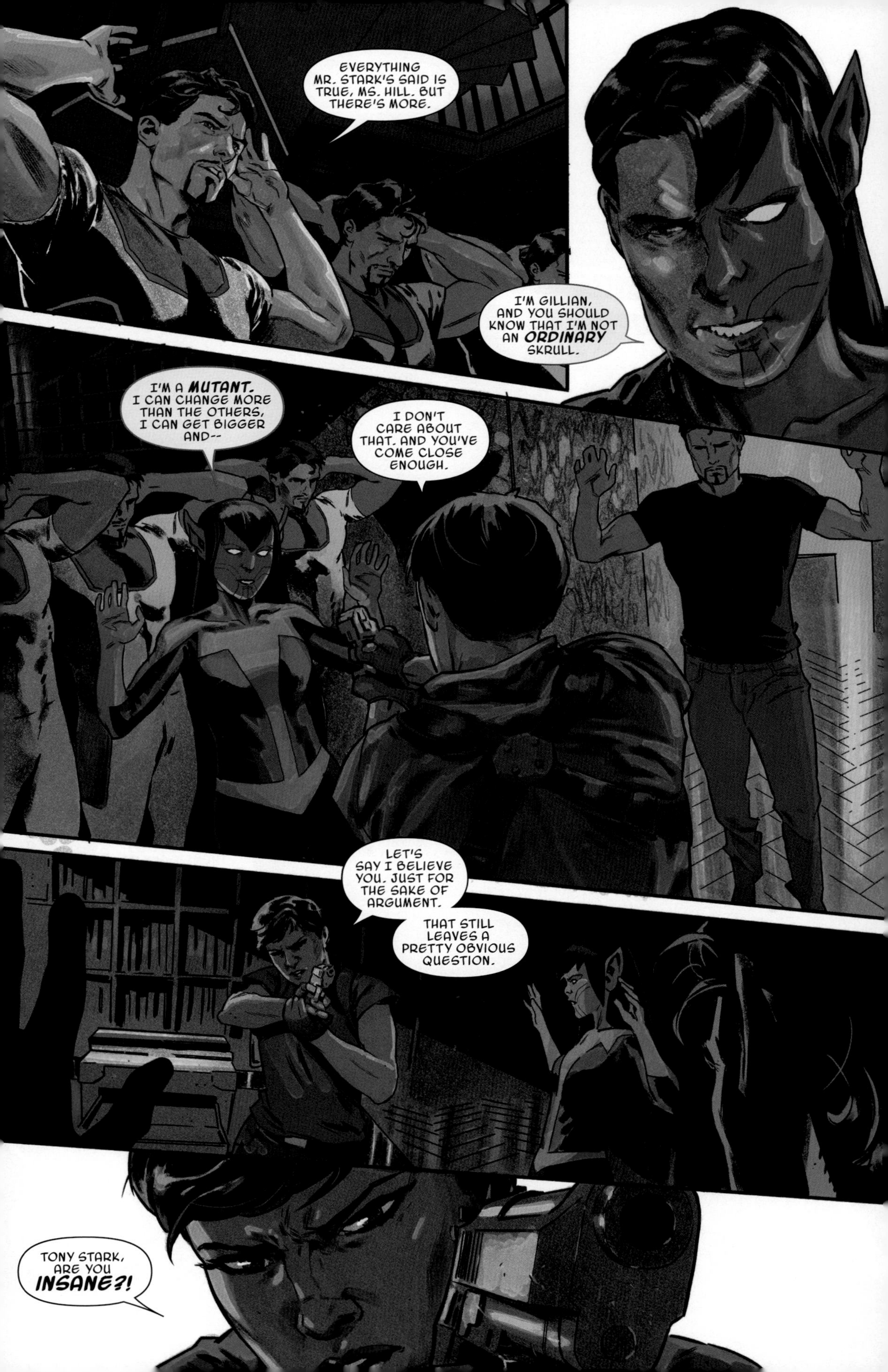
EVERYTHING MR. STARK'S SAID IS TRUE, MS. HILL. BUT THERE'S MORE.
I'M GILLIAN, AND YOU SHOULD KNOW THAT I'M NOT AN ORDINARY SKRULL.
I'M A MUTANT. I CAN CHANGE MORE THAN THE OTHERS, I CAN GET BIGGER AND--
I DON'T CARE ABOUT THAT. AND YOU'VE COME CLOSE ENOUGH.
LET'S SAY I BELIEVE YOU. JUST FOR THE SAKE OF ARGUMENT.
THAT STILL LEAVES A PRETTY OBVIOUS QUESTION.
TONY STARK, ARE YOU INSANE?!

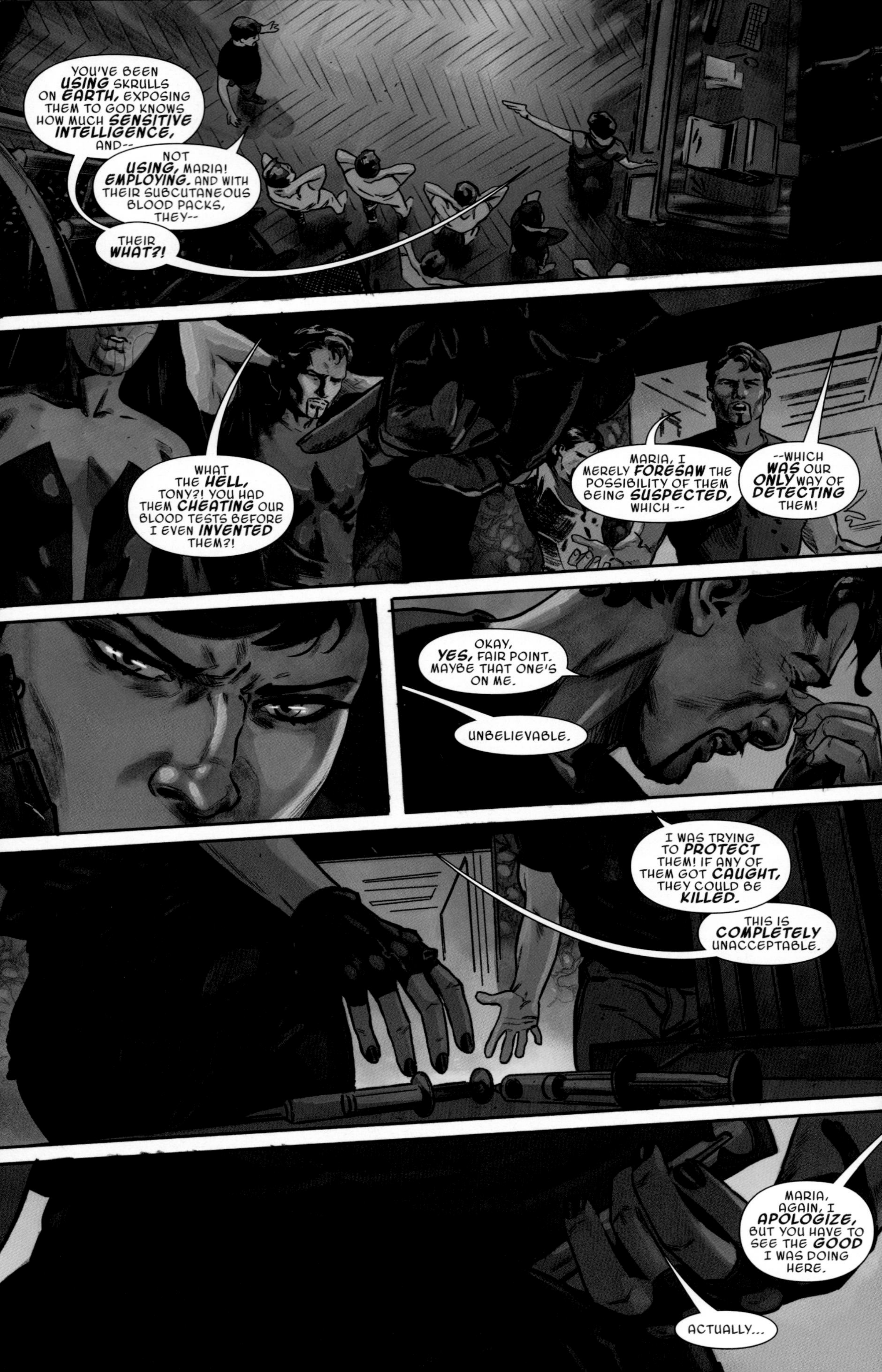
YOU'VE BEEN USING SKRULLS ON EARTH, EXPOSING THEM TO GOD KNOWS HOW MUCH SENSITIVE INTELLIGENCE, AND--
NOT USING, MARIA! EMPLOYING. AND WITH THEIR SUBCUTANEOUS BLOOD PACKS, THEY--
THEIR WHAT?!
WHAT THE HELL, TONY?! YOU HAD THEM CHEATING OUR BLOOD TESTS BEFORE I EVEN INVENTED THEM?!
MARIA, I MERELY FORESAW THE POSSIBILITY OF THEM BEING SUSPECTED, WHICH --
--WHICH WAS OUR ONLY WAY OF DETECTING THEM!
OKAY, YES, FAIR POINT. MAYBE THAT ONE'S ON ME.
UNBELIEVABLE.
I WAS TRYING TO PROTECT THEM! IF ANY OF THEM GOT CAUGHT, THEY COULD BE KILLED.
THIS IS COMPLETELY UNACCEPTABLE.
MARIA, AGAIN, I APOLOGIZE, BUT YOU HAVE TO SEE THE GOOD I WAS DOING HERE.
ACTUALLY...

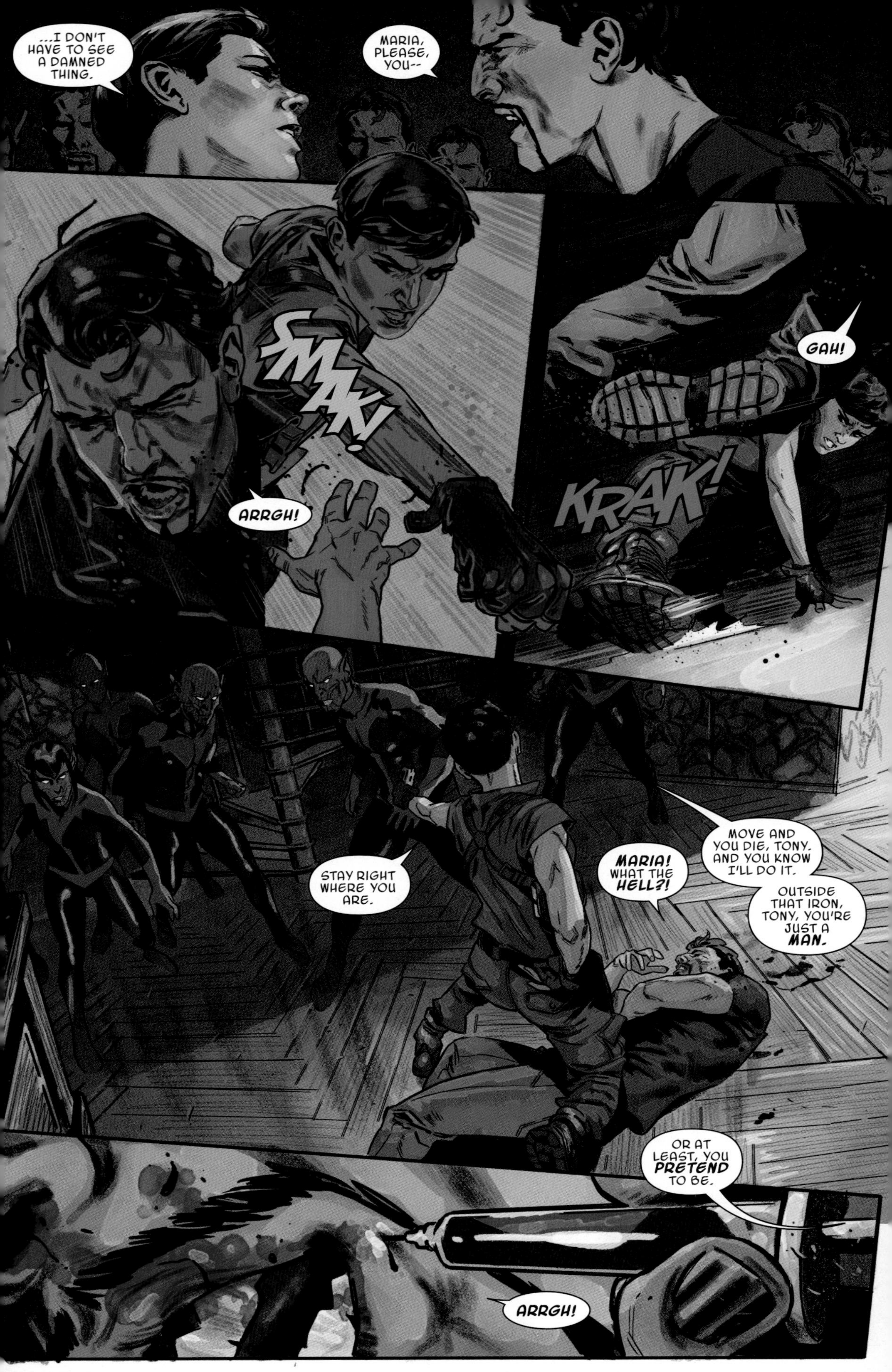
...I DON'T HAVE TO SEE A DAMNED THING.
MARIA, PLEASE, YOU--
SMAK!
ARRGH!
GAH!
KRAK!
STAY RIGHT WHERE YOU ARE.
MARIA! WHAT THE HELL?!
MOVE AND YOU DIE, TONY. AND YOU KNOW I'LL DO IT.
OUTSIDE THAT IRON, TONY, YOU'RE JUST A MAN.
OR AT LEAST, YOU PRETEND TO BE.
ARRGH!

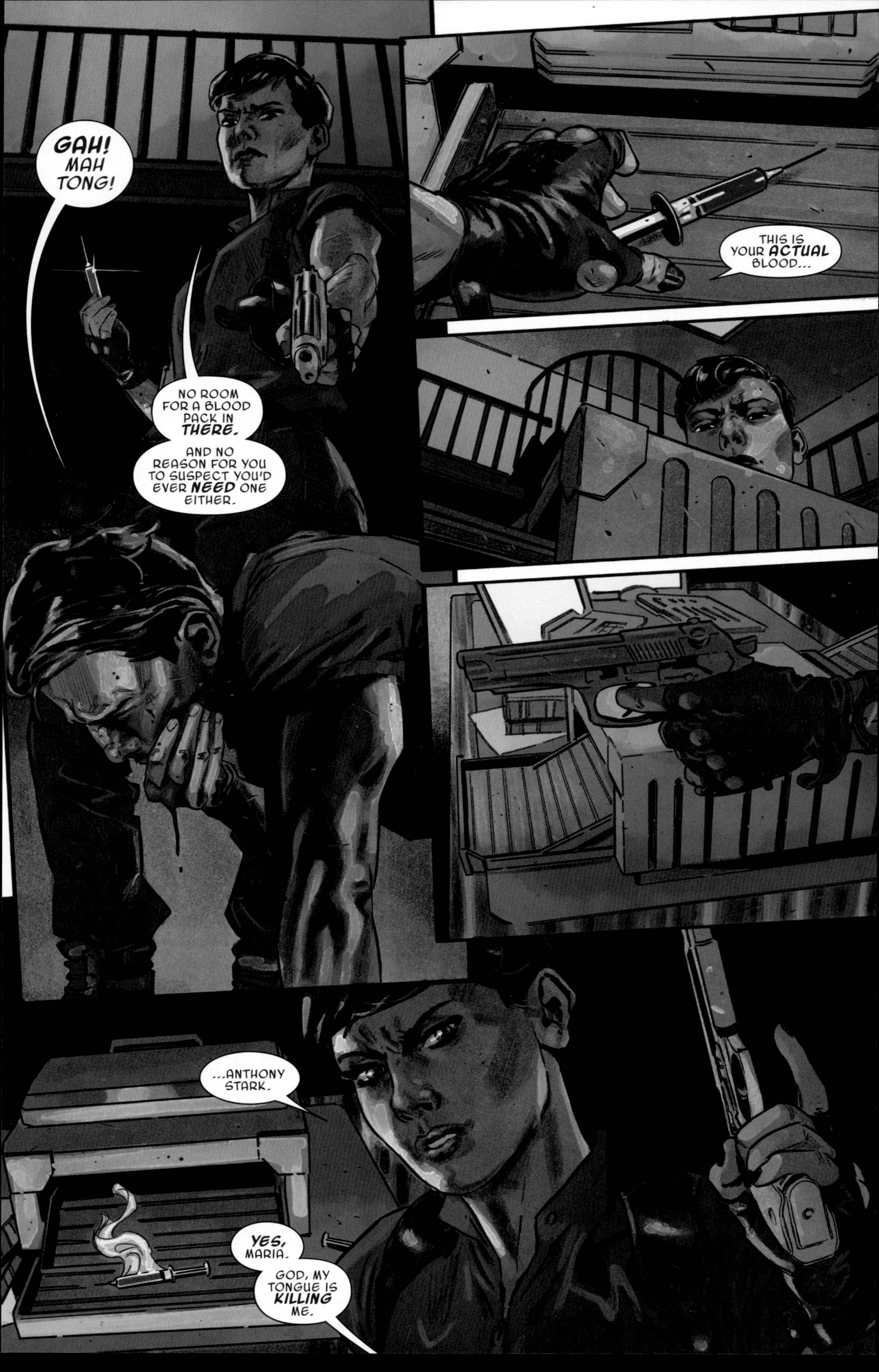
GAH! MAH TONG!
NO ROOM FOR A BLOOD PACK IN THERE.
AND NO REASON FOR YOU TO SUSPECT YOU'D EVER NEED ONE EITHER.
THIS IS YOUR ACTUAL BLOOD...
...ANTHONY STARK.
YES, MARIA.
GOD, MY TONGUE IS KILLING ME.

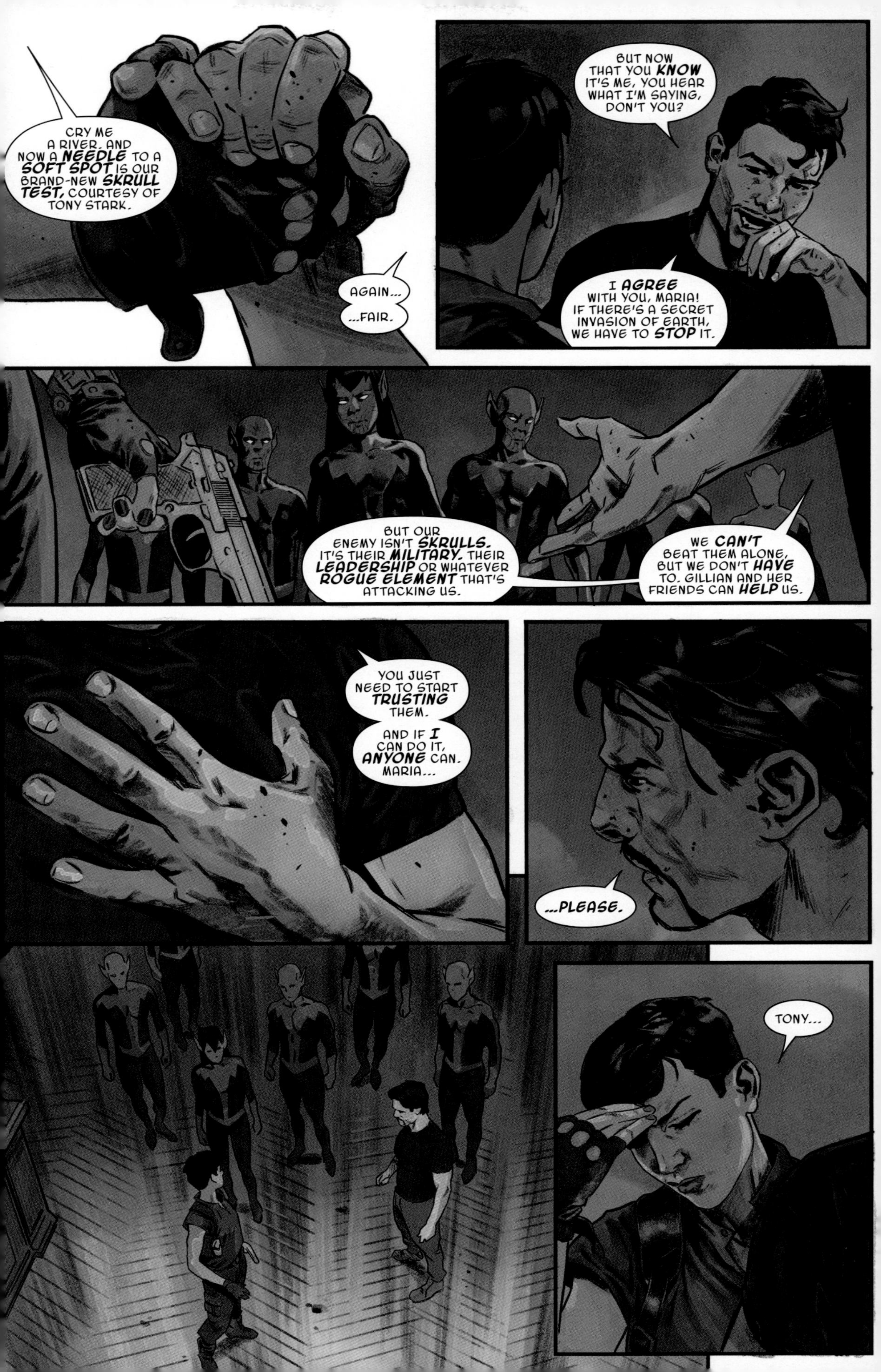

CRY ME A RIVER. AND NOW A NEEDLE TO A SOFT SPOT IS OUR BRAND-NEW SKRULL TEST, COURTESY OF TONY STARK.
AGAIN...
...FAIR.
BUT NOW THAT YOU KNOW IT'S ME, YOU HEAR WHAT I'M SAYING, DON'T YOU?
I AGREE WITH YOU, MARIA! IF THERE'S A SECRET INVASION OF EARTH, WE HAVE TO STOP IT.
BUT OUR ENEMY ISN'T SKRULLS. IT'S THEIR MILITARY. THEIR LEADERSHIP OR WHATEVER ROGUE ELEMENT THAT'S ATTACKING US.
WE CAN'T BEAT THEM ALONE, BUT WE DON'T HAVE TO. GILLIAN AND HER FRIENDS CAN HELP US.
YOU JUST NEED TO START TRUSTING THEM.
AND IF I CAN DO IT, ANYONE CAN. MARIA...
...PLEASE.
TONY...

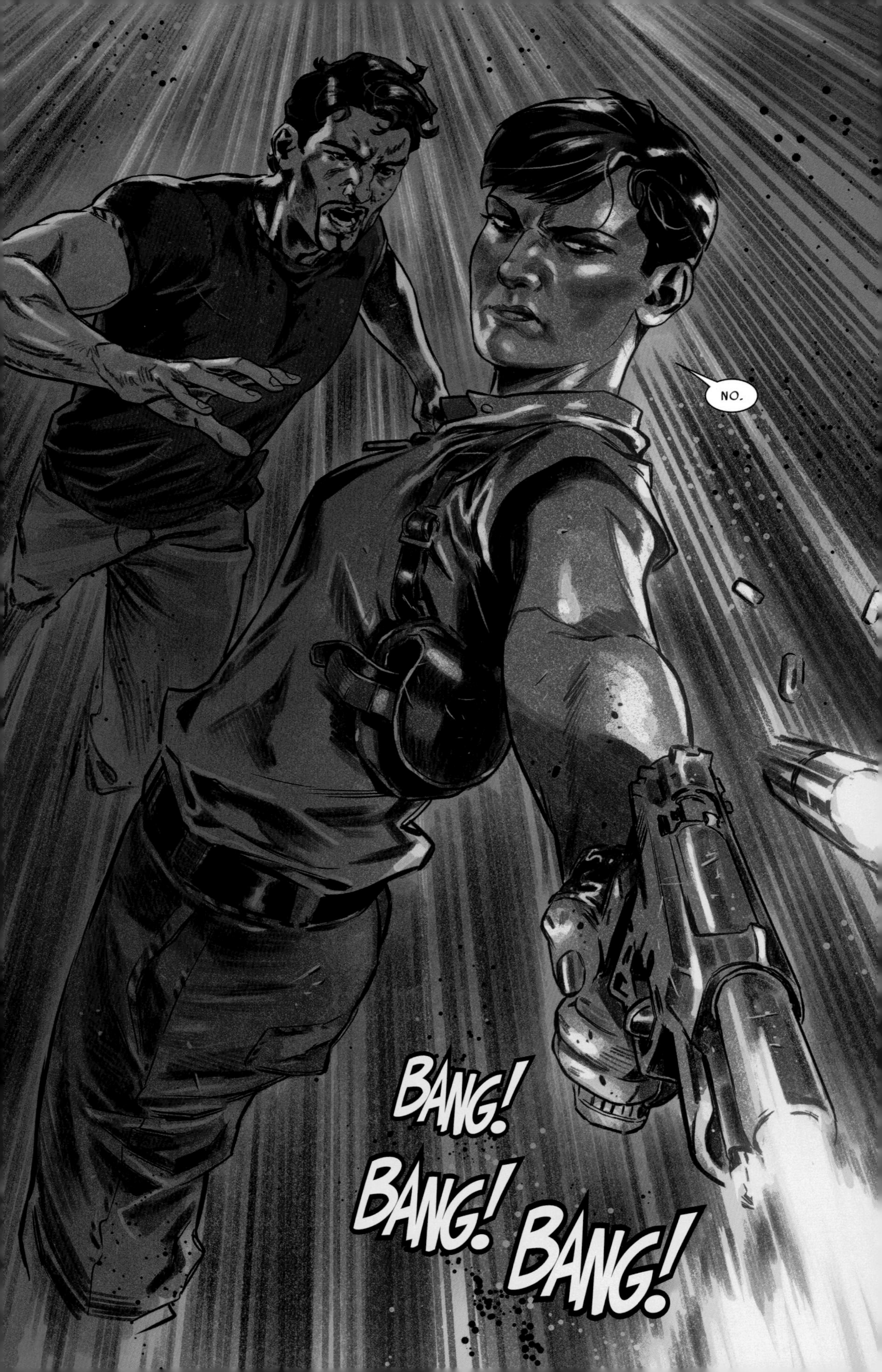
NO.
BANG!
BANG!
BANG!

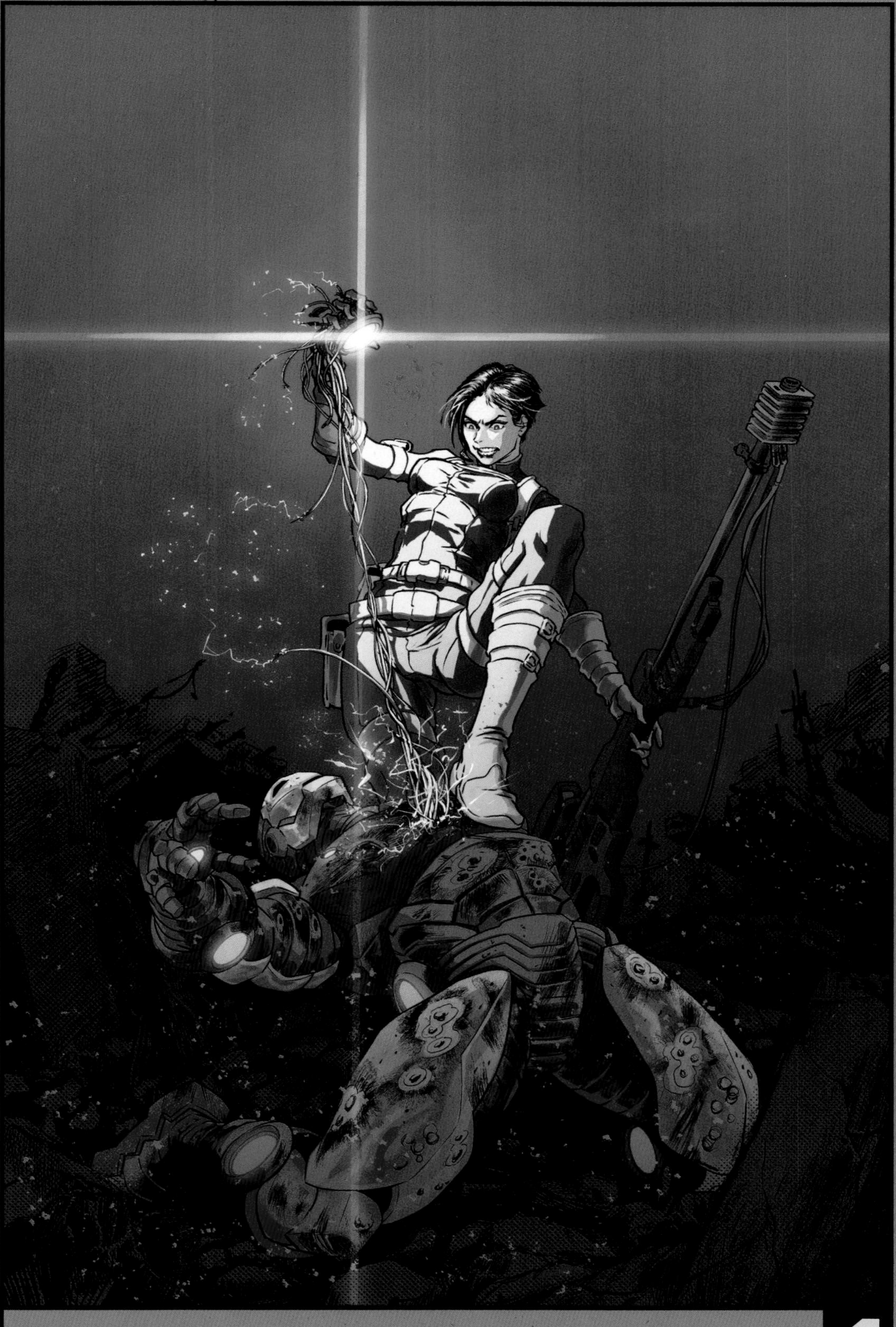

4

"We Got Her"

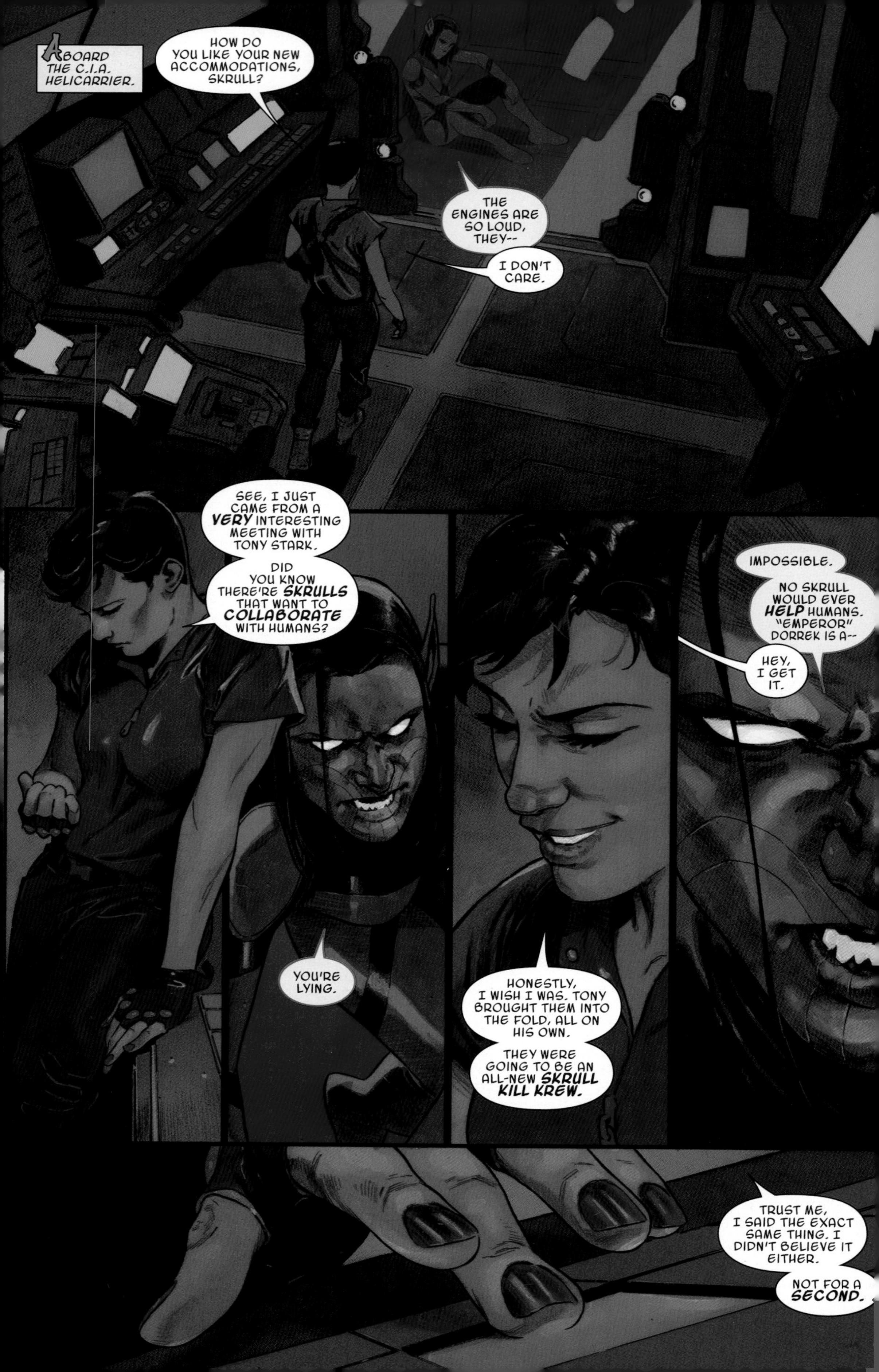
ABOARD THE C.I.A. HELICARRIER.
HOW DO YOU LIKE YOUR NEW ACCOMMODATIONS, SKRULL?
THE ENGINES ARE SO LOUD, THEY--
I DON'T CARE.
SEE, I JUST CAME FROM A VERY INTERESTING MEETING WITH TONY STARK.
DID YOU KNOW THERE'RE SKRULLS THAT WANT TO COLLABORATE WITH HUMANS?
YOU'RE LYING.
HONESTLY, I WISH I WAS. TONY BROUGHT THEM INTO THE FOLD, ALL ON HIS OWN.
THEY WERE GOING TO BE AN ALL-NEW SKRULL KILL KREW.
IMPOSSIBLE.
NO SKRULL WOULD EVER HELP HUMANS. "EMPEROR" DORREK IS A--
HEY, I GET IT.
TRUST ME, I SAID THE EXACT SAME THING. I DIDN'T BELIEVE IT EITHER.
NOT FOR A SECOND.

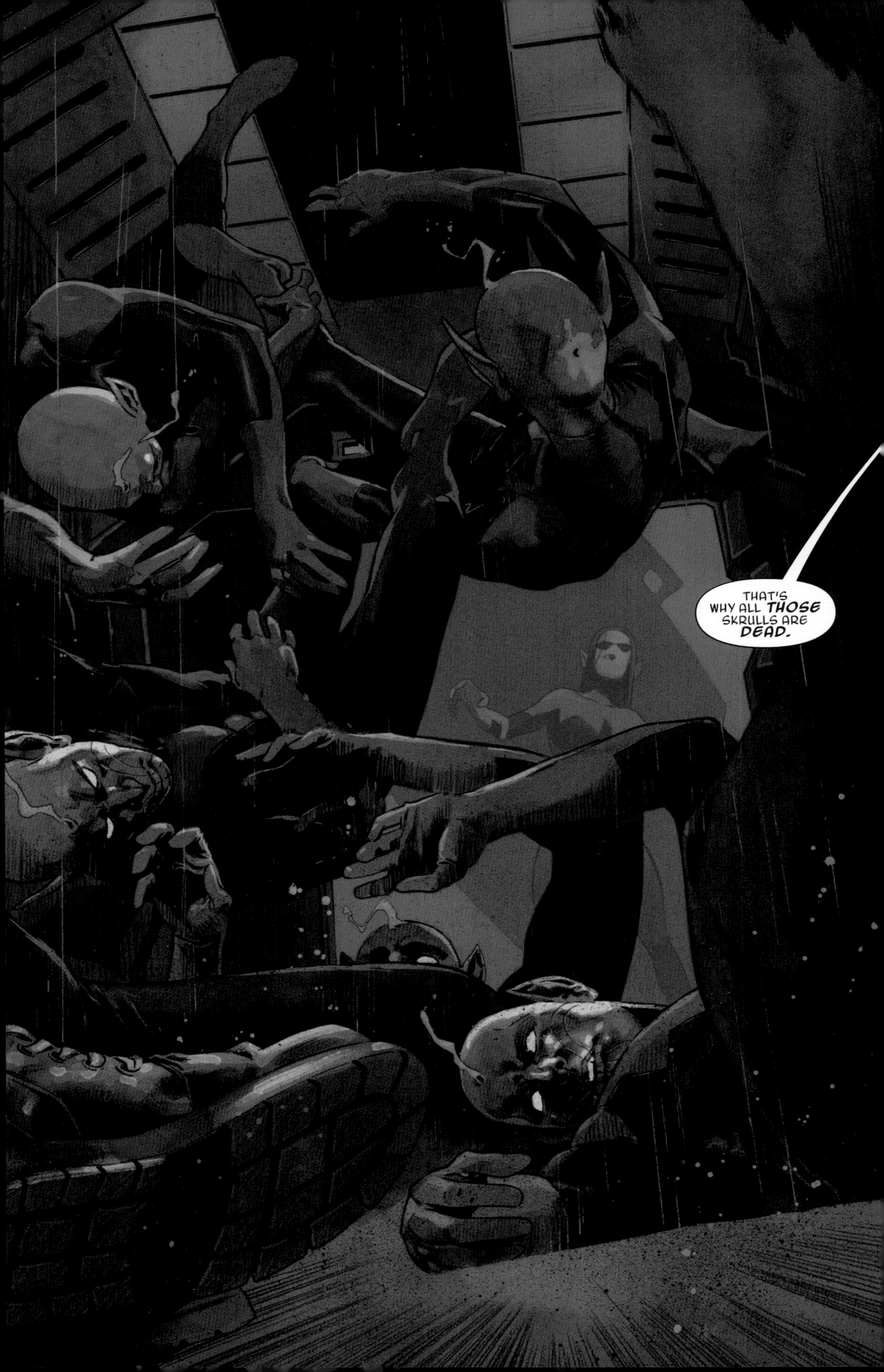
THAT'S WHY ALL **THOSE** SKRULLS ARE **DEAD.**

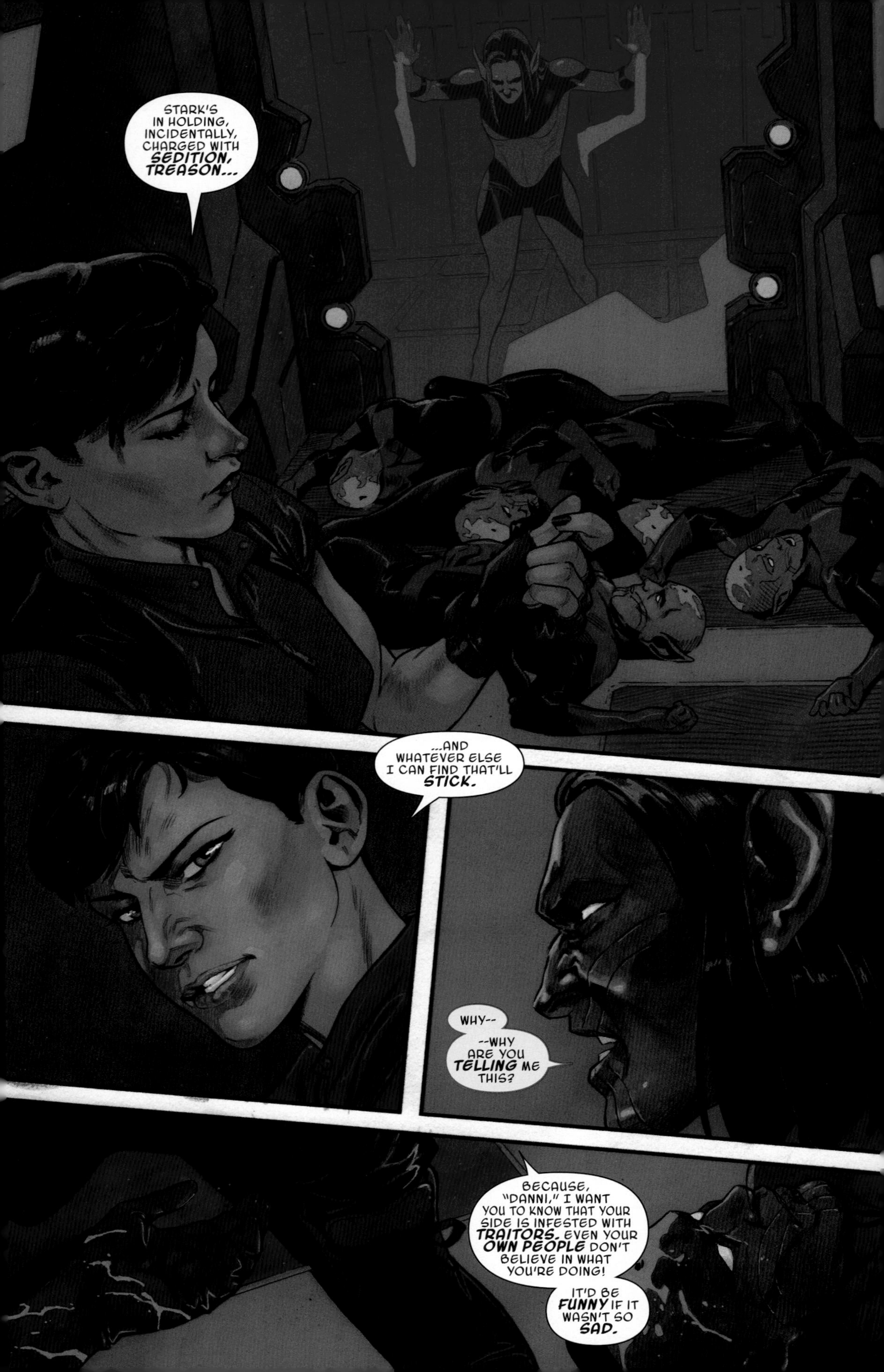
STARK'S IN HOLDING, INCIDENTALLY, CHARGED WITH SEDITION, TREASON...
...AND WHATEVER ELSE I CAN FIND THAT'LL STICK.
WHY--
--WHY ARE YOU TELLING ME THIS?
BECAUSE, "DANNI," I WANT YOU TO KNOW THAT YOUR SIDE IS INFESTED WITH TRAITORS. EVEN YOUR OWN PEOPLE DON'T BELIEVE IN WHAT YOU'RE DOING!
IT'D BE FUNNY IF IT WASN'T SO SAD.

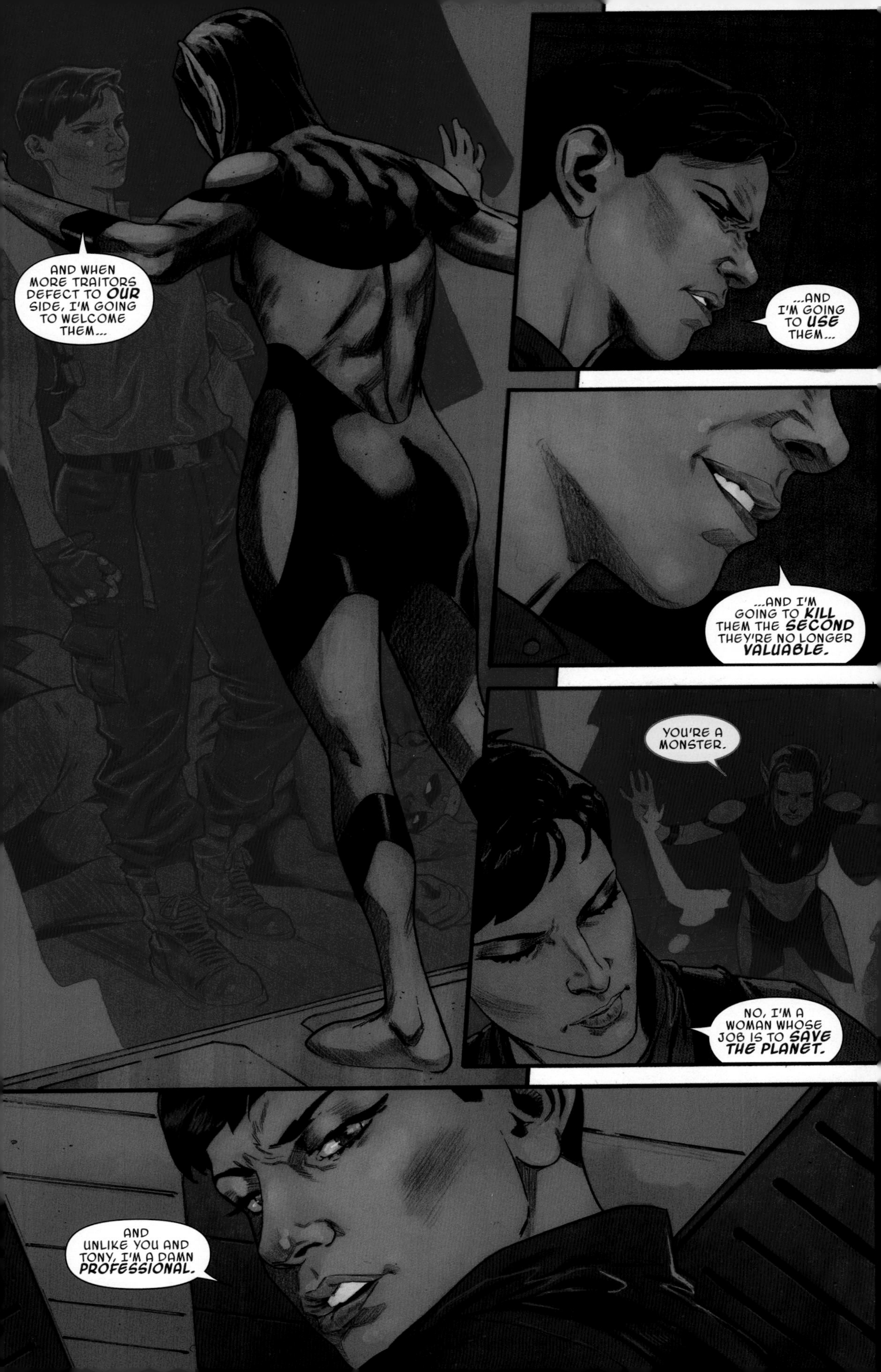
AND WHEN MORE TRAITORS DEFECT TO OUR SIDE, I'M GOING TO WELCOME THEM...
...AND I'M GOING TO USE THEM...
...AND I'M GOING TO KILL THEM THE SECOND THEY'RE NO LONGER VALUABLE.
YOU'RE A MONSTER.
NO, I'M A WOMAN WHOSE JOB IS TO SAVE THE PLANET.
AND UNLIKE YOU AND TONY, I'M A DAMN PROFESSIONAL.

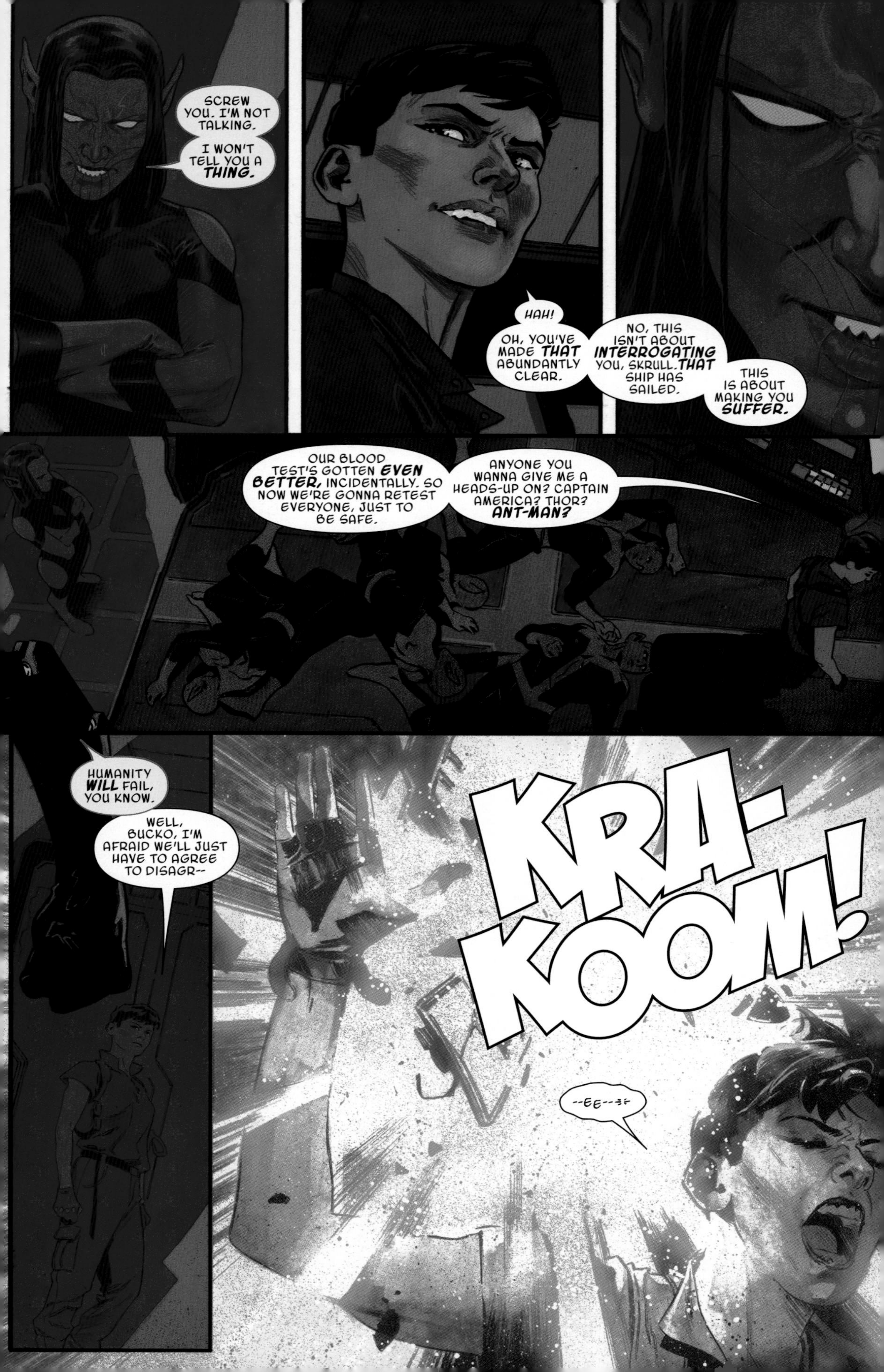

SCREW YOU. I'M NOT TALKING.
I WON'T TELL YOU A **THING.**
HAH!
OH, YOU'VE MADE **THAT** ABUNDANTLY CLEAR.
NO, THIS ISN'T ABOUT **INTERROGATING** YOU, SKRULL. **THAT** SHIP HAS SAILED.
THIS IS ABOUT MAKING YOU **SUFFER.**
OUR BLOOD TEST'S GOTTEN **EVEN BETTER,** INCIDENTALLY. SO NOW WE'RE GONNA RETEST EVERYONE, JUST TO BE SAFE.
ANYONE YOU WANNA GIVE ME A HEADS-UP ON? CAPTAIN AMERICA? THOR? **ANT-MAN?**
HUMANITY **WILL** FAIL, YOU KNOW.
WELL, BUCKO, I'M AFRAID WE'LL JUST HAVE TO AGREE TO DISAGR--
KRA-KOOM!
--EE--

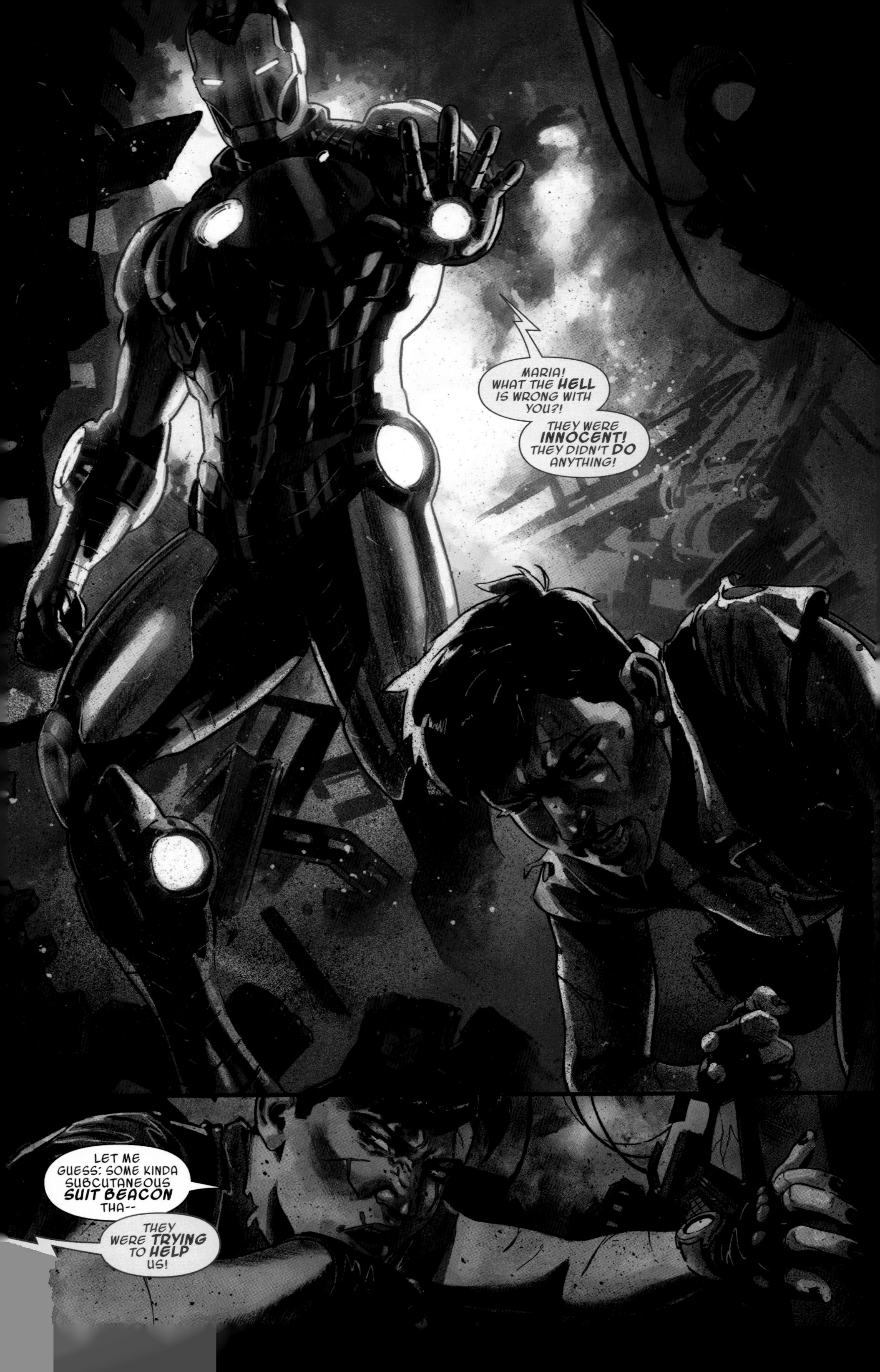
MARIA! WHAT THE HELL IS WRONG WITH YOU?!
THEY WERE INNOCENT! THEY DIDN'T DO ANYTHING!
LET ME GUESS: SOME KINDA SUBCUTANEOUS SUIT BEACON THA--
THEY WERE TRYING TO HELP US!

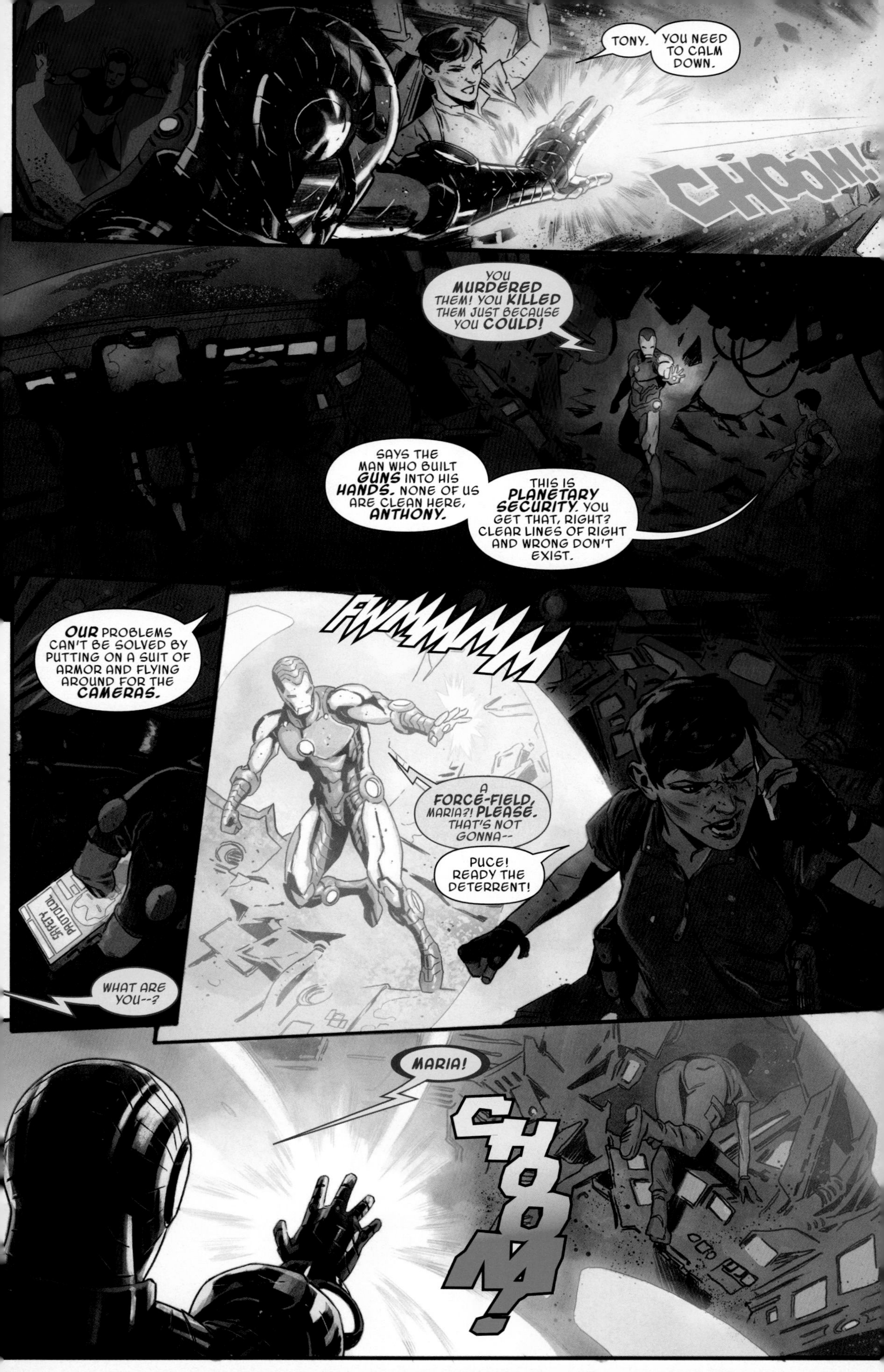

TONY.
YOU NEED TO CALM DOWN.
CHOOM!
YOU MURDERED THEM! YOU KILLED THEM JUST BECAUSE YOU COULD!
SAYS THE MAN WHO BUILT GUNS INTO HIS HANDS. NONE OF US ARE CLEAN HERE, ANTHONY.
THIS IS PLANETARY SECURITY. YOU GET THAT, RIGHT? CLEAR LINES OF RIGHT AND WRONG DON'T EXIST.
OUR PROBLEMS CAN'T BE SOLVED BY PUTTING ON A SUIT OF ARMOR AND FLYING AROUND FOR THE CAMERAS.
FWMMMMM
A FORCE-FIELD, MARIA?! PLEASE. THAT'S NOT GONNA--
PUCE! READY THE DETERRENT!
SAFETY PROTOCOL
WHAT ARE YOU--?
MARIA!
CHOOM!

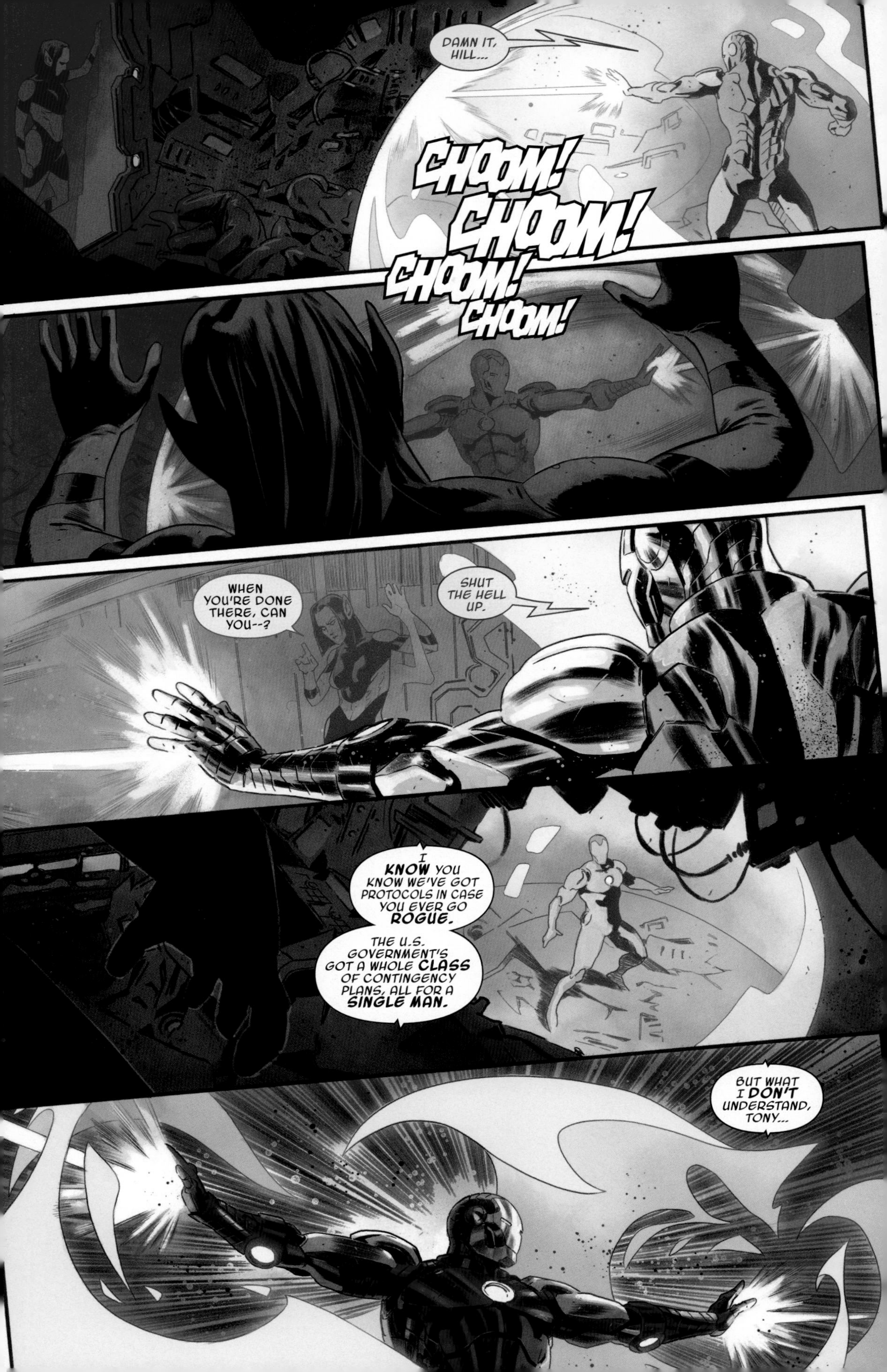
DAMN IT, HILL...
CHOOM! CHOOM! CHOOM! CHOOM!
WHEN YOU'RE DONE THERE, CAN YOU--?
SHUT THE HELL UP.
I KNOW YOU KNOW WE'VE GOT PROTOCOLS IN CASE YOU EVER GO ROGUE.
THE U.S. GOVERNMENT'S GOT A WHOLE CLASS OF CONTINGENCY PLANS, ALL FOR A SINGLE MAN.
BUT WHAT I DON'T UNDERSTAND, TONY...

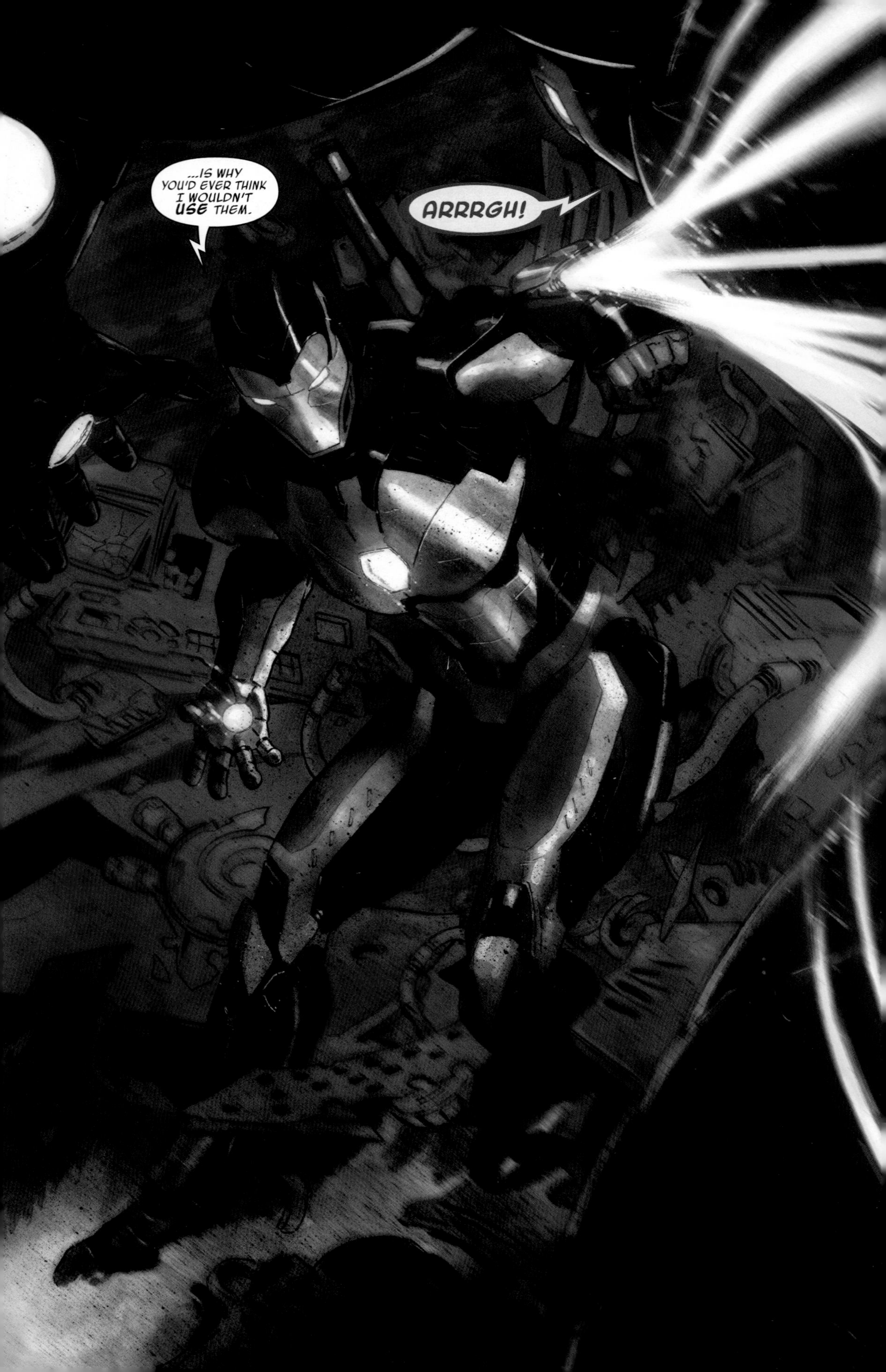
...IS WHY YOU'D EVER THINK I WOULDN'T USE THEM.
ARRRGH!

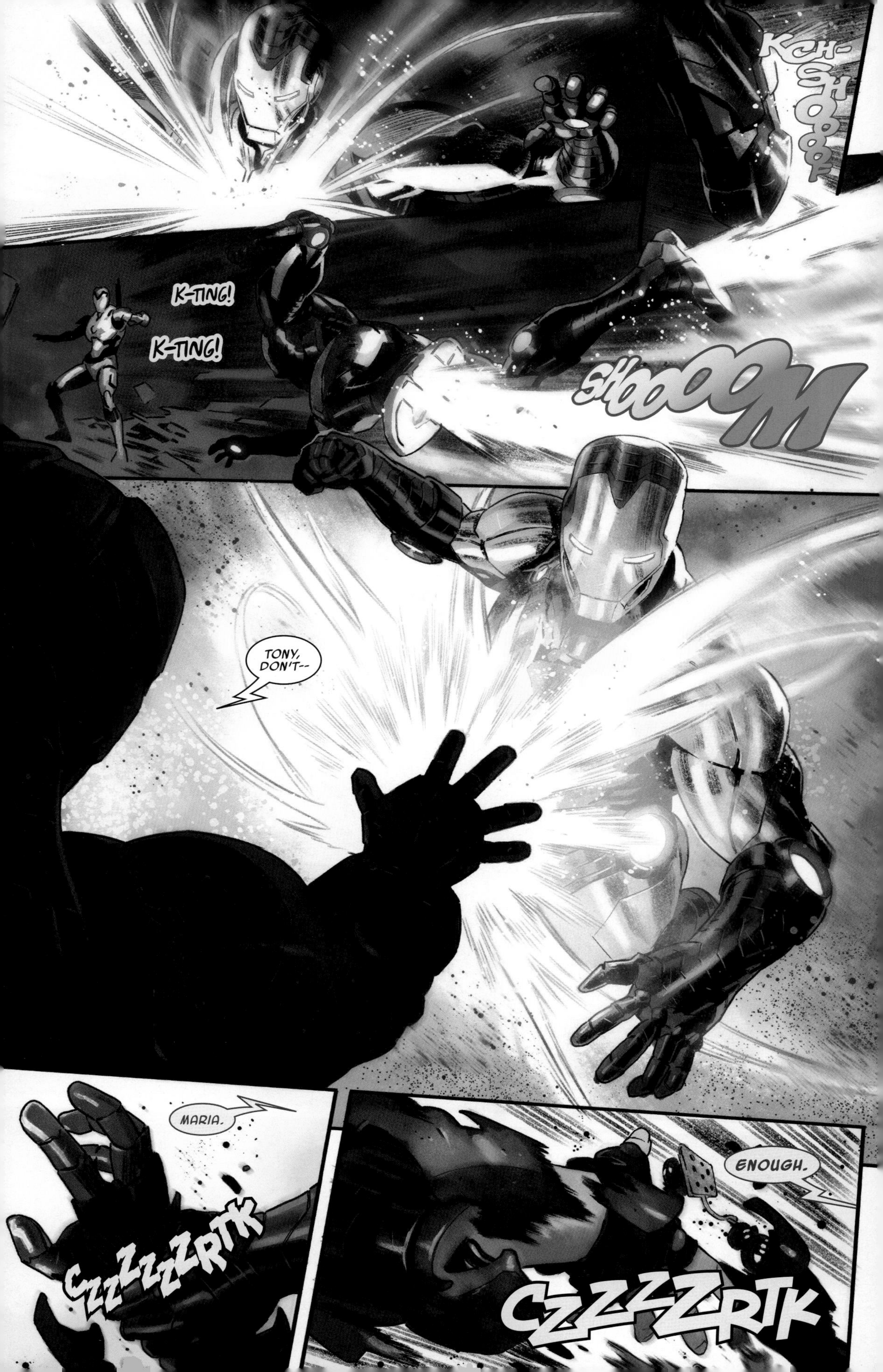
KCH-SHOOOOF
K-TING!
K-TING!
SHOOOOOM
TONY, DON'T--
MARIA.
CZZZZZZZRTK
ENOUGH.
CZZZZZRTK

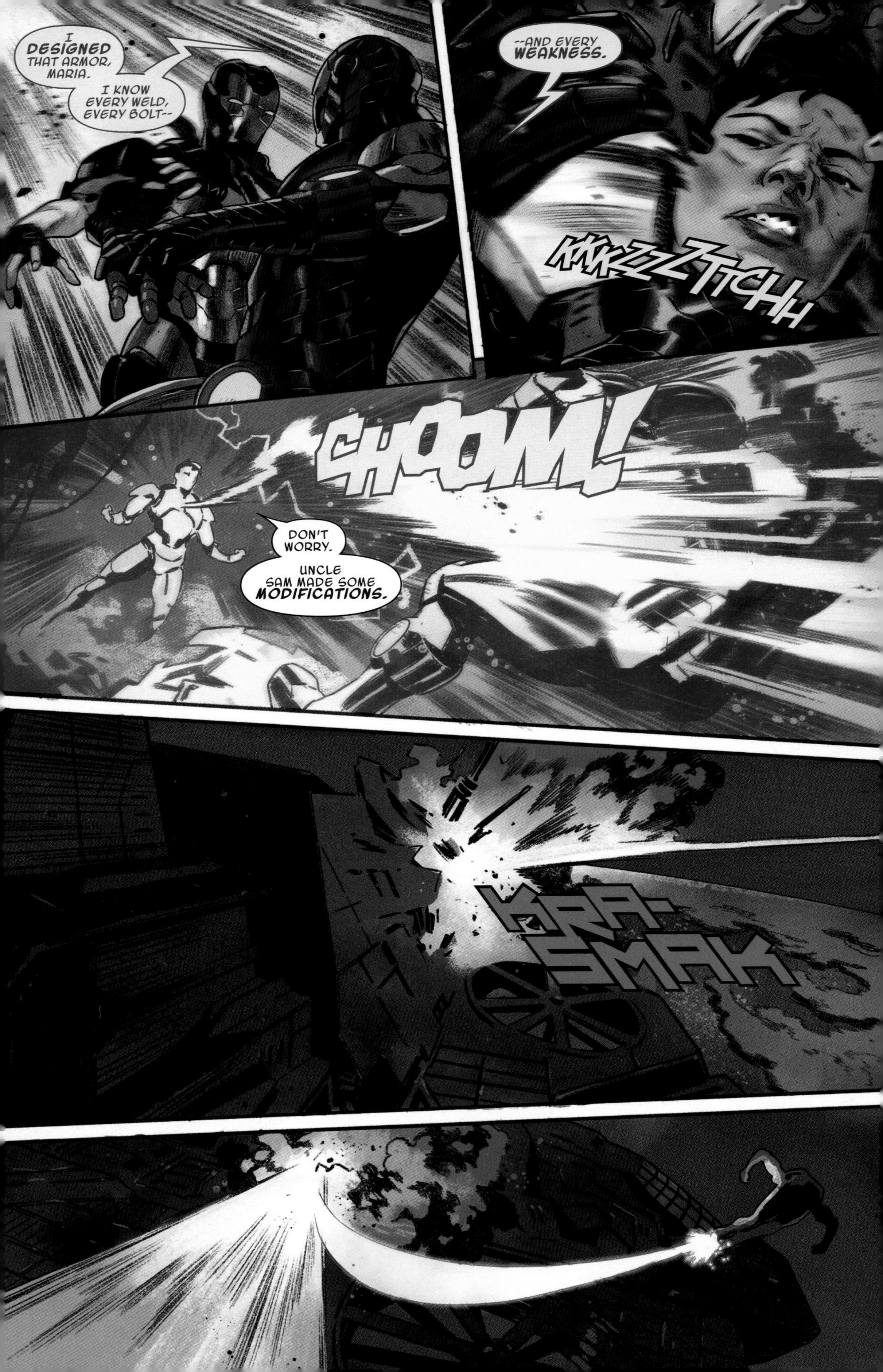
I DESIGNED THAT ARMOR, MARIA.
I KNOW EVERY WELD, EVERY BOLT--
--AND EVERY WEAKNESS.
KKKZZZTTCHH
CHOOM!
DON'T WORRY.
UNCLE SAM MADE SOME MODIFICATIONS.
KRA-SMAK

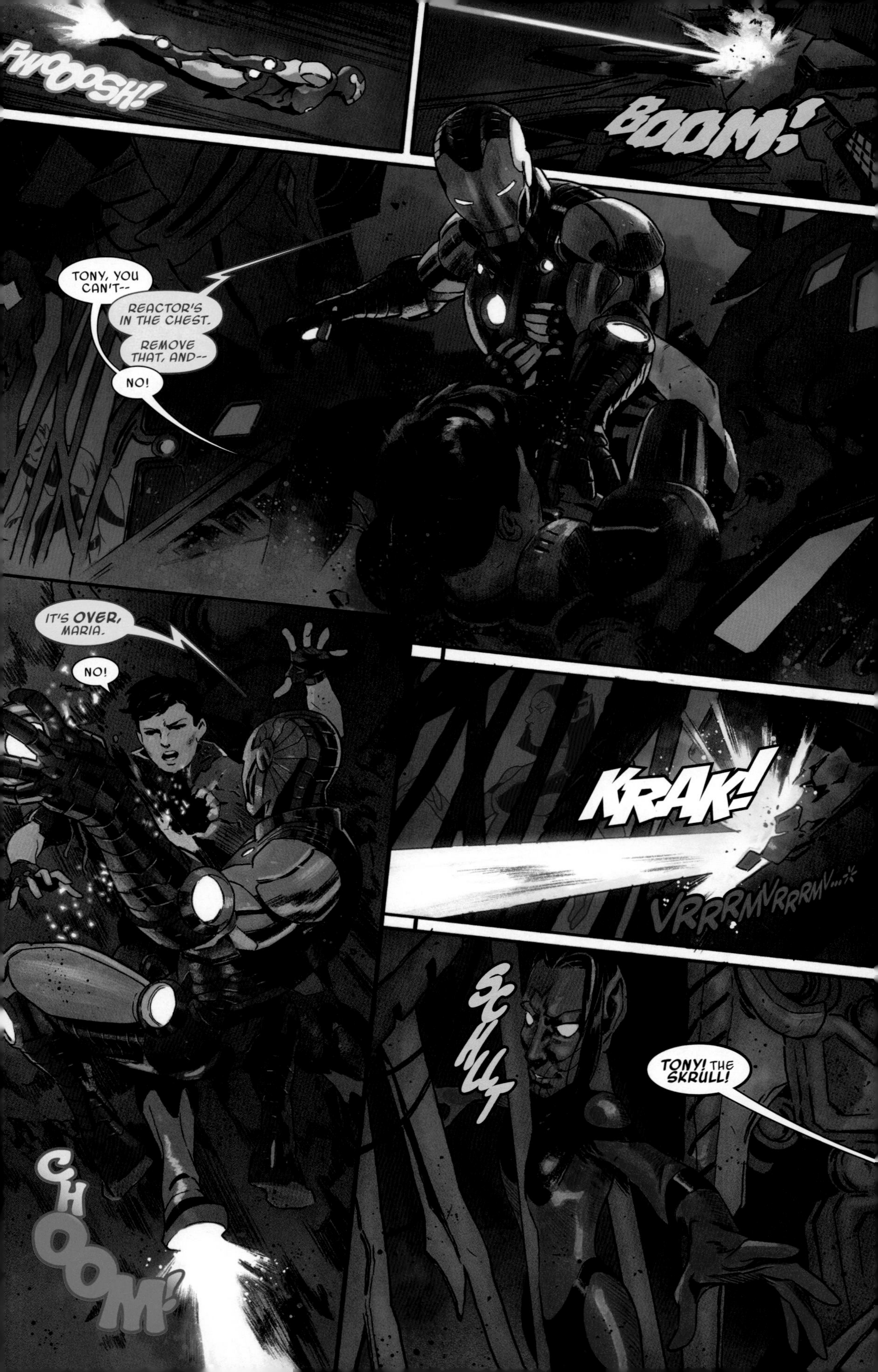
FWOOOSH!
BOOM!
TONY, YOU CAN'T--
REACTOR'S IN THE CHEST.
REMOVE THAT, AND--
NO!
IT'S OVER, MARIA.
NO!
KRAK!
VRRRMVRRRMV...
SCHUK
TONY! THE SKRULL!
CHOOOM!

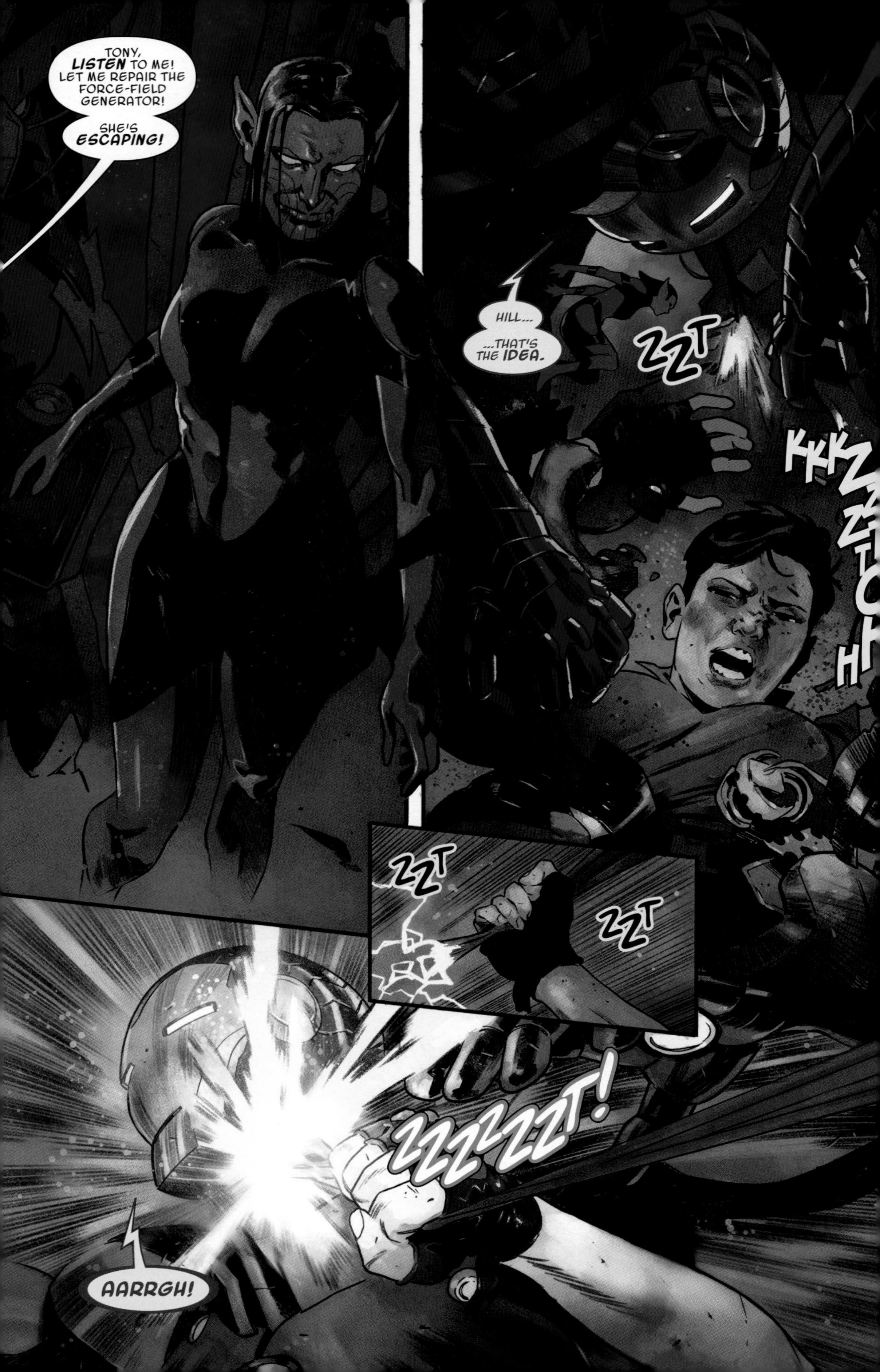
TONY, LISTEN TO ME! LET ME REPAIR THE FORCE-FIELD GENERATOR!
SHE'S ESCAPING!
HILL...
...THAT'S THE IDEA.
ZZT
KKKZZZTCHH
ZZT
ZZT
ZZZZZZZT!
AARRGH!

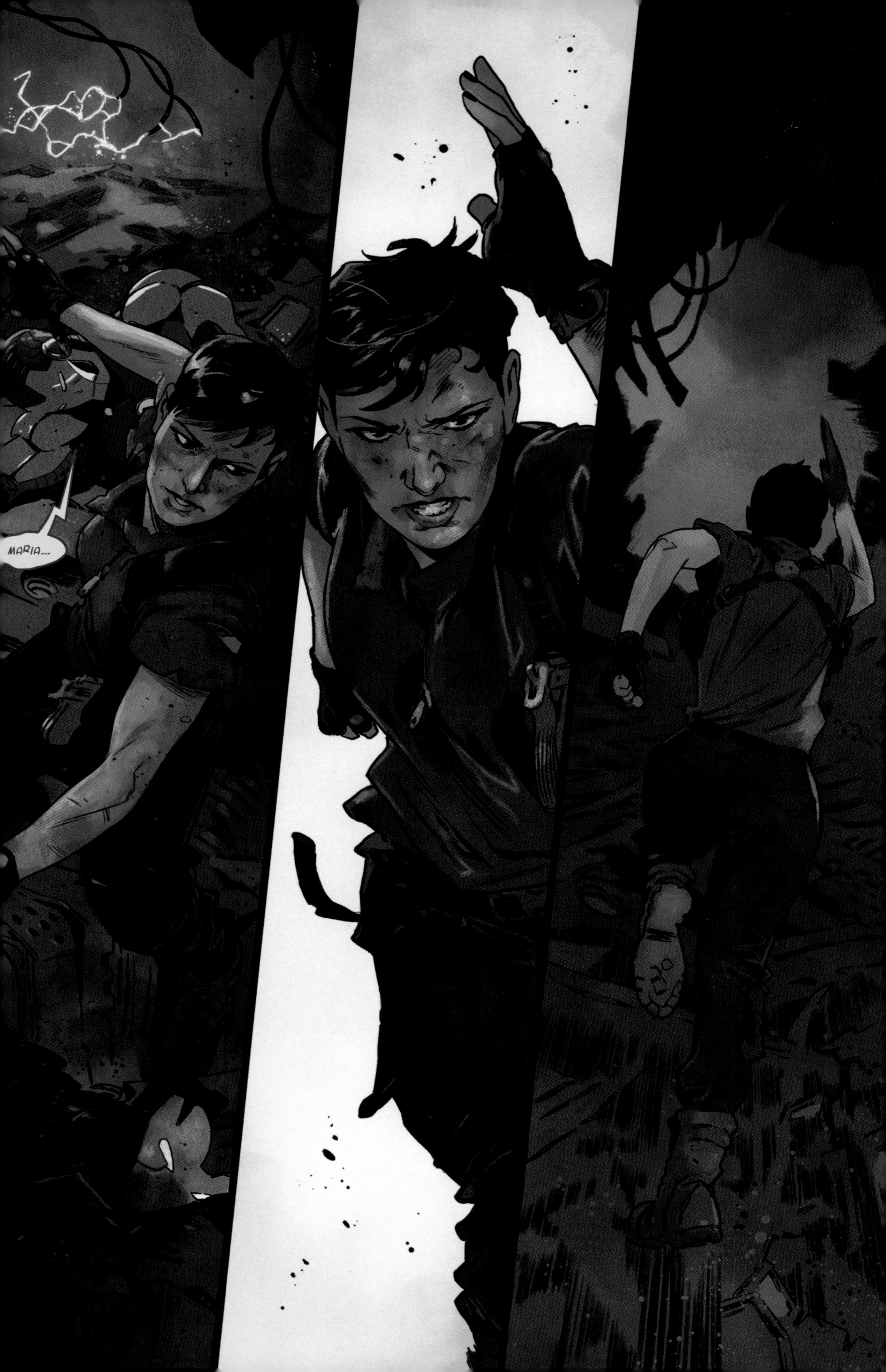
MARIA...

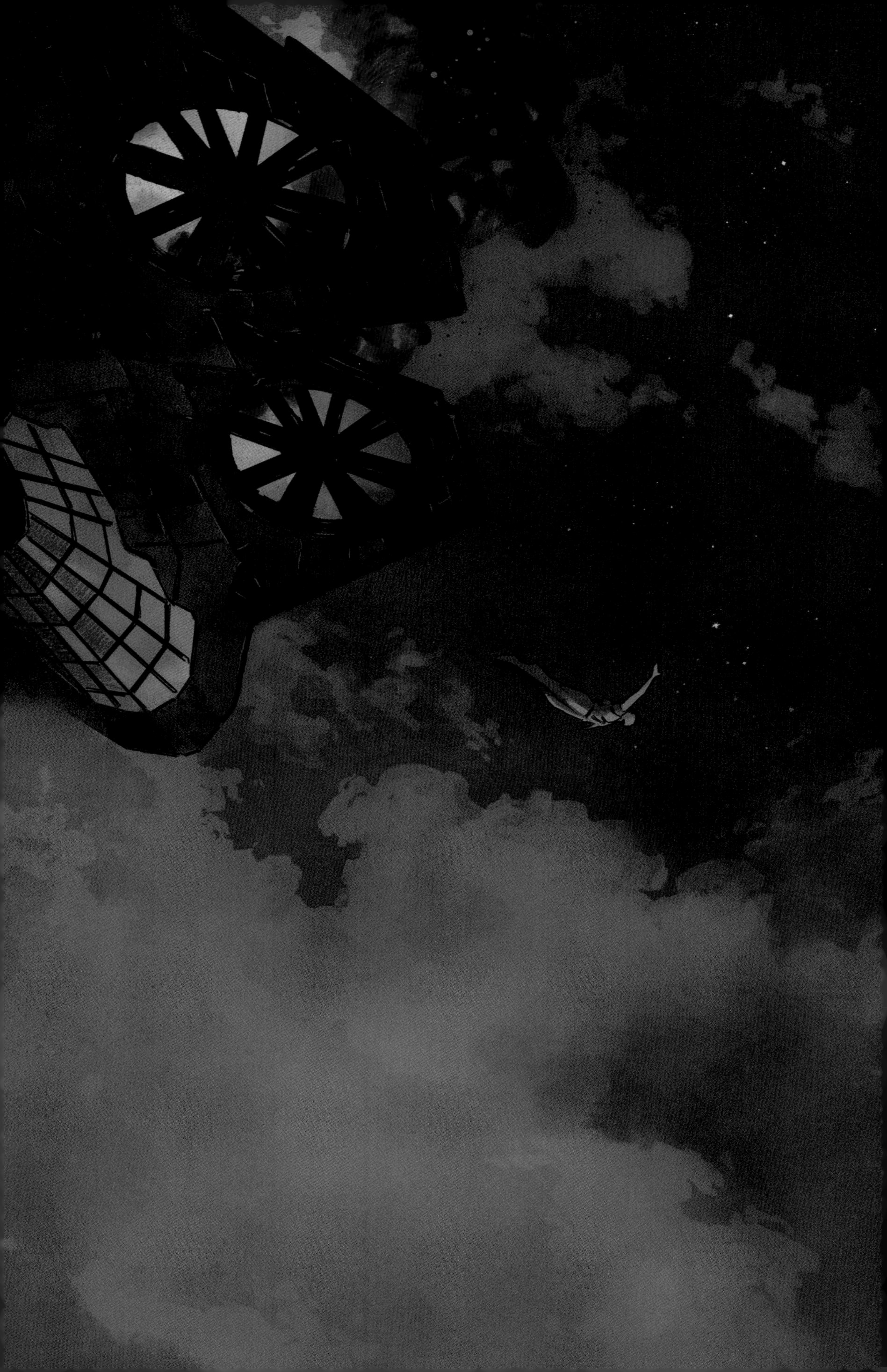

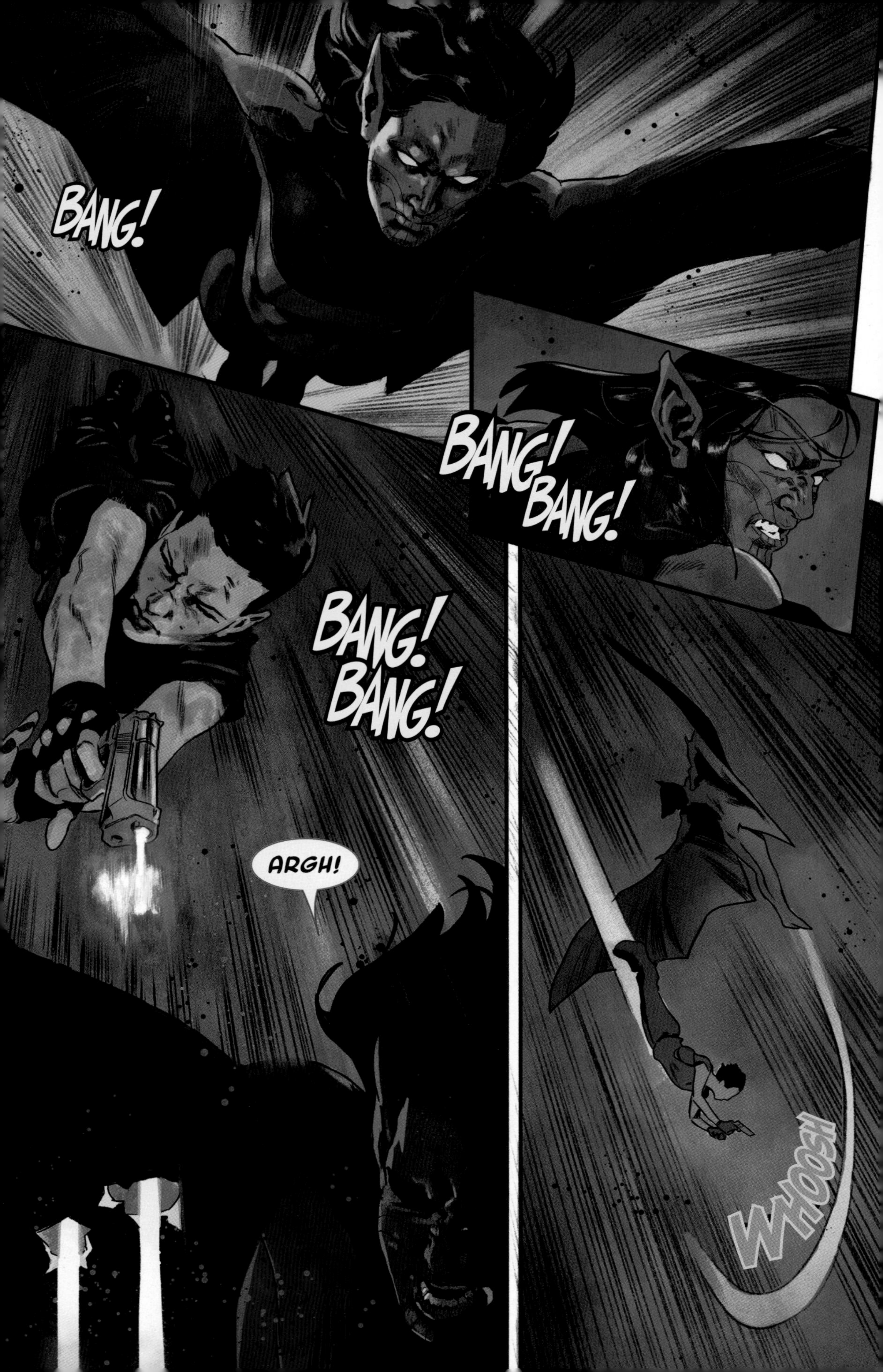
BANG!
BANG!
BANG!
BANG!
BANG!
ARGH!
WHOOSH

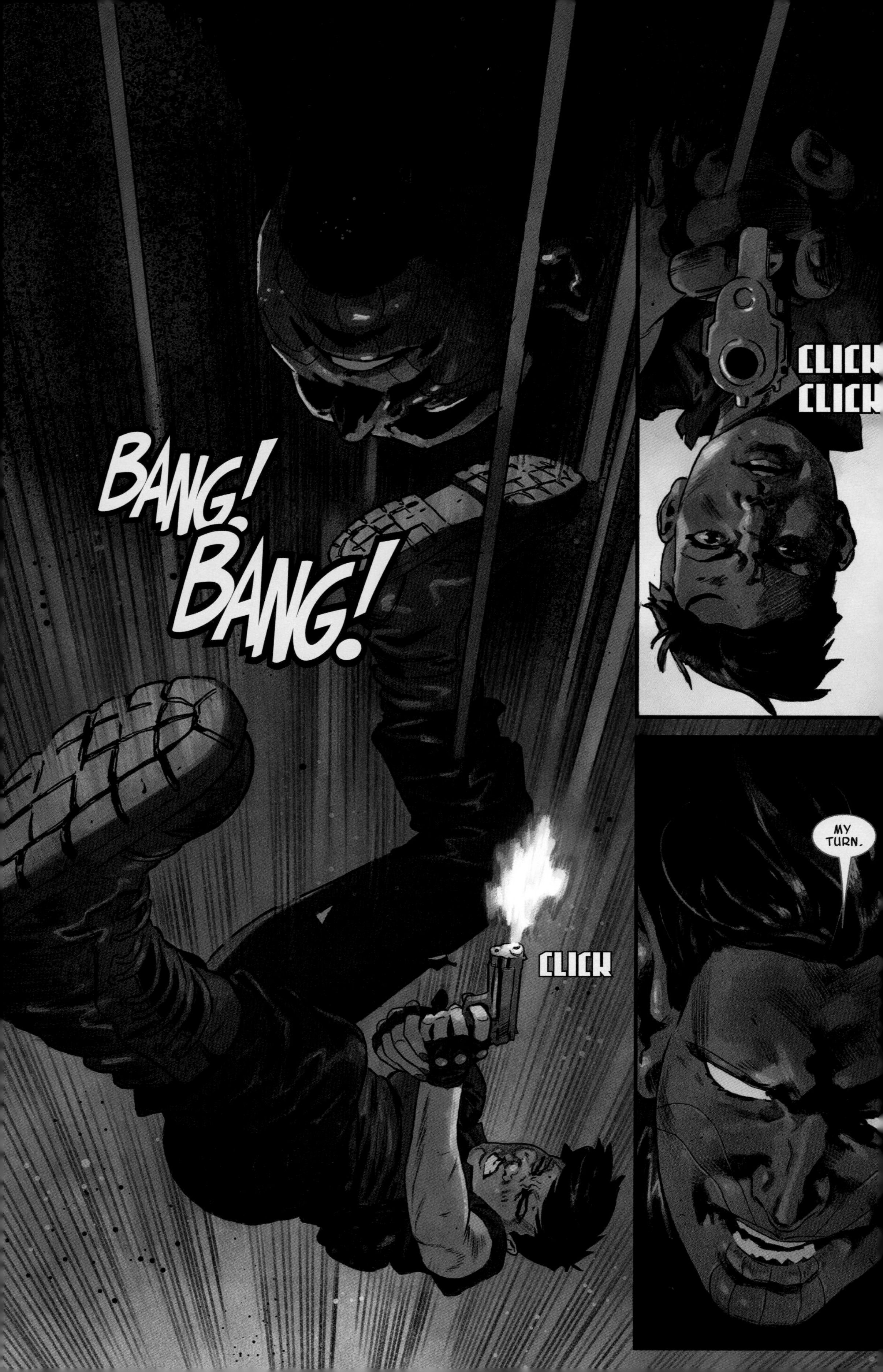
BANG! BANG!
CLICK
CLICK
CLICK
MY TURN.

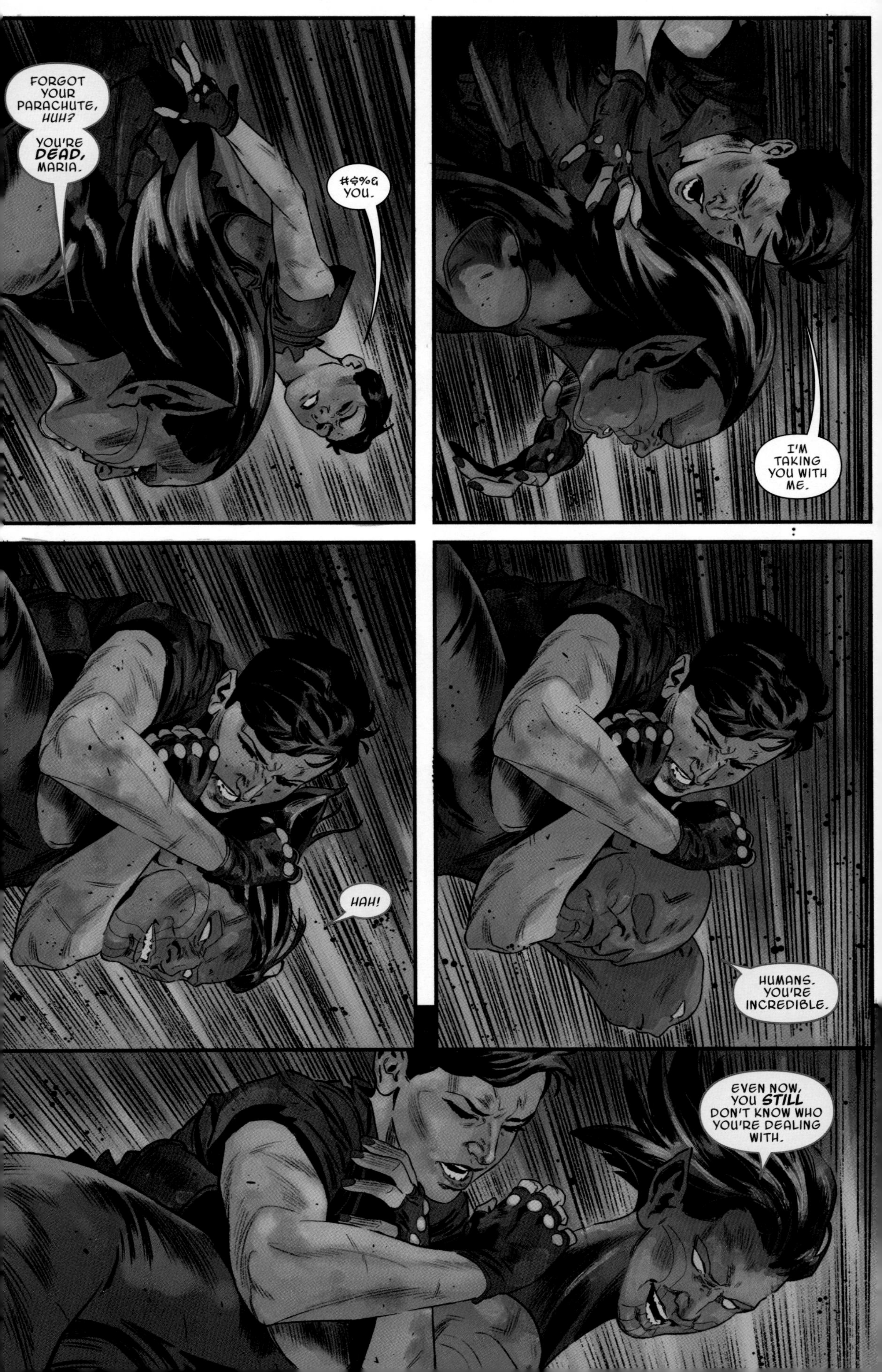
FORGOT YOUR PARACHUTE, HUH?
YOU'RE DEAD, MARIA.
#$%& YOU.
I'M TAKING YOU WITH ME.
HAH!
HUMANS. YOU'RE INCREDIBLE.
EVEN NOW, YOU STILL DON'T KNOW WHO YOU'RE DEALING WITH.

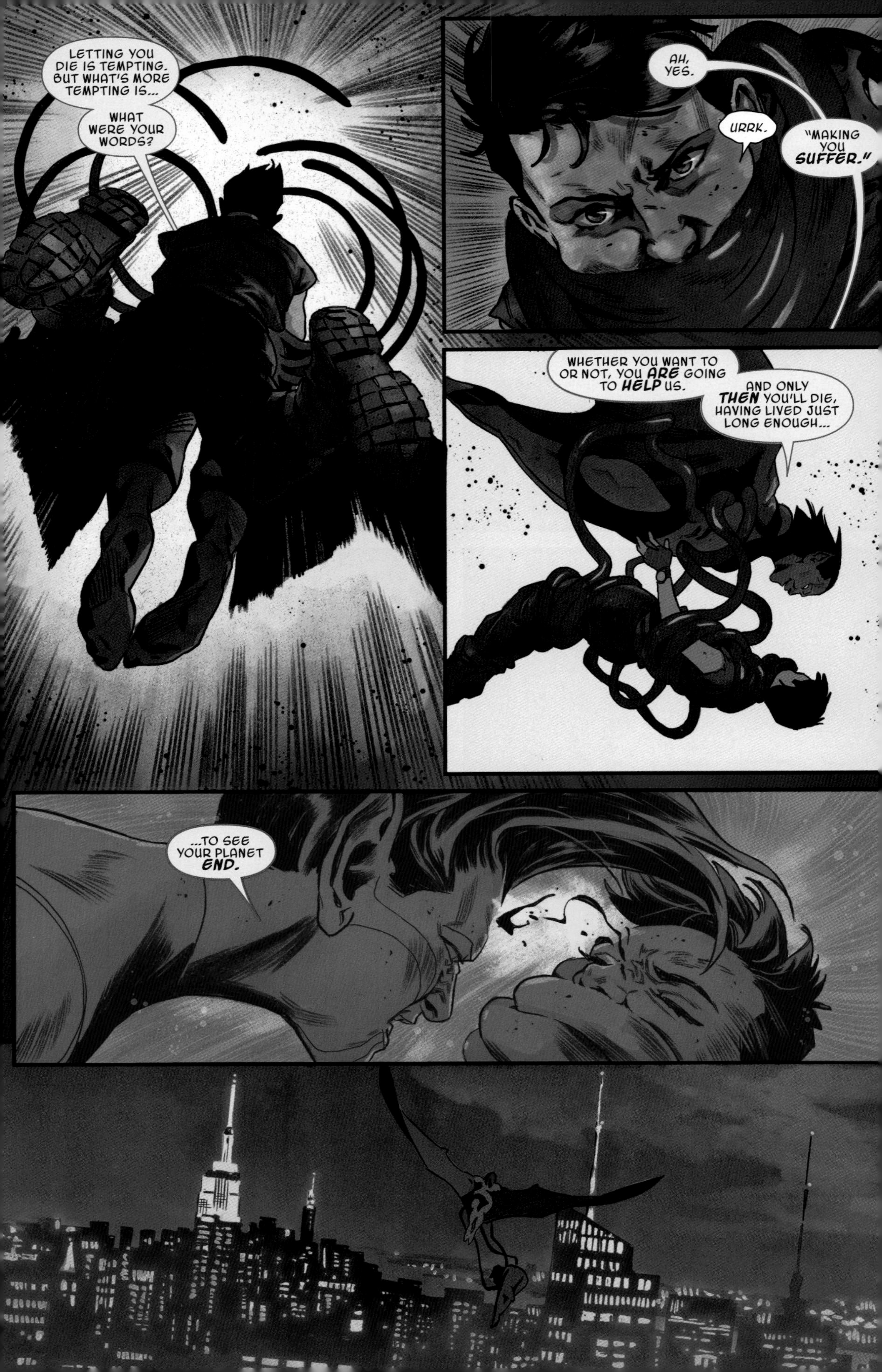
LETTING YOU DIE IS TEMPTING. BUT WHAT'S MORE TEMPTING IS...
WHAT WERE YOUR WORDS?
AH, YES.
URRK.
"MAKING YOU SUFFER."
WHETHER YOU WANT TO OR NOT, YOU ARE GOING TO HELP US.
AND ONLY THEN YOU'LL DIE, HAVING LIVED JUST LONG ENOUGH...
...TO SEE YOUR PLANET END.

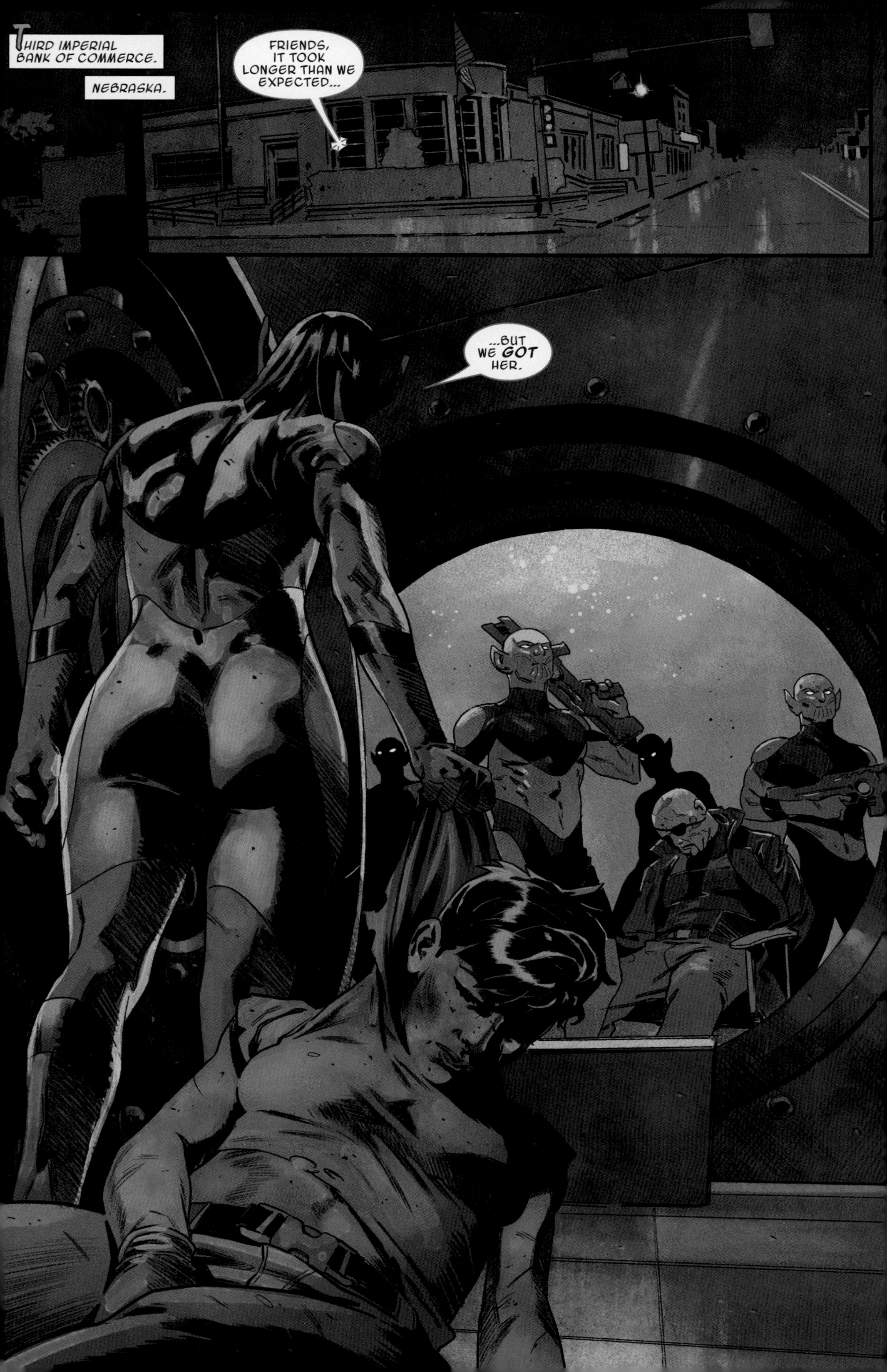
THIRD IMPERIAL BANK OF COMMERCE.
NEBRASKA.
FRIENDS, IT TOOK LONGER THAN WE EXPECTED...
...BUT WE GOT HER.

5

"Everywhere We Need To Be"

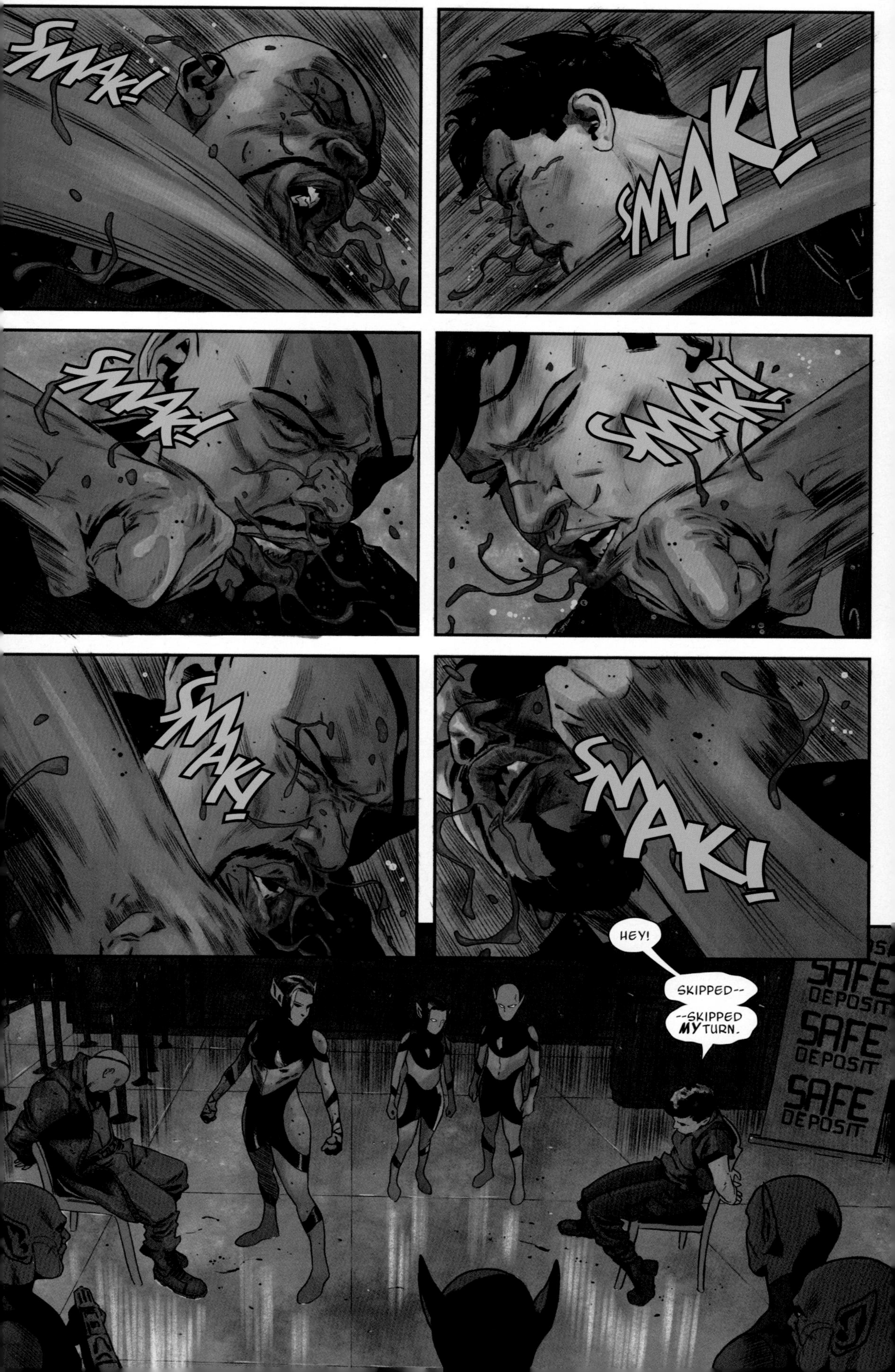
SMAK!
SMAK!
SMAK!
SMAK!
SMAK!
SMAK!
HEY!
SKIPPED--
--SKIPPED MY TURN.
SAFE DEPOSIT
SAFE DEPOSIT
SAFE DEPOSIT

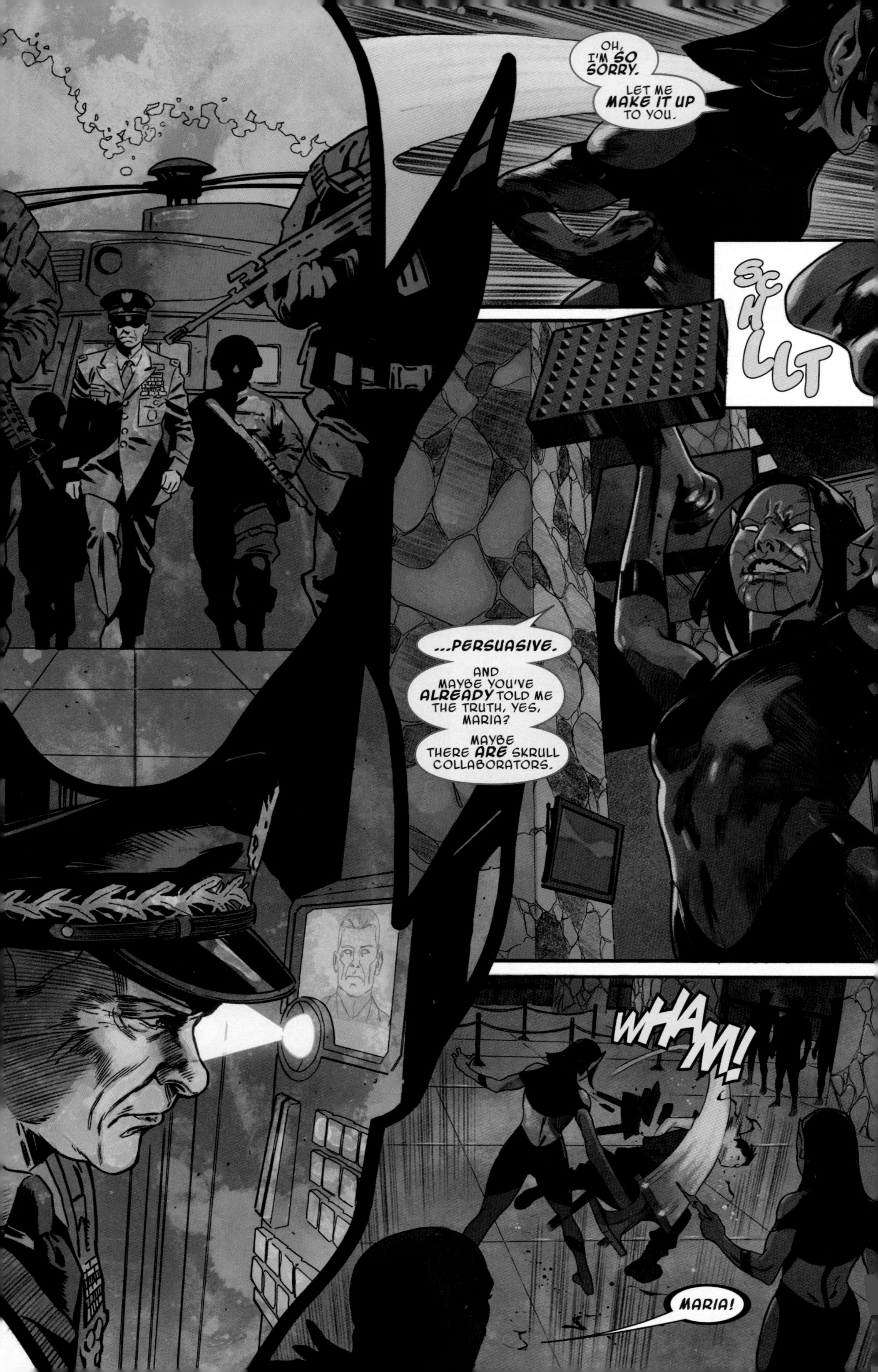
OH, I'M SO SORRY.
LET ME MAKE IT UP TO YOU.
SCHLLT
...PERSUASIVE.
AND MAYBE YOU'VE ALREADY TOLD ME THE TRUTH, YES, MARIA?
MAYBE THERE ARE SKRULL COLLABORATORS.
WHAM!
MARIA!

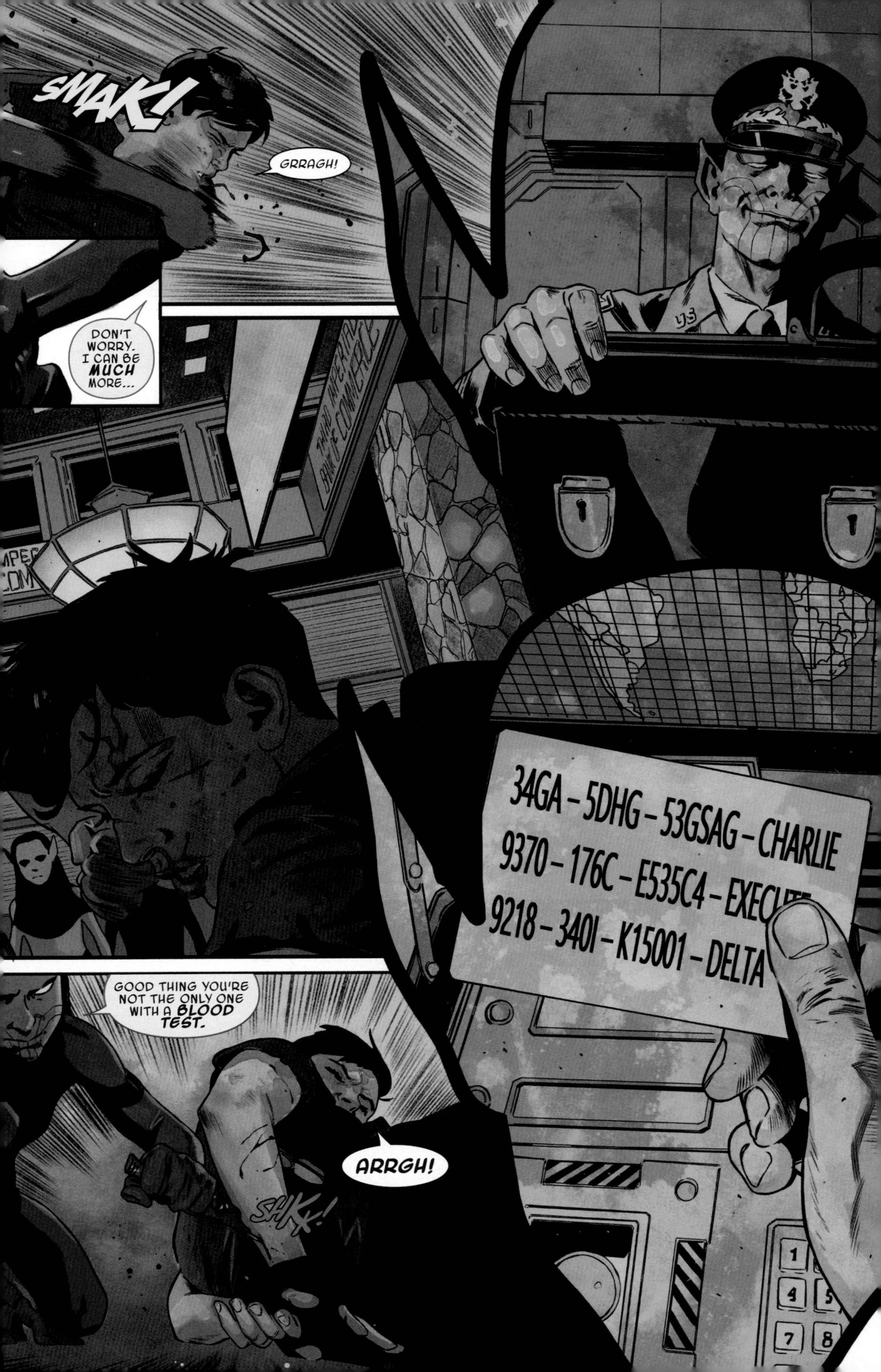
SMAK!
GRRAGH!
DON'T WORRY. I CAN BE MUCH MORE...
THIRD IMPERIAL BANK OF COMMERCE
34GA – 5DHG – 53GSAG – CHARLIE
9370 – 176C – E535C4 – EXECUTE
9218 – 340I – K15001 – DELTA
GOOD THING YOU'RE NOT THE ONLY ONE WITH A BLOOD TEST.
ARRGH!
SHKK!

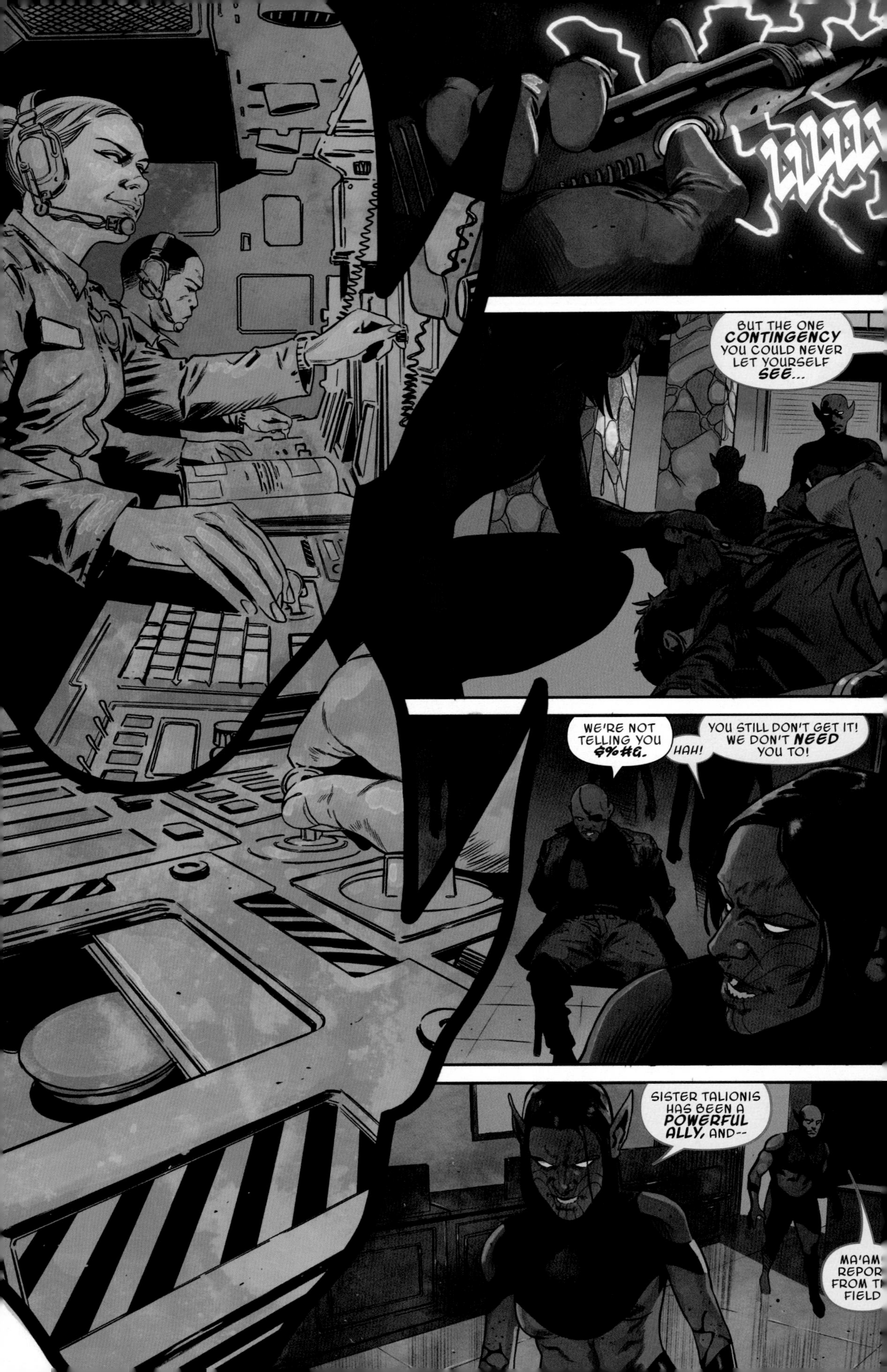
ZZZZZT
BUT THE ONE CONTINGENCY YOU COULD NEVER LET YOURSELF SEE...
WE'RE NOT TELLING YOU $%#G.
HAH!
YOU STILL DON'T GET IT! WE DON'T NEED YOU TO!
SISTER TALIONIS HAS BEEN A POWERFUL ALLY, AND--

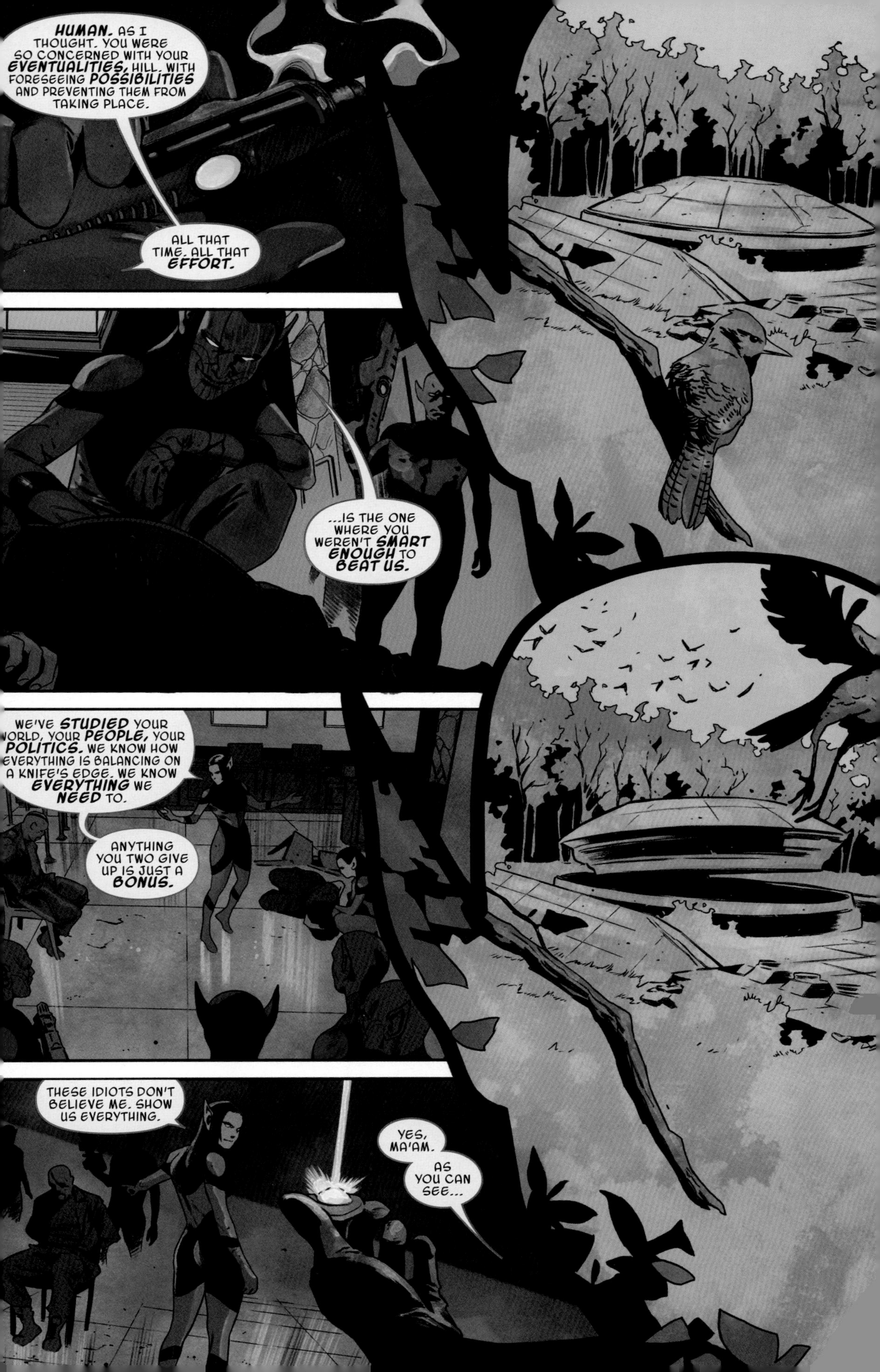
HUMAN. AS I THOUGHT. YOU WERE SO CONCERNED WITH YOUR EVENTUALITIES, HILL. WITH FORESEEING POSSIBILITIES AND PREVENTING THEM FROM TAKING PLACE.
ALL THAT TIME. ALL THAT EFFORT.
...IS THE ONE WHERE YOU WEREN'T SMART ENOUGH TO BEAT US.
WE'VE STUDIED YOUR WORLD, YOUR PEOPLE, YOUR POLITICS. WE KNOW HOW EVERYTHING IS BALANCING ON A KNIFE'S EDGE. WE KNOW EVERYTHING WE NEED TO.
ANYTHING YOU TWO GIVE UP IS JUST A BONUS.
THESE IDIOTS DON'T BELIEVE ME. SHOW US EVERYTHING.
YES, MA'AM.
AS YOU CAN SEE...

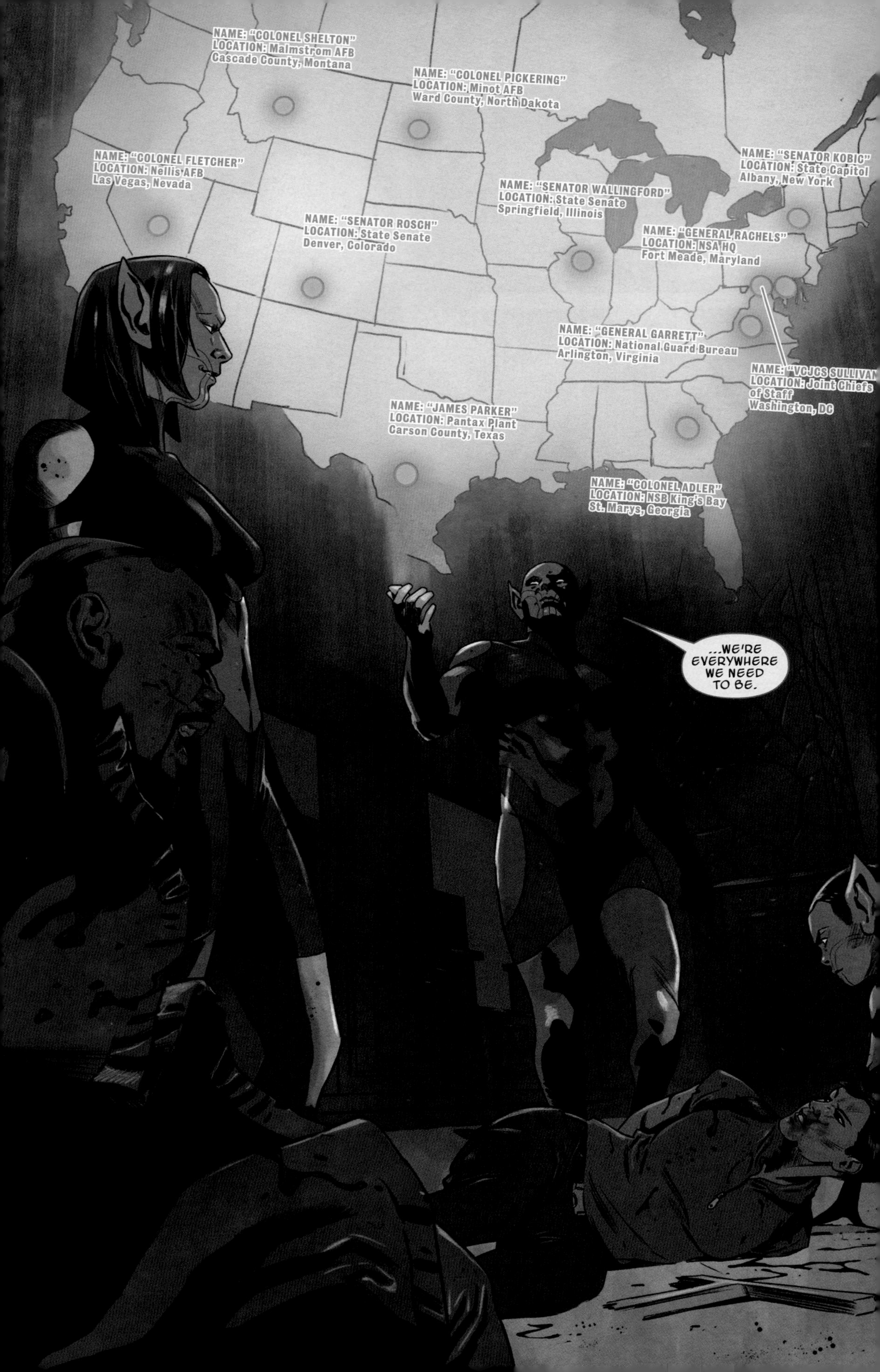

NAME: "COLONEL SHELTON"
LOCATION: Malmstrom AFB
Cascade County, Montana
NAME: "COLONEL PICKERING"
LOCATION: Minot AFB
Ward County, North Dakota
NAME: "COLONEL FLETCHER"
LOCATION: Nellis AFB
Las Vegas, Nevada
NAME: "SENATOR KOBIC"
LOCATION: State Capitol
Albany, New York
NAME: "SENATOR WALLINGFORD"
LOCATION: State Senate
Springfield, Illinois
NAME: "SENATOR ROSCH"
LOCATION: State Senate
Denver, Colorado
NAME: "GENERAL RACHELS"
LOCATION: NSA HQ
Fort Meade, Maryland
NAME: "GENERAL GARRETT"
LOCATION: National Guard Bureau
Arlington, Virginia
NAME: "VCJCS SULLIVAN
LOCATION: Joint Chiefs
of Staff
Washington, DC
NAME: "JAMES PARKER"
LOCATION: Pantax Plant
Carson County, Texas
NAME: "COLONEL ADLER"
LOCATION: NSB King's Bay
St. Marys, Georgia
...WE'RE EVERYWHERE WE NEED TO BE.

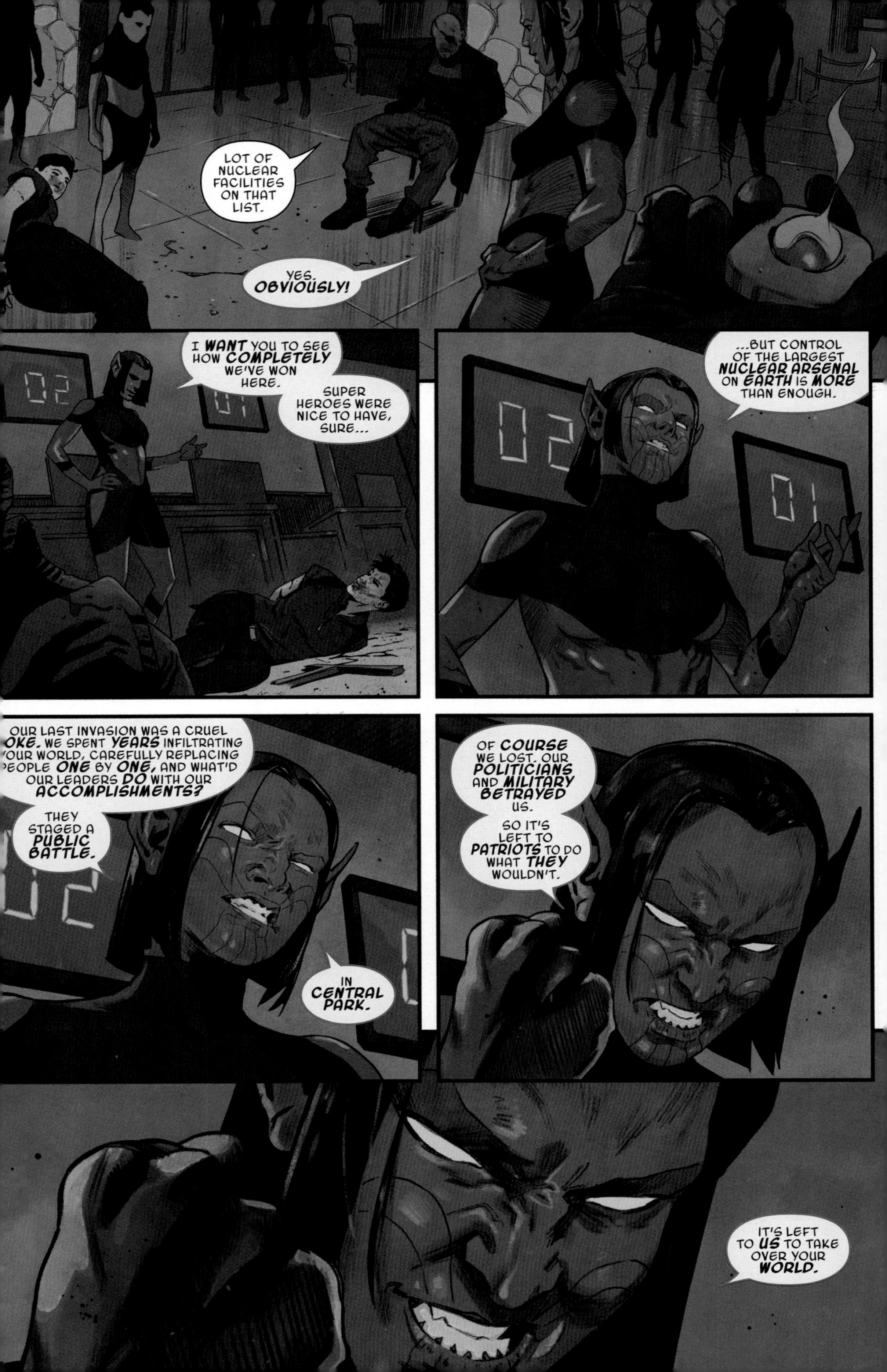

LOT OF NUCLEAR FACILITIES ON THAT LIST.
YES. OBVIOUSLY!
I WANT YOU TO SEE HOW COMPLETELY WE'VE WON HERE.
SUPER HEROES WERE NICE TO HAVE, SURE...
...BUT CONTROL OF THE LARGEST NUCLEAR ARSENAL ON EARTH IS MORE THAN ENOUGH.
OUR LAST INVASION WAS A CRUEL OKE. WE SPENT YEARS INFILTRATING OUR WORLD, CAREFULLY REPLACING PEOPLE ONE BY ONE, AND WHAT'D OUR LEADERS DO WITH OUR ACCOMPLISHMENTS?
THEY STAGED A PUBLIC BATTLE.
IN CENTRAL PARK.
OF COURSE WE LOST. OUR POLITICIANS AND MILITARY BETRAYED US.
SO IT'S LEFT TO PATRIOTS TO DO WHAT THEY WOULDN'T.
IT'S LEFT TO US TO TAKE OVER YOUR WORLD.

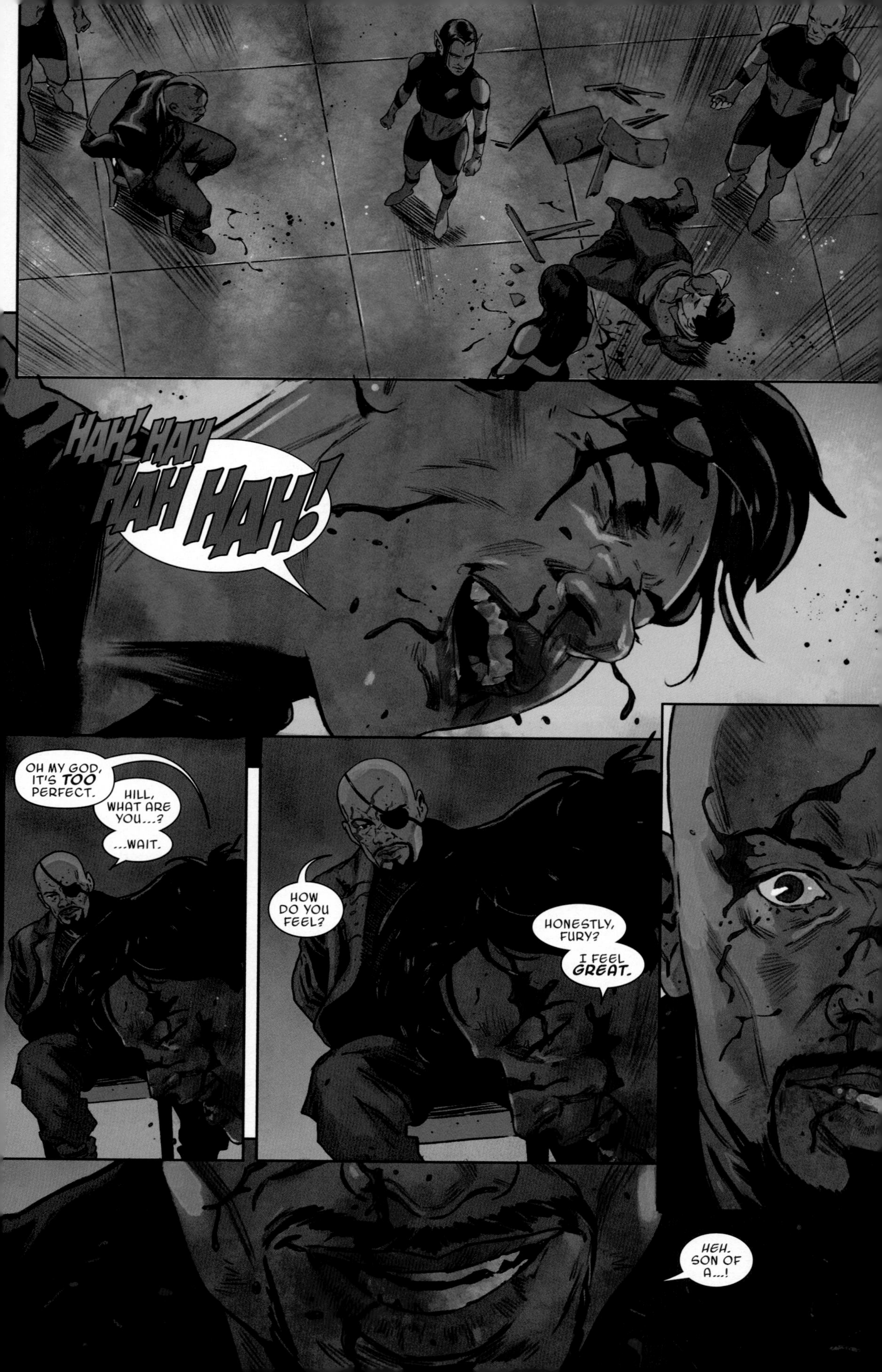
HAH! HAH HAH HAH!
OH MY GOD, IT'S TOO PERFECT.
HILL, WHAT ARE YOU...?
...WAIT.
HOW DO YOU FEEL?
HONESTLY, FURY?
I FEEL GREAT.
HEH. SON OF A...!

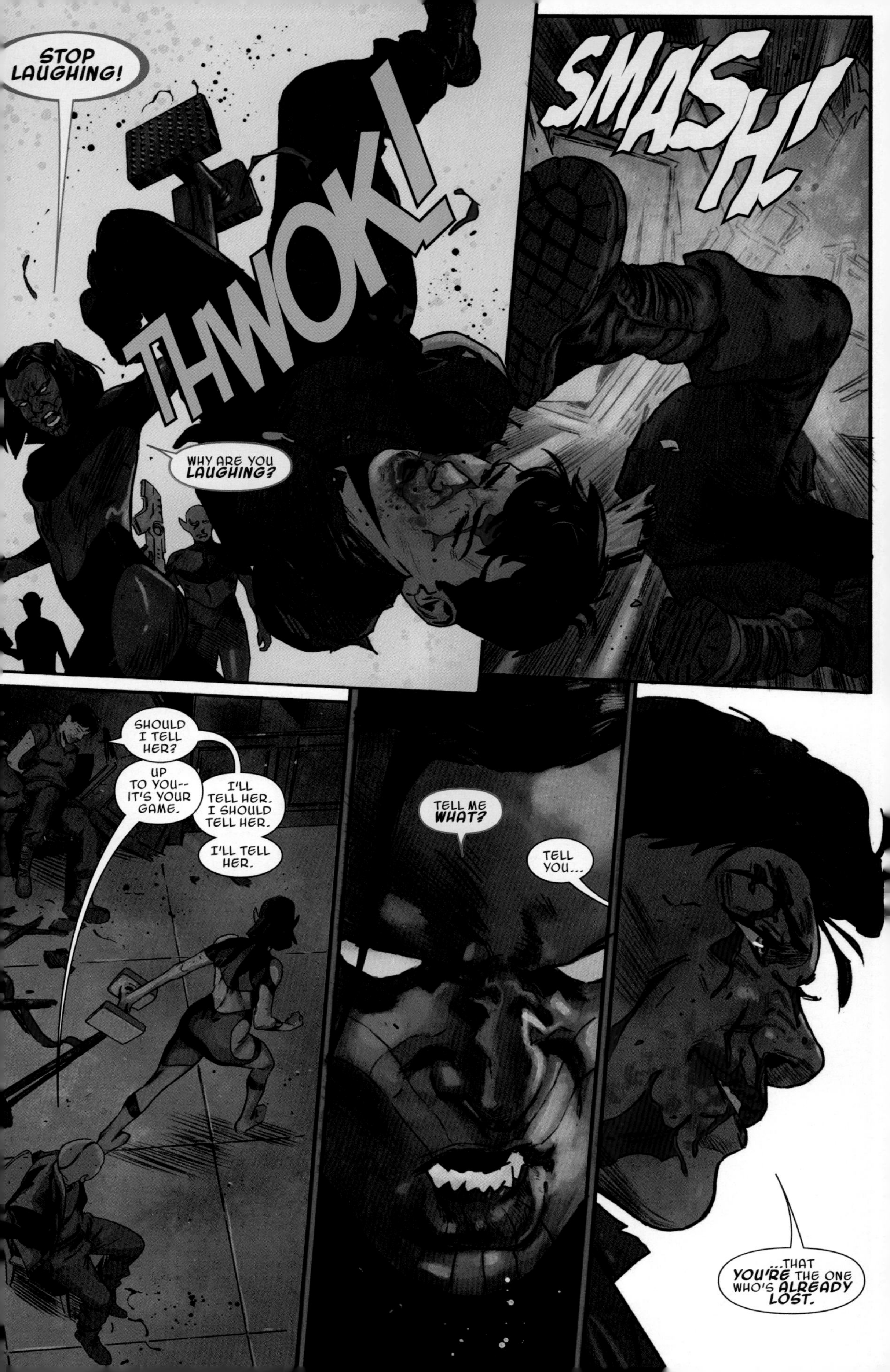
STOP LAUGHING!
THWOK!
SMASH!
WHY ARE YOU LAUGHING?
SHOULD I TELL HER?
UP TO YOU-- IT'S YOUR GAME.
I'LL TELL HER. I SHOULD TELL HER.
I'LL TELL HER.
TELL ME WHAT?
TELL YOU...
...THAT YOU'RE THE ONE WHO'S ALREADY LOST.

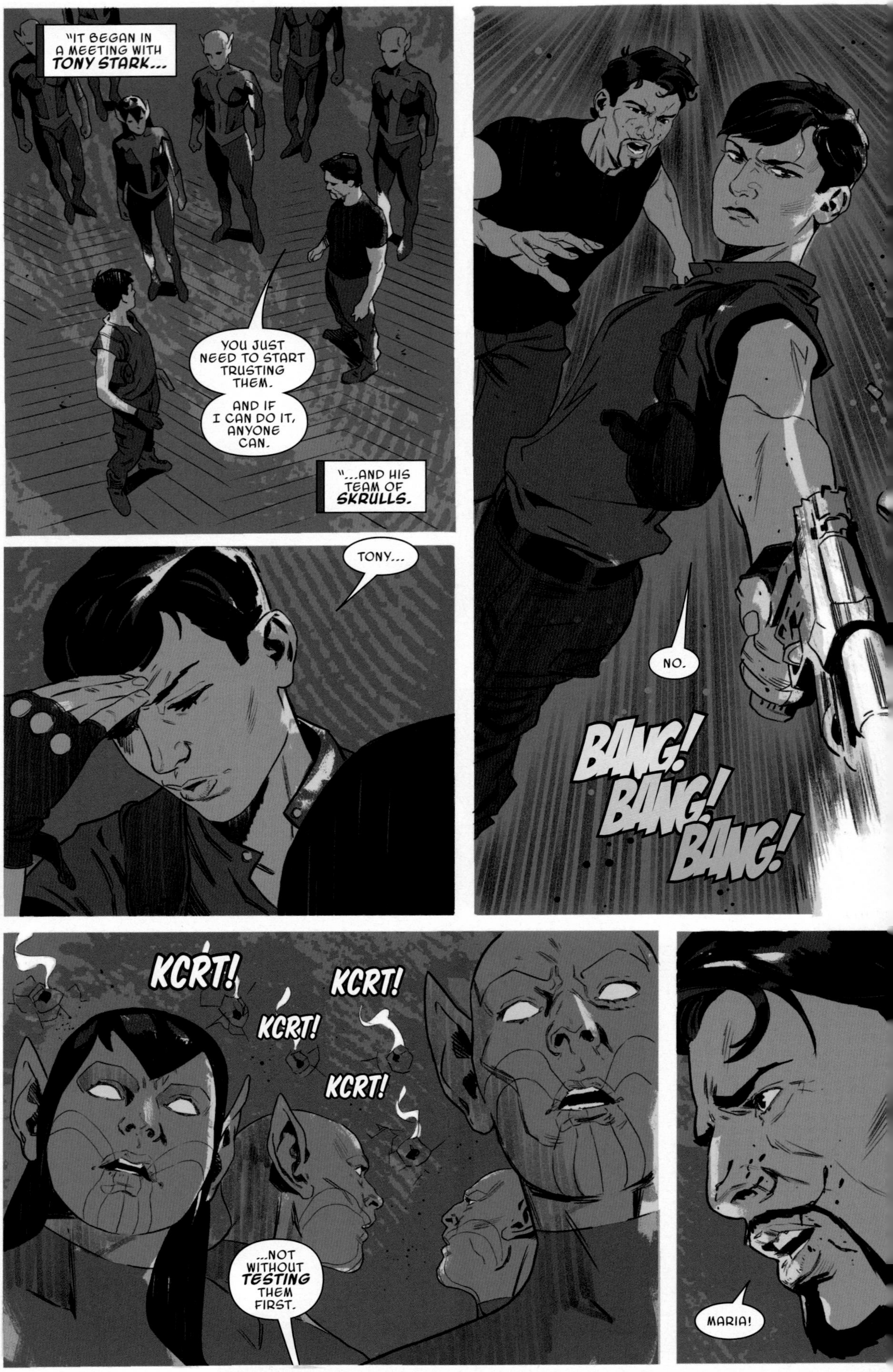
"IT BEGAN IN A MEETING WITH TONY STARK...
YOU JUST NEED TO START TRUSTING THEM.
AND IF I CAN DO IT, ANYONE CAN.
"...AND HIS TEAM OF SKRULLS.
TONY...
NO.
BANG! BANG! BANG!
KCRT!
KCRT!
KCRT!
KCRT!
...NOT WITHOUT TESTING THEM FIRST.
MARIA!

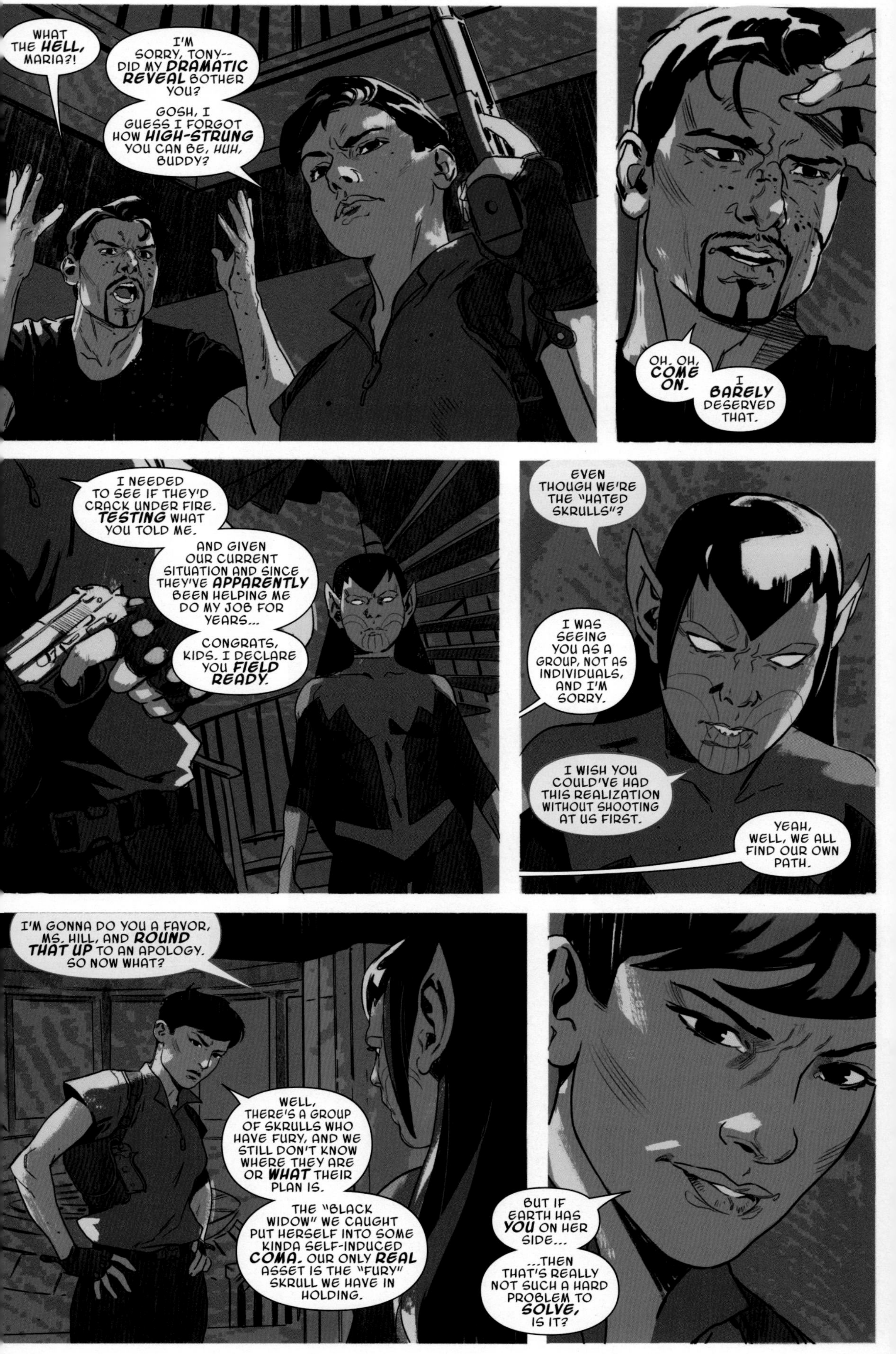
WHAT THE HELL, MARIA?!
I'M SORRY, TONY-- DID MY DRAMATIC REVEAL BOTHER YOU?
GOSH, I GUESS I FORGOT HOW HIGH-STRUNG YOU CAN BE, HUH, BUDDY?
OH, OH, COME ON.
I BARELY DESERVED THAT.
I NEEDED TO SEE IF THEY'D CRACK UNDER FIRE. TESTING WHAT YOU TOLD ME.
AND GIVEN OUR CURRENT SITUATION AND SINCE THEY'VE APPARENTLY BEEN HELPING ME DO MY JOB FOR YEARS...
CONGRATS, KIDS. I DECLARE YOU FIELD READY.
EVEN THOUGH WE'RE THE "HATED SKRULLS"?
I WAS SEEING YOU AS A GROUP, NOT AS INDIVIDUALS, AND I'M SORRY.
I WISH YOU COULD'VE HAD THIS REALIZATION WITHOUT SHOOTING AT US FIRST.
YEAH, WELL, WE ALL FIND OUR OWN PATH.
I'M GONNA DO YOU A FAVOR, MS. HILL, AND ROUND THAT UP TO AN APOLOGY. SO NOW WHAT?
WELL, THERE'S A GROUP OF SKRULLS WHO HAVE FURY, AND WE STILL DON'T KNOW WHERE THEY ARE OR WHAT THEIR PLAN IS.
THE "BLACK WIDOW" WE CAUGHT PUT HERSELF INTO SOME KINDA SELF-INDUCED COMA. OUR ONLY REAL ASSET IS THE "FURY" SKRULL WE HAVE IN HOLDING.
BUT IF EARTH HAS YOU ON HER SIDE...
...THEN THAT'S REALLY NOT SUCH A HARD PROBLEM TO SOLVE, IS IT?

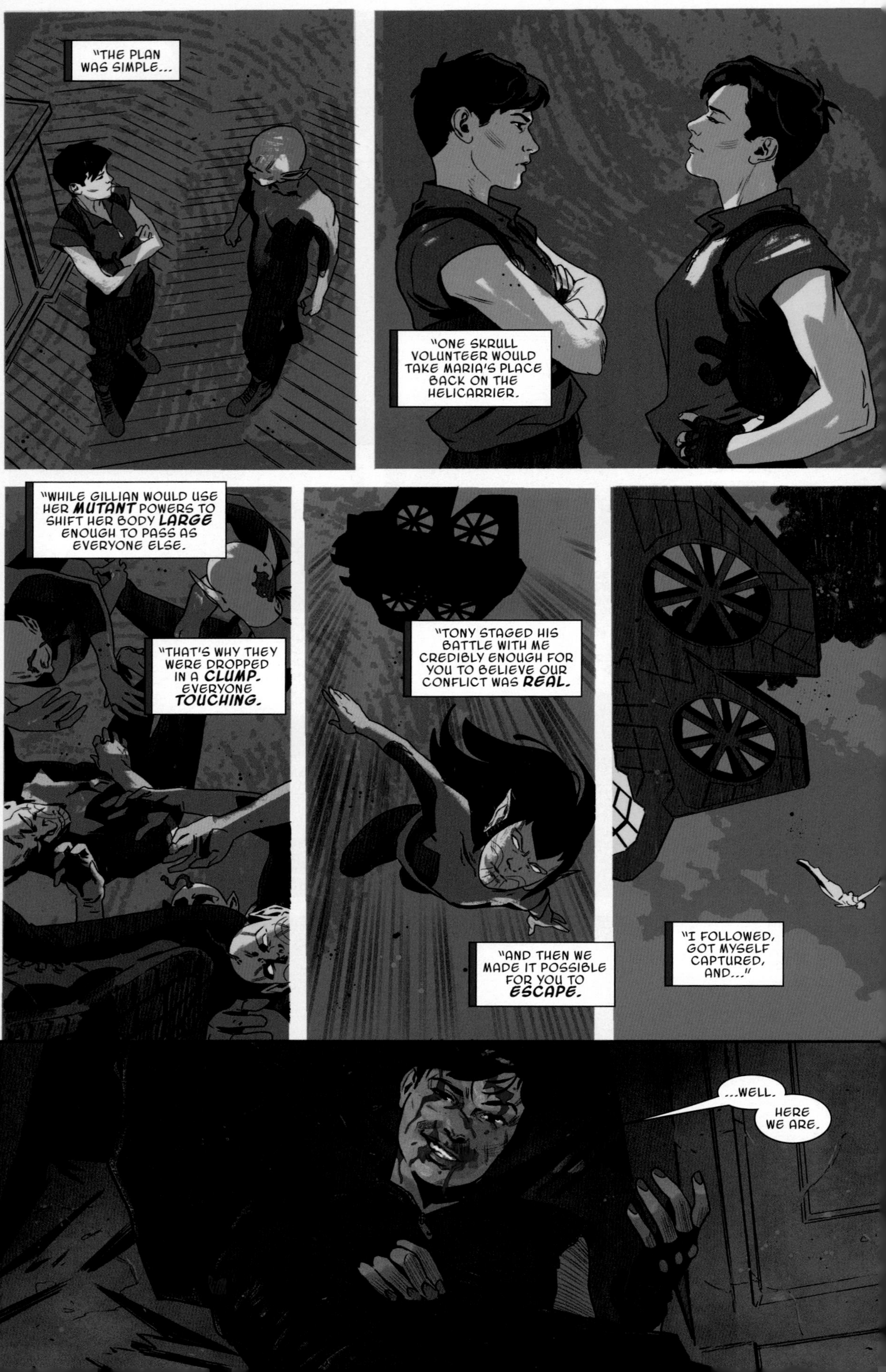
"THE PLAN WAS SIMPLE...
"ONE SKRULL VOLUNTEER WOULD TAKE MARIA'S PLACE BACK ON THE HELICARRIER.
"WHILE GILLIAN WOULD USE HER MUTANT POWERS TO SHIFT HER BODY LARGE ENOUGH TO PASS AS EVERYONE ELSE.
"THAT'S WHY THEY WERE DROPPED IN A CLUMP. EVERYONE TOUCHING.
"TONY STAGED HIS BATTLE WITH ME CREDIBLY ENOUGH FOR YOU TO BELIEVE OUR CONFLICT WAS REAL.
"AND THEN WE MADE IT POSSIBLE FOR YOU TO ESCAPE.
"I FOLLOWED, GOT MYSELF CAPTURED, AND..."
...WELL.
HERE WE ARE.

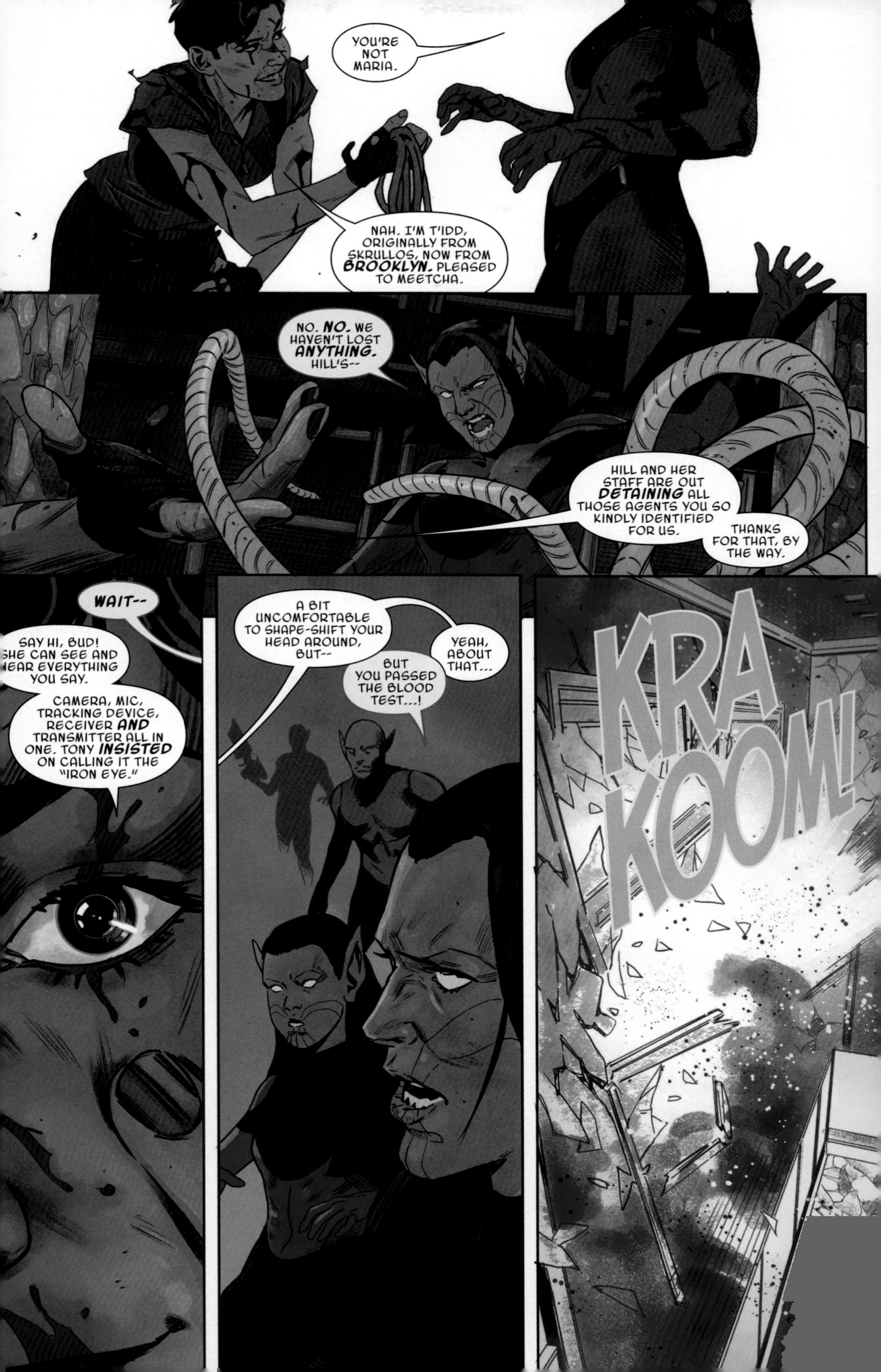
YOU'RE NOT MARIA.
NAH. I'M T'IDD, ORIGINALLY FROM SKRULLOS, NOW FROM BROOKLYN. PLEASED TO MEETCHA.
NO. NO. WE HAVEN'T LOST ANYTHING. HILL'S--
HILL AND HER STAFF ARE OUT DETAINING ALL THOSE AGENTS YOU SO KINDLY IDENTIFIED FOR US.
THANKS FOR THAT, BY THE WAY.
WAIT--
SAY HI, BUD! SHE CAN SEE AND HEAR EVERYTHING YOU SAY.
CAMERA, MIC, TRACKING DEVICE, RECEIVER AND TRANSMITTER ALL IN ONE. TONY INSISTED ON CALLING IT THE "IRON EYE."
BUT YOU PASSED THE BLOOD TEST...!
YEAH, ABOUT THAT...
A BIT UNCOMFORTABLE TO SHAPE-SHIFT YOUR HEAD AROUND, BUT--
KRA KOOM!

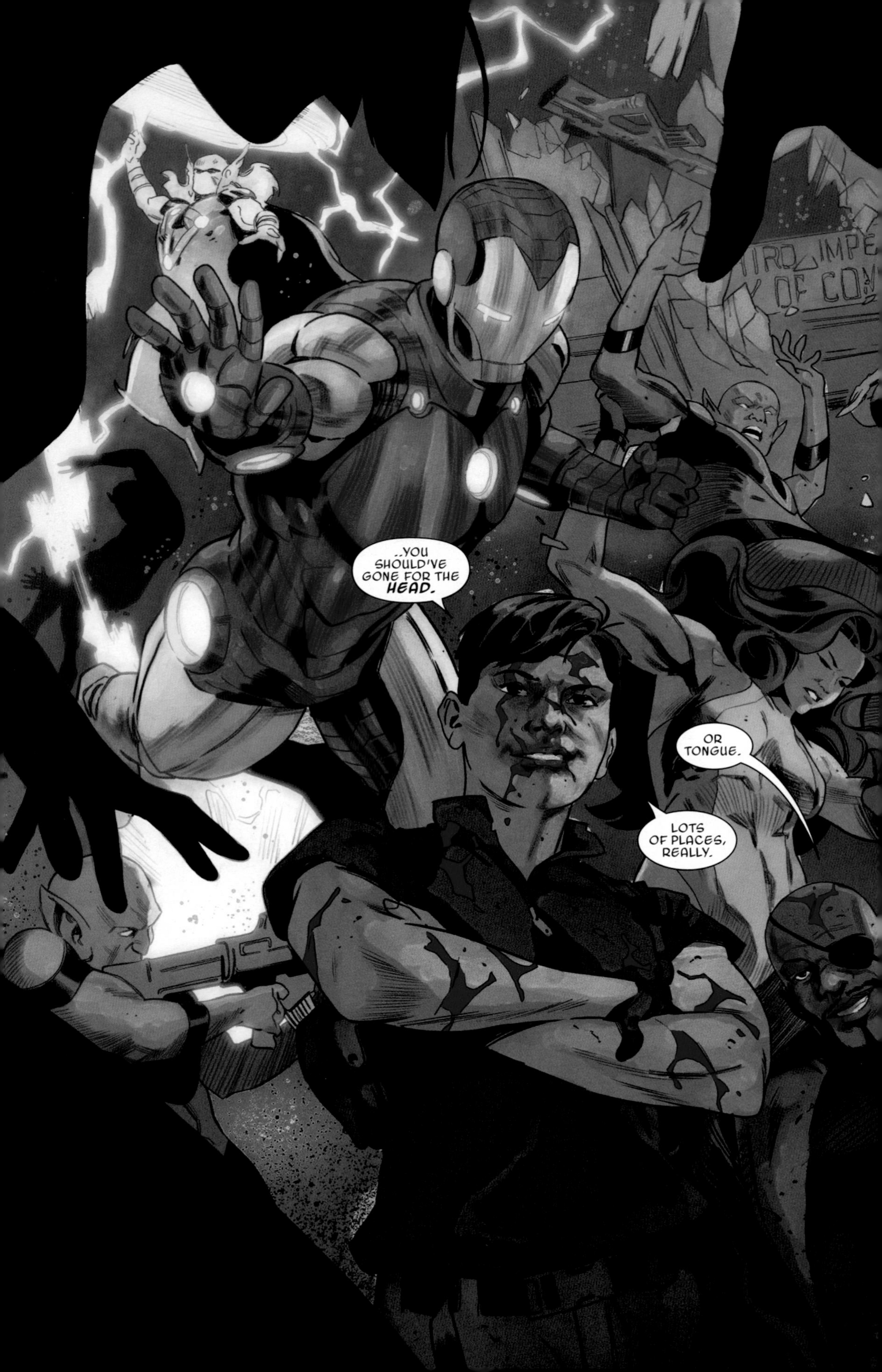
..YOU SHOULD'VE GONE FOR THE HEAD.
OR TONGUE.
LOTS OF PLACES, REALLY.

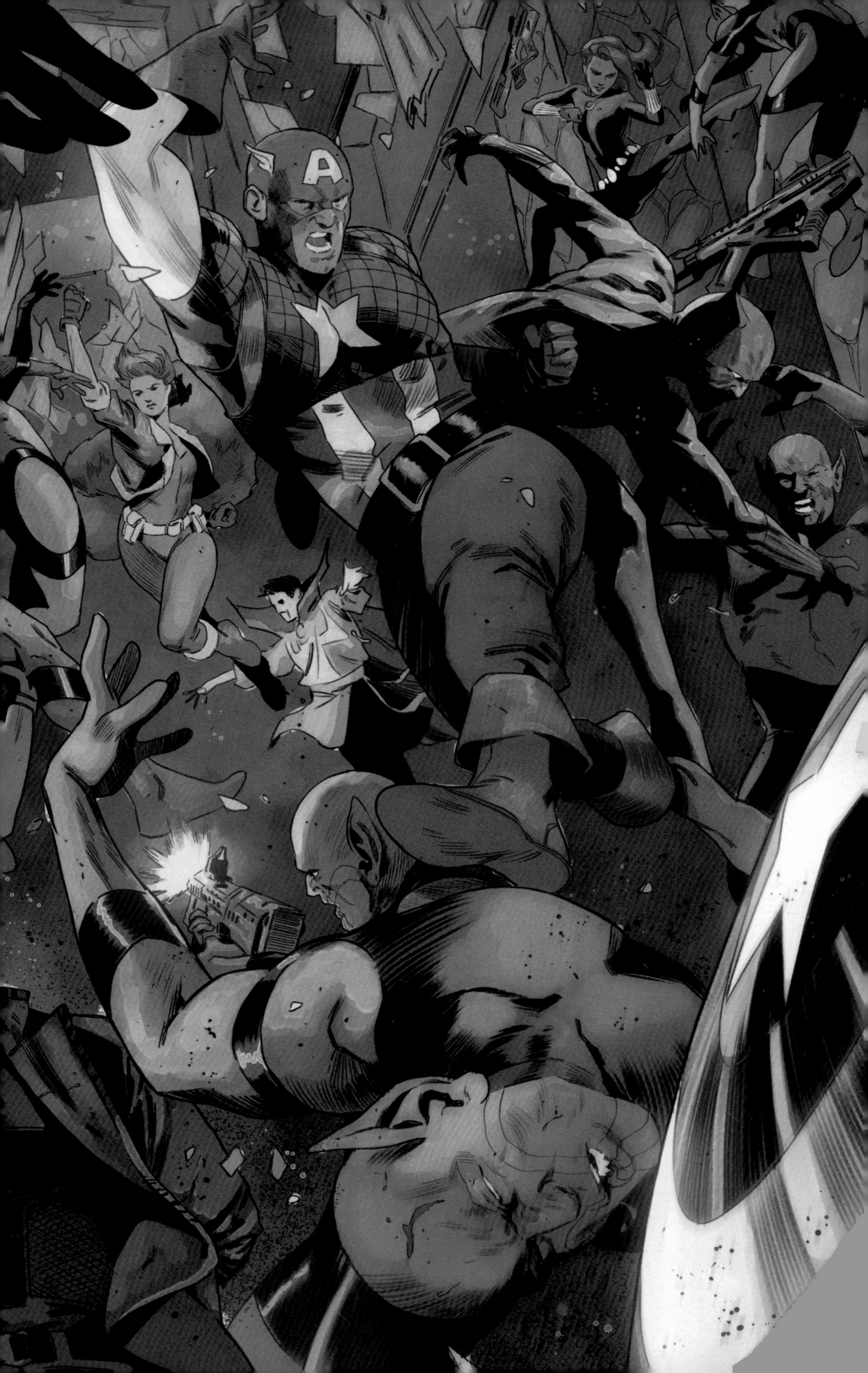

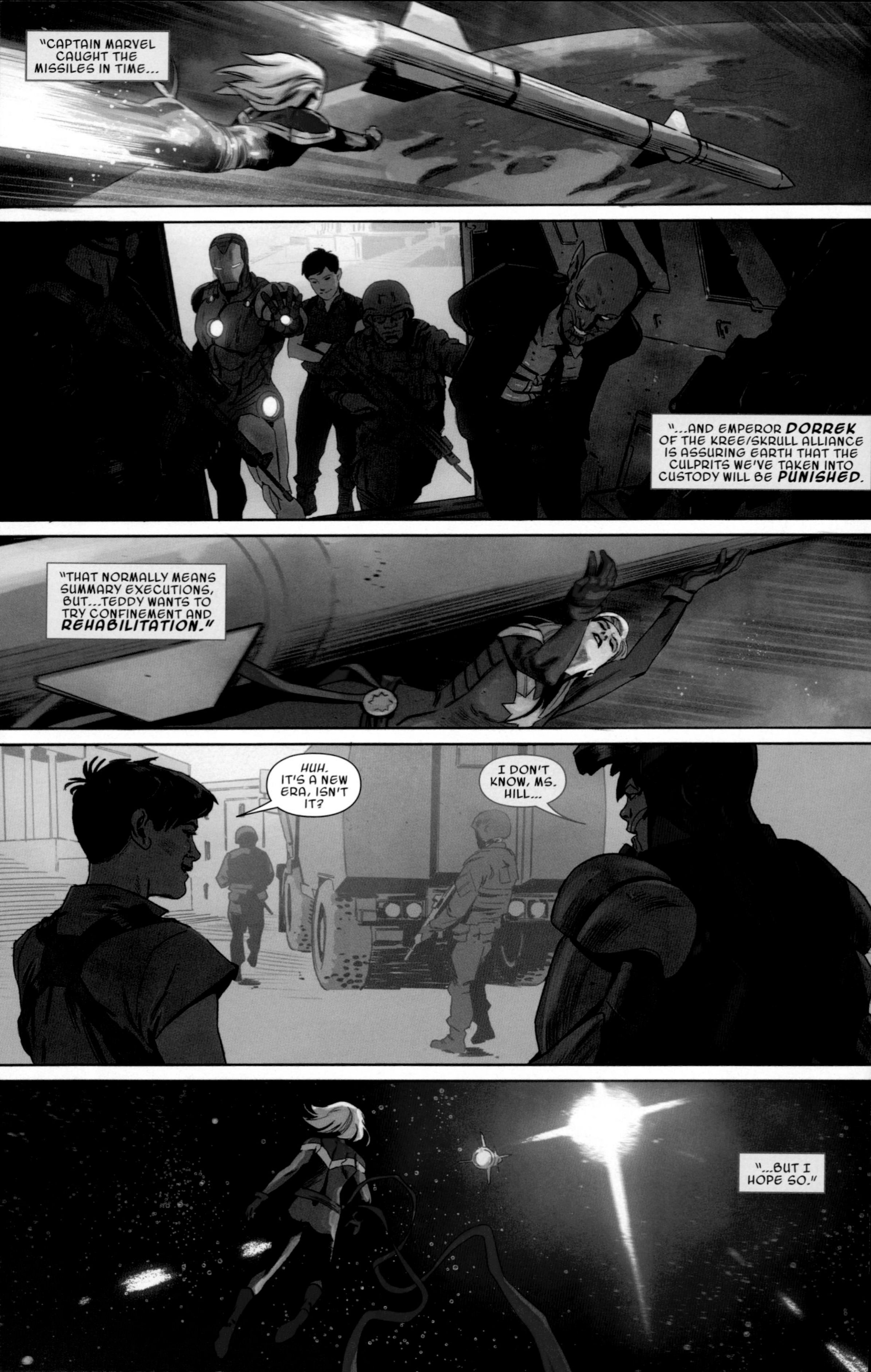
"CAPTAIN MARVEL CAUGHT THE MISSILES IN TIME...
"...AND EMPEROR DORREK OF THE KREE/SKRULL ALLIANCE IS ASSURING EARTH THAT THE CULPRITS WE'VE TAKEN INTO CUSTODY WILL BE PUNISHED.
"THAT NORMALLY MEANS SUMMARY EXECUTIONS, BUT...TEDDY WANTS TO TRY CONFINEMENT AND REHABILITATION."
HUH. IT'S A NEW ERA, ISN'T IT?
I DON'T KNOW, MS. HILL...
"...BUT I HOPE SO."

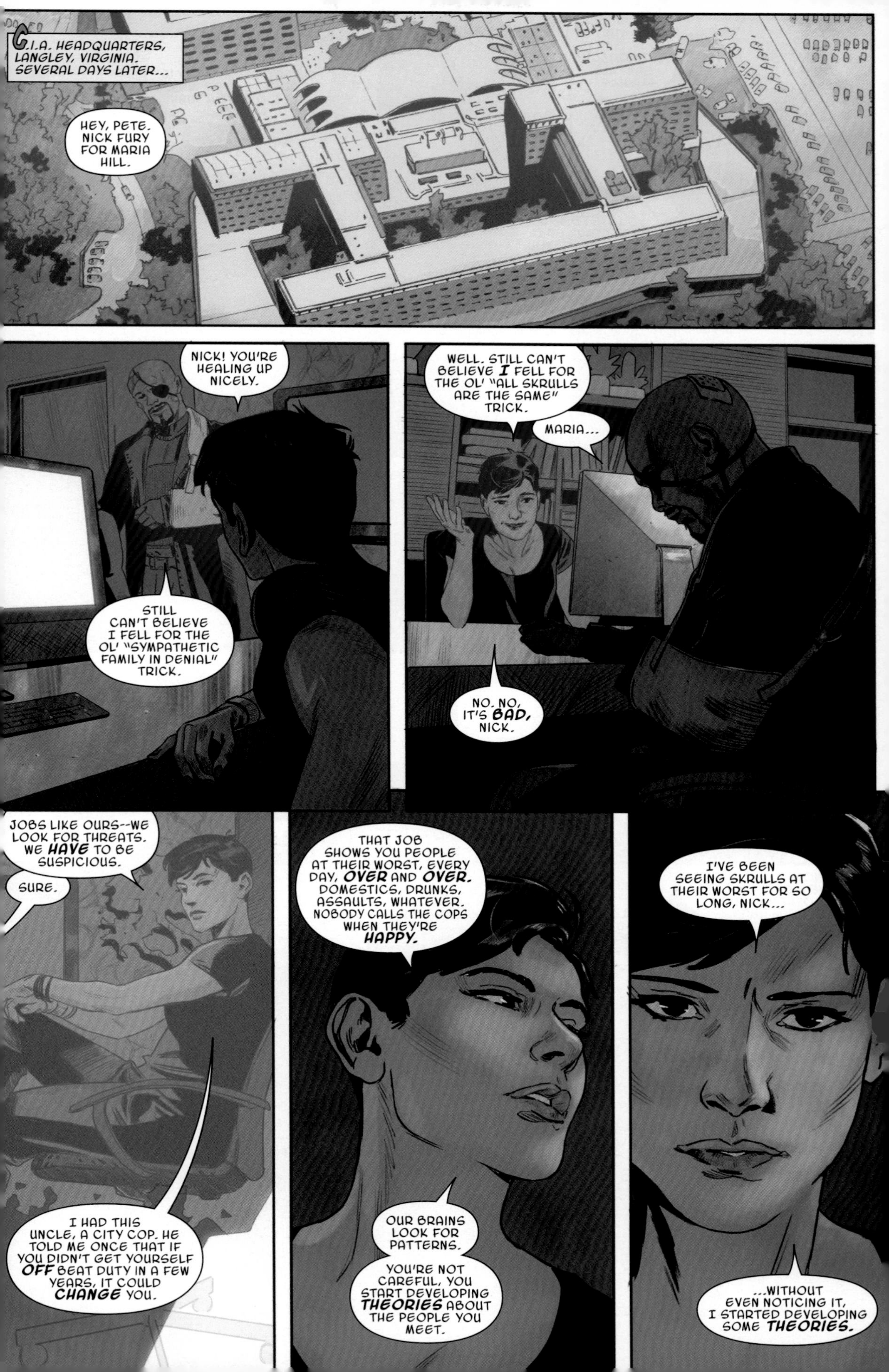
C.I.A. HEADQUARTERS, LANGLEY, VIRGINIA. SEVERAL DAYS LATER...
HEY, PETE. NICK FURY FOR MARIA HILL.
NICK! YOU'RE HEALING UP NICELY.
STILL CAN'T BELIEVE I FELL FOR THE OL' "SYMPATHETIC FAMILY IN DENIAL" TRICK.
WELL. STILL CAN'T BELIEVE I FELL FOR THE OL' "ALL SKRULLS ARE THE SAME" TRICK.
MARIA...
NO. NO, IT'S BAD, NICK.
JOBS LIKE OURS--WE LOOK FOR THREATS. WE HAVE TO BE SUSPICIOUS.
SURE.
I HAD THIS UNCLE, A CITY COP. HE TOLD ME ONCE THAT IF YOU DIDN'T GET YOURSELF OFF BEAT DUTY IN A FEW YEARS, IT COULD CHANGE YOU.
THAT JOB SHOWS YOU PEOPLE AT THEIR WORST, EVERY DAY, OVER AND OVER. DOMESTICS, DRUNKS, ASSAULTS, WHATEVER. NOBODY CALLS THE COPS WHEN THEY'RE HAPPY.
OUR BRAINS LOOK FOR PATTERNS.
YOU'RE NOT CAREFUL, YOU START DEVELOPING THEORIES ABOUT THE PEOPLE YOU MEET.
I'VE BEEN SEEING SKRULLS AT THEIR WORST FOR SO LONG, NICK...
...WITHOUT EVEN NOTICING IT, I STARTED DEVELOPING SOME THEORIES.

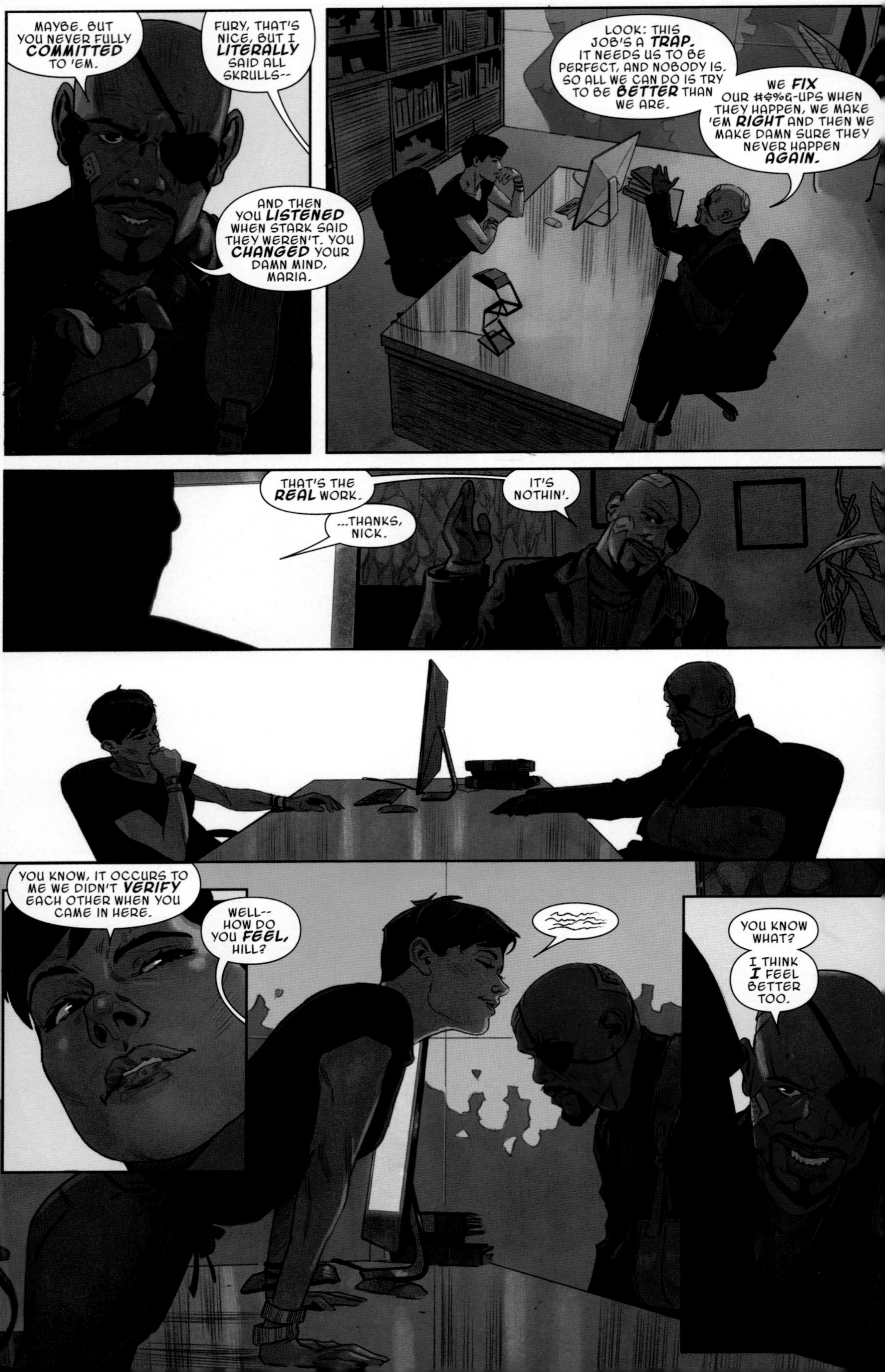
MAYBE. BUT YOU NEVER FULLY COMMITTED TO 'EM.
FURY, THAT'S NICE, BUT I LITERALLY SAID ALL SKRULLS--
AND THEN YOU LISTENED WHEN STARK SAID THEY WEREN'T. YOU CHANGED YOUR DAMN MIND, MARIA.
LOOK: THIS JOB'S A TRAP. IT NEEDS US TO BE PERFECT, AND NOBODY IS. SO ALL WE CAN DO IS TRY TO BE BETTER THAN WE ARE.
WE FIX OUR #$%&-UPS WHEN THEY HAPPEN, WE MAKE 'EM RIGHT AND THEN WE MAKE DAMN SURE THEY NEVER HAPPEN AGAIN.
THAT'S THE REAL WORK.
...THANKS, NICK.
IT'S NOTHIN'.
YOU KNOW, IT OCCURS TO ME WE DIDN'T VERIFY EACH OTHER WHEN YOU CAME IN HERE.
WELL-- HOW DO YOU FEEL, HILL?
YOU KNOW WHAT?
I THINK I FEEL BETTER TOO.

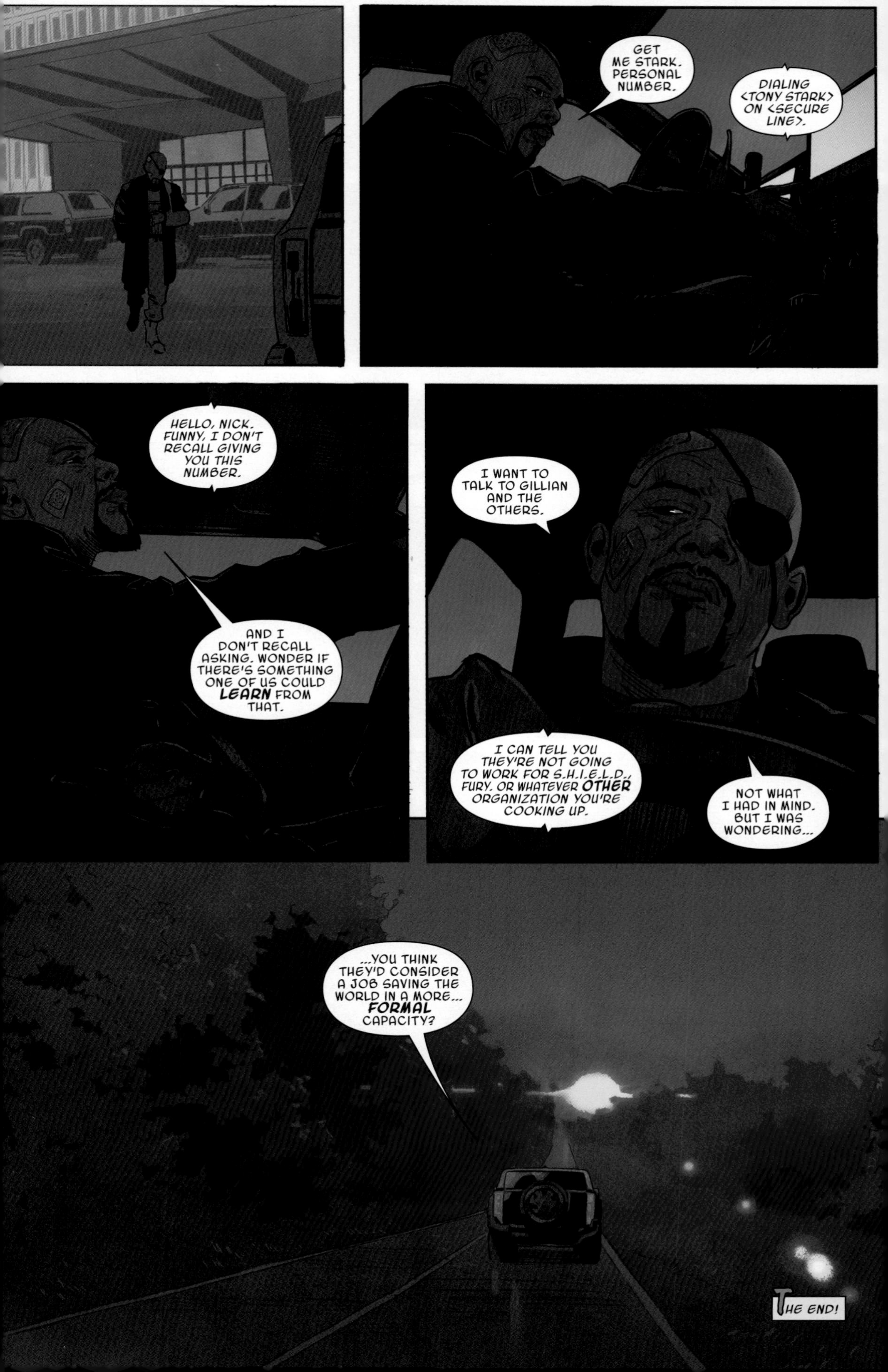
GET ME STARK. PERSONAL NUMBER.
DIALING <TONY STARK> ON <SECURE LINE>.
HELLO, NICK. FUNNY, I DON'T RECALL GIVING YOU THIS NUMBER.
AND I DON'T RECALL ASKING. WONDER IF THERE'S SOMETHING ONE OF US COULD LEARN FROM THAT.
I WANT TO TALK TO GILLIAN AND THE OTHERS.
I CAN TELL YOU THEY'RE NOT GOING TO WORK FOR S.H.I.E.L.D., FURY. OR WHATEVER OTHER ORGANIZATION YOU'RE COOKING UP.
NOT WHAT I HAD IN MIND. BUT I WAS WONDERING...
...YOU THINK THEY'D CONSIDER A JOB SAVING THE WORLD IN A MORE... FORMAL CAPACITY?
THE END!

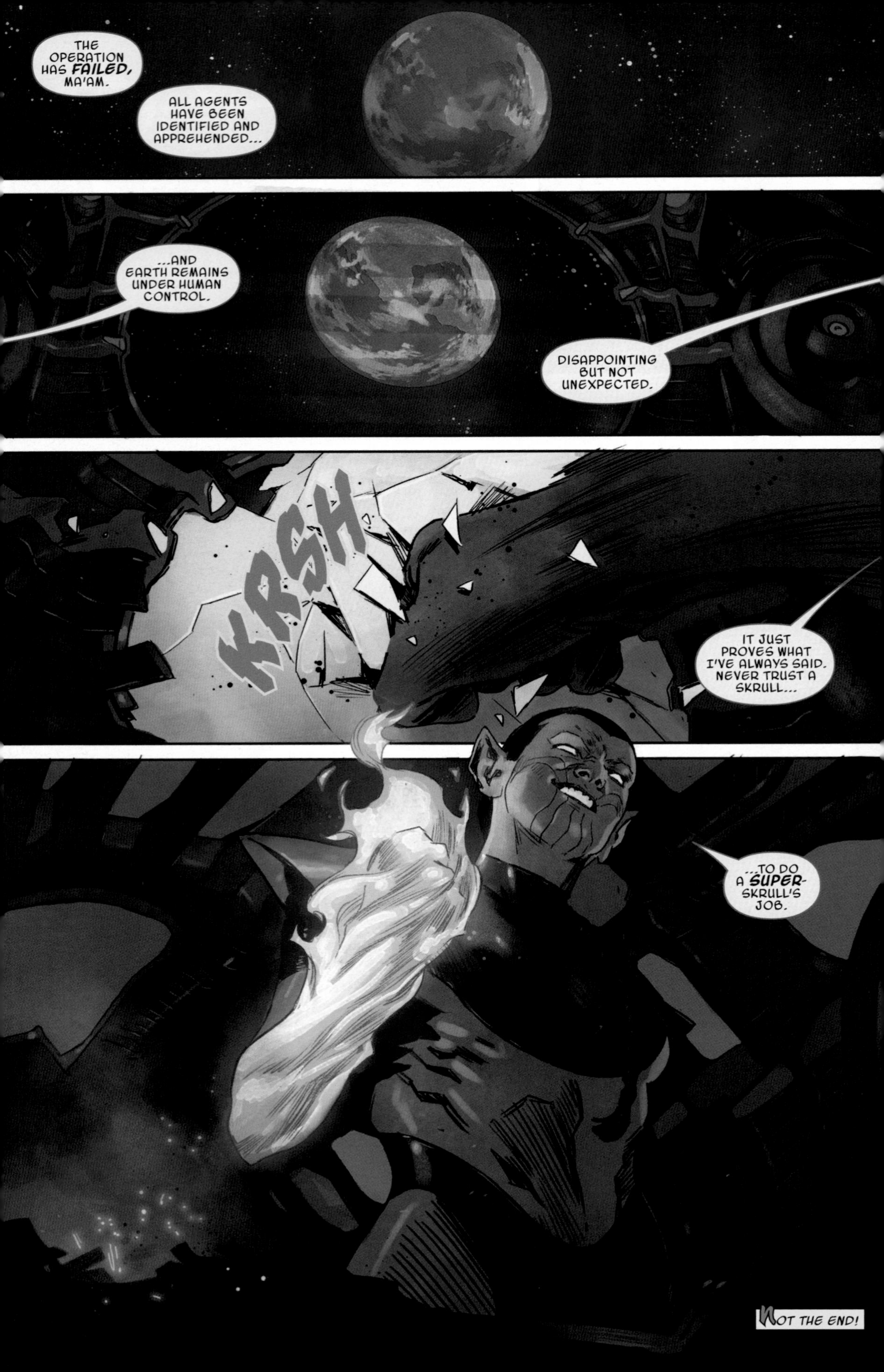
THE OPERATION HAS FAILED, MA'AM.
ALL AGENTS HAVE BEEN IDENTIFIED AND APPREHENDED...
...AND EARTH REMAINS UNDER HUMAN CONTROL.
DISAPPOINTING BUT NOT UNEXPECTED.
KRSH
IT JUST PROVES WHAT I'VE ALWAYS SAID. NEVER TRUST A SKRULL...
...TO DO A SUPER-SKRULL'S JOB.
NOT THE END!